Using Literature in the Middle School Curriculum

By Carol Otis Hurst and Rebecca Otis

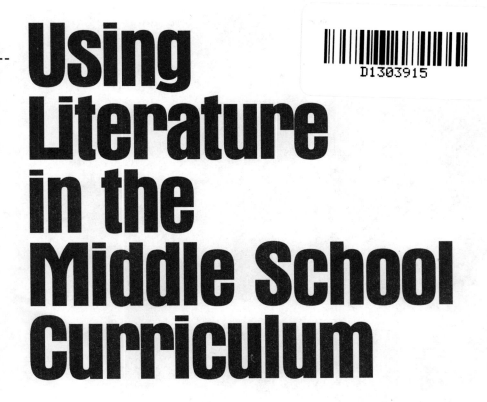

PROFESSIONAL GROWTH SERIES®

A Publication of THE BOOK REPORT & LIBRARY TALK
Professional Growth Series

Linworth Publishing, Inc.
Worthington, Ohio

Library of Congress Cataloging-in-Publication Data

Hurst, Carol Otis.
    Using literature in the middle school curriculum / by Carol Otis
Hurst and Rebecca Otis
        p.   cm. -- (Professional growth series)
    ISBN 0-938865-73-0
    1. Middle schools--United States--Curricula.   2. Literature--Study
and teaching (Middle school)--United States.   3. Young adult
literature.   4. Interdisciplinary approach in education--United
States.   I. Otis, Rebecca.   II. Title.   III. Series.
    LB1628.5.H87   1999
    373.19--dc21   98-54106
                                                          CIP

Published by Linworth Publishing, Inc.
480 East Wilson Bridge Road, Suite L
Worthington, Ohio 43085

Copyright©1999 by Linworth Publishing, Inc.

Series Information:
        From The Professional Growth Series

ISBN 0-938865-73-0

5 4 3 2 1

Table of Contents

Table of Contents continued

Introduction

In this book we have brought together some of the research, methods, and philosophy supporting the use of trade book literature in the curriculum for middle schools with an exploration of some of the specific novels, picture books, and nonfiction to be used in those classrooms. Although the books we use and describe in this book are not the only good books available today, we have culled our choices from a cast of thousands. We have described or summarized their content and suggested some of the ways these books can be used as an integral part of the curriculum without destroying their integrity.

The star ratings for the books are as follows:

★ = good
★★ = very good
★★★ = excellent
★★★★ = outstanding

We start off with a Literature in the Content Areas: Curriculum Cross Reference Chart. Although the main thrust of each of the themes and focus books is literature, the chart shows other curriculum strengths of each theme and focus book. The book consists of four main parts:

CLASSROOM TECHNIQUES

This is an investigation and description of some classroom organizational and management systems and techniques to facilitate the use of literature as a basis of study. There is an emphasis here on connecting literature with the rest of the curriculum.

THEMES & GENRES

This section contains themes and topics around which to organize reading, research, and writing inquiry. Some of these are clearly curriculum-related, and others relate to common interests. These subjects can be used as a master plan for a unit or as a means of making connections from one area of the curriculum to another while pursuing individual or class interests. Each theme encourages teachers to start out with a picture book; suggests some possible activities for approaching the theme or genre; and lists good to outstanding fiction and nonfiction books on the topic, activities, connections to further topics, resources for inquiry, and connections to cross curriculum subjects.

Introduction (continued)

▨ LITERARY STUDY

This section is intended to help teachers lead students to an analytical level in their reading and writing. How do authors use characterization, symbolism, and various techniques to communicate? Citations are made for books that demonstrate symbolism, character development, uses of foreshadowing, flashbacks, and point of view.

▨ FOCUS BOOKS

In this section we take some of the best works for middle school students and focus on each of them individually. For each title we give a summary of the book, important things to notice and question or debate, activities, related nonfiction subjects, and related books. In effect, each of these focus books can become a unit or theme for further exploration.

A further word of warning belongs here, however. We have listed many activities and questions under the "Taking It Deeper" part for each focus book. They are meant to be topics for dialogue or further exploration. Care must be taken not to use these as tests or questions at the end of the chapter for students to answer correctly.

About the Authors

Carol Otis Hurst is a nationally known storyteller, author and language arts consultant. She has taught grade levels from pre-school through grade three and was a school librarian for many years before becoming a free-lance consultant and writer. Carol is the author of fourteen books for teachers and librarians. A teaching editor for *TeachingK8 Magazine*, Carol writes two columns a month for that magazine and has done so since 1973. Carol Otis Hurst has two daughters, one of whom is the co-author of this book, and two grandsons. She lives in Westfield, Massachusetts.

Rebecca Otis is the co-author of several books for teachers including "In Times Past: An Encyclopedia for Integrating US History with Literature in Grades 3-8" and "Picturing Math: Using Picture Books in the Math Curriculum," both available from McGraw Learning. She also runs "Carol Hurst's Children's Literature Site" on the Internet at http://www.carolhurst.com and publishes the quarterly newsletter Carol Hurst's Children's' Literature Newsletter. The mother of two sons, Rebecca lives in Colrain, Massachusetts

Literature in the Content Areas: Curriculum Cross Reference Chart

Themes

Title	Science	History	Sociology	Art	Music	Physical Ed	Mathematics
Slavery		●		●	●		
Going West			●	●			
Native Americans			●	●			
The Holocaust			●	●			
Immigration			●	●			
Protest & Rebellion			●	●		●	
Biography	●	●	●	●	●	●	●
The Rive	●	●		●	●		
Survival	●	●					
Music	●	●	●	●	●		●
Picture Books				●			
Appalachia		●	●	●	●		
Mythology	●			●	●		
Animal Stories	●		●				
Sports	●	●	●	●	●	●	●
Humor			●				
Quests	●	●					
Poetry				●	●		

Focus Books

Title	Science	History	Sociology	Art	Music	Physical Ed	Mathematics
Watership Down	●	●	●				
Nothing But the Truth			●				
Heartlight	●		●				●
Truth to Tell			●				
The Moves Make the Man	●		●			●	
The Cry of the Wolf	●	●					
After the First Death		●	●				
Catherine, Called Birdy	●	●		●	●		
Sees Behind Trees	●	●	●				
The Tulip Touch			●				
The Borning Room		●		●	●		
Dateline: Troy		●			●		
Out of the DUst		●	●				
Kinship		●	●				
Alan & Naomi	●	●	●				
The Giver		●	●				
The Wall		●	●				
Good Night, Mr. Tom			●				
Letters from Inside			●		●		
I Will Call It Goergie's Blues	●	●					
LyddieStrays Like Us	●		●				
Freak the Mighty			●				
Words by Heart		●	●				
Wringer	●		●				
The Ramsay Scallop		●		●	●		
Taste of Salt		●	●				
Belle Prater's Boy			●				
Only Opal		●		●			

Section 1:
Classroom Techniques

READING AND LITERATURE

It wasn't so long ago that most literature programs in middle and high schools consisted of selections from an anthology produced by a textbook company. That, together with a grammar text, some composition workbooks, and a testing program, was the reading, English, and literature curriculum in many schools. Later years have produced some changes; multiple copies of some novels have been working their way into the program with the result that teachers and kids make a more intimate, in-depth exploration of a work of literature.

Nancy Atwell's book **In the Middle** suggested using reading and writing workshops with a wider range of choices for students and teachers. The writing process work of Donald Graves and Lucy Calkins has made inroads into the field, encouraging middle school students to consider themselves authentic writers. In her book **Seeking Diversity: Language Arts with Adolescents**, Linda Rief describes the increasing use of trade books as the basis of her language arts program.

Many of us now embrace the philosophy that students learn best when they are given as much control over learning as possible. When they are immersed in reading and writing for a purpose to which they are committed, students feel a sense of ownership and are apt to become motivated learners. In order to become literate, students need access to print in its many forms: books, letters, magazine articles, ads, comics, lists, and signs and symbols which combine to become their reading/writing texts. In many classrooms, teachers and students are recognizing the playfulness of learning and sharing what they have learned without robbing the subjects of their academic intent. Activities are learner-centered rather than teacher- or curriculum-driven. The language arts, as well as other curriculum areas, are seen as a forum for "seeing what is."

Group projects and problems in which reading, writing, and listening activities have a valid and apparent purpose invite students to work together toward their exploration and solutions, using their unique perspectives and creative abilities. By ascertaining what they already know, what they need to know, and how they might go about obtaining further information, students become researchers with commitment and purpose.

This does not mean that skills or strategies are not taught or learned, but that these techniques are explored in the context of reading and writing relevant material, and these strategies are taught to seek mastery in order to proceed in their areas of investigation.

CROSSING DISCIPLINES

Some cross disciplines make wonderful combinations for using literature in the classroom. History and English are particularly good allies because so many good books are historical in nature. Look through the table of contents in any history textbook with literature in mind. A suggested source for history-related literature and its use in the classroom is **In Times Past** by Otis and Hurst (SRA/McGraw-Hill).

Add art and music to the above duo of history and literature and you've got an opportunity for integration on a broad spectrum. Work back and forth between works of art and the history and literature of the time, the subject, or the area. For instance, see page 93, where Brueghel's painting is used in conjunction with Auden's poem about the fall of Icarus. The myth itself can be read alone or can be connected to the other myths about the labyrinth and about Daedalus himself. The myth can lead to other novels, poems, and stories about man's reach exceeding his grasp. Look at page 160 for connections between a painting by Van Eyck and Karen Cushman's story, **Catherine, Called Birdy**.

Work the other way and find musical and artistic ways of responding to the literature. Research the lives of the artists and find out the events that influenced those lives, and you're back to the history again. Using novels set in the same times or places or on the same subjects will lead you into literature.

The point to all this cross disciplining is obvious: it leads students away from tunnel learning, away from the idea that events exist as single items without being influenced by other factors or events. Each book read individually or in groups can lead students to an area of study in a discipline that they might otherwise have ignored or not fully appreciated. Teachers from several disciplines can exchange ideas, learn from each other, share or alleviate exasperation with humor or sympathy. They become part of the classroom learning community.

▶ CLASS DISCUSSIONS AND LITERATURE GROUPS

Facilitating group discussions is one part of our job as teachers. A well-facilitated discussion models the skills necessary for students to conduct their own discussions: sharing views without discounting those of others; commenting on someone's ideas without causing offense while still speaking the truth. These are not inborn skills, yet they are some of the most essential skills for group learning and living.

Ralph Peterson in **Life in a Crowded Place** (Heinemann, 1992 ISBN 0 435 08736 3) differentiates between conversation and dialogue in a way useful to those of us working with books, ideas, and middle school students. Peterson says: "Conversation is combustible and can take off in an unanticipated direction without notice. Dialogue, on the other hand, has a focus, and participants join for the purpose of understanding, disclosing, and

constructing meaning." It is dialogue, that higher level of discourse and communication, which most of us want to encourage during group activities. Dialogue involves both careful listening and critical thinking, and it should bring out the best of both.

It is obvious then, that the best of teacher/student, as well as small or large group, communication is dialogue. Through dialogue rather than discourse or lecture, a bigger meaning can be achieved and greater learning can occur. Peterson also points out, however, that this does not mean that the teacher holds back information that might be helpful to understanding this dialogue. The teacher is an informed member of the dialogue (sometimes, but not always, better informed than the student), divulging information whenever it seems pertinent or helpful to those searching for meaning.

Setting up a dialogue session doesn't mean that the teacher has the answer and is leading the kids through a series of questions to discover that answer. The teacher, if participating in the dialogue, has to be as honest as the others in the group in negotiating meaning from the text.

We know that, while assigned reading results in less commitment on the part of the readers, it does make things easier to manage. When students are off in their own directions, reading whatever appeals or has relevance to their goals, the problems of organizing class or small group dialogue, conferences, and assessment can become prohibitive. Members of the community, including the teacher, may need some concrete setups and ideas for discussion format for using multiple texts. These will not become restrictive if the focus is on the goal of having free and open dialogue in the classroom.

Here are some techniques to start a dialogue. After students have used the formats several times, techniques can usually be abandoned, as students will have developed their own protocols. Jerry Harste and Kathy Short developed the first four of these.

► Say Something

Students read a piece of material in teams of two. They divide the material into short chunks, marking stopping points in the margin before reading. After reading a small section of the material aloud or silently, the readers stop, look at each other, and say something about the material they've read. After each has spoken and been listened to, regardless of the amount of time it takes, they then go on to the next section.

► Written Conversation

Instead of speaking aloud to each other as in "Say Something," the readers conduct a conversation about the book in writing, using the same sheet of paper as they pass it back and forth for comments.

► Stretch and Sketch

After reading a piece of literature, each student draws or sketches something which symbolizes to him or her something about the meaning of the selection. On the back of the sketch, students write down why they chose that particular object. Readers share their sketches and their motives in the dialogue.

► Save the Last Word for Me

On an index card, readers write a quote from the material that pleases, puzzles, or is in some other way special to them. On the back of their card, they write down why. In the group, each person reads his or her quote and opens it up for discussion. After the group has had its say, the original quoter has the last word about it.

► Hey! Listen to This!

Each reader brings to the dialogue a short section from his or her book to read aloud. The reasons for that selection can be its humor, its unusual or eloquent language, its murkiness, or any other bona fide excuse. After the first reading, other members of the group talk about the way their books differ from or resemble it before going on to the next selection.

► They Should Have Called It . . .

Readers bring to the dialogue table alternate titles for a piece of work that they think would better inform or intrigue readers. Discussions of the author or editor's choice of the title as particularly appropriate or inappropriate put readers in the writer's place.

► Branching Out

One reader makes a web of his or her reading selection and posts it. Other readers look for a commonality with their reading and come to the discussion prepared to link the two selections.

► And for Best Supporting Role

Students look for well-developed minor or supporting characters in a work. The dialogue includes such matters as: Why are they there? What role do they play in the plot: a sounding board? A barrier or support for the main character's goal? To add color? Humor? Diversion?

► It Was a Dark and Stormy Night

Students read aloud the opening paragraphs of a book. First lines and first paragraphs of a piece of writing are the author's attempts to draw in the reader. Some are more successful than others. See page 133 for some interesting first paragraphs. Encourage readers to add their nominations for best first words.

▶ Introducing . . . —Character Development

Readers use a bookmark for a period of time during which they note on their bookmark the page number when a character is introduced. After everyone, or almost everyone, has one citation noted and the class is together, those passages are reread silently. Have a few books with passages marked ready for students who do not have one of their own available.

Students can read to the group some character introductions from their selections. Try changing some adjectives and other descriptive words. How many word possibilities for that spot can you find? How and why might the author have chosen that word? How do the new words change the reader's experience of that sentence and of that character?

▶ Roles in Dialogue

Another way of setting up a dialogue about literature is to assign roles for the participants. They do the required reading knowing that, during the ensuing dialogue, they will have these role assignments. Some possible roles are: moderator, extender (person brings related information to add to the discussion), definer (person has researched meanings of important words or concepts), recorder, summarizer, and questioner (person comes to the discussion with one or more questions to stimulate the dialogue). These roles should be changed for each dialogue for variety of viewpoint. The need for the assignment of roles usually diminishes as students take over later dialogues.

▷ MINI-LESSON—GROUP READING OF FIRST PARAGRAPHS

Bob and Marlene McCracken suggest a technique using beginning paragraphs that makes a good mini-lesson. Because many poor readers are often unable to use the technique that better readers use unconsciously—interacting with the text, making and discarding predictions as they affirm or negate them—the McCrackens suggest reproducing on an overhead the first few paragraphs of a book unfamiliar to the students. The reading difficulty of the book should be slightly below that of the average reader in the class.

The selection is read aloud by all the students in unison at a fairly fluent pace. This eliminates problems in deciphering for some students. Students are then asked to respond to "What do we know" questions, some of which are directly stated while others are implied by the text: What time might this be? Is it day or night? What is so and so feeling? What might be happening here? Who appears sinister or afraid?

Because no one knows the "right" answers, speculation is encouraged and no one is about to be proven wrong. After milking the first paragraphs of the first chapter for all they are worth, do the same thing with the first paragraphs of the second chapter. Obviously, much has occurred that we don't know about, but some of those events can be gleaned by the beginning paragraphs of the next chapter. Also, some of the predictions from the first chapter can be affirmed or thrown out. When those are guessed at and more predictions made, do the same with opening paragraphs from chapter three. After that, the lesson is concluded.

Obviously, not all books can be used in this way. Some authors use a chapter setup which is not sequential. Others don't give enough information with which to play in this way. Some students may well choose to read the whole book, because the exercise does often create interest in the plot, but that is not your primary purpose. What has happened is that poorer readers have worked successfully with print, and better readers have not been held back in the process but have instead practiced using successful techniques of interacting with text.

⟫ READING ALOUD

If we want to get the kids in our classrooms excited about books, we've got to be sure that they have constant access to a wide variety of books. Our classrooms have to have so many books that we run out of shelf room. Students have to have instant access to the library so that no matter the subject, the chances are great that a nearby book will tell them more. Our curriculum has to be constructed so that reading and writing are at the core of most subjects and at least tangential to the others.

However, the most efficient way to get a classroom full of students to care about books is for the person who is best at reading aloud in that classroom to do so frequently and enthusiastically. That person, in most classrooms, is you, the teacher. This means that almost every day you should read aloud to your students. The length of selections for reading aloud will vary and so will the genre, but the reading will occur.

Read-aloud programs open doors. For one thing, by reading a book aloud you provide a common plot, set of characters, scene, and theme to which individually read books can be compared and contrasted. As the pile of shared selections grows, the comparisons become easier and more meaningful.

Sometimes student readers get hooked on a particular genre or author. They are interested only in horse books or science fiction or the work of Stephen King. We should be careful with those students. When we attack or look down upon a person's reading choice, we're on dangerous ground. In this day and age, we are lucky to have students who read at all. Showing a lack of respect for their choices may cause students to stop all recreational reading. However, with a read aloud program, we have no threats, no condescension, no bribery—just a teacher's choice of material that he or she thinks the students will like, and this

can broaden the choices for individual students' recreational reading.

Read-aloud programs should be as well-planned as any other vital part of the curriculum. Although there will be some spontaneous choices, for the most part, the read-aloud should be carefully constructed. Start with books you love, but chart new territory in future selections. Because of time constraints, it doesn't make sense to read aloud books the kids are already reading or that were read aloud to them in previous years. It is important that the books in the read-aloud program cover many genres and touch on many subjects. Use novels, biographies, humorous and thoughtful essays, poems, and works of nonfiction.

From your reading, students hear language as it should sound. The language flows, and sometimes they actively listen for plot; other times they drift on a single thought or phrase. They react together to the humor and the action of the story. They love or hate or tolerate characters. Vocabulary development is intrinsic to the read-aloud experience. So are making inferences, making predictions, and affirming or negating their predictions. Many, if not all, of the subskills sometimes taught in isolation can be mastered orally and aurally in the read-aloud experience.

Remember, however, that it's just as possible to bore people or frustrate them with a book read aloud as it is with a reading assignment. You can't jump your audience from Beverly Cleary to Jane Austen. Take small steps. If all the kids are reading horror stories, read a short story such as "The Monkey's Paw" or "The Telltale Heart" aloud. If here-and-now teenage romances are the only thing being read by your kids, read Joan Paton Walsh's **Fireweed** (Farrar, 1988 ISBN 0 374 42316 4), a romance that starts in the night bombing of London during World War II. Try Harry Mazer's

City Light (Scholastic, 1988 ISBN 0 590 40511 X), a romance we hear about through the wry voice of George, rejected but unbowed.

Find a selection that won't bore those who are not fond of horror stories or romances or whatever genre you've selected. Often this means selections that are particularly well-written because they are most apt to have strong, well-developed characters and intricacies of plot that can capture the interest of students who were lukewarm about that genre. The point is to entice them into further and slightly deeper reading.

Remember that one of the perks of hearing a book read aloud is that students get a new author, new topic, new series, new genre to follow. If you read aloud Brian Jacques' **Redwall** (Putnam, 1987 ISBN 0 399 21424 0), and they like it, don't read the many sequels aloud. The reading of that series is the new path some students may follow. There is no need to take full class time (and those books are long) to read the rest of the series or sequels aloud.

Your read-aloud program should lead the students to expect more of books. A good read-aloud program has depth and breadth and ample time for dialogue as a result of the reading. Decisions are made by the main character that need to be talked about. Some things are stated as fact that may be opinion, necessitating further discussion. Inevitably, comparisons are made with other readings and with one's own experiences. Books threaten and challenge old thinking. They are dangerous and exciting, and by making good read-aloud choices, you can help the students dig deeper into literature.

Section 2:
Themes and Topics

CHAPTER 1

Slavery

COMMENTS

Although the study of slavery is often done within the context of the Civil War, it doesn't have to stay there. It can be approached from the perspective of World History or within the context of the labor movement. No matter what the context, the literature abounds with good books on the subject.

Perhaps a word of caution belongs here before we immerse ourselves in this theme. The subject of Slavery is and should be a very emotional one to investigate. Students and teachers alike may need help handling some of the information that such an investigation turns up. It's important that teachers be aware of this and provide opportunities for students to talk and write about the experiences, or even to receive counseling if the need arises. Offering students a variety of ways in which to express their feelings is very important with this theme. Suggest writing, music, and art activities as possible ways to deal with the subject. The Internet is a good source for ways in which this has been done by others.

PICTURE BOOK STARTER

Jacob Lawrence's book **Harriet and the Promised Land** (Simon and Schuster, 1968 ISBN 0 671 86673 7 Grades 2-9) is an interesting picture book about Harriet Tubman. Opening this picture book, one finds that stylized, poster-like illustrations in bold, primary colors dominate the book and should provoke discussion. Notice the illustrator's enlargement of Harriet's hands as she scrubs the endless, wooden floor, and as she urges the escaping slaves toward the northern star.

Read aloud the forward by Lawrence telling why he did the book and the people he honors with it. Let students decide on the way the poetry/prose text should be read aloud and which words should be stressed:

> "Harriet, clean;
> Harriet, sweep.
> Harriet, rock
> The child to sleep."

Speculate on the words the author chose not to use as well as those he did use. The words are simple but quite powerful.

Because Harriet Tubman was often compared to Moses, and because many middle school students are only vaguely aware of that biblical figure, it might be beneficial to take the time to find out about Moses so that they can better understand the analogy.

ACTIVITIES

Students can compile a list of "facts" about the subject—statements they think they know to be true. Because most of us have misinformation and facts intermingled in our memories, this process often starts heated discussions. Encourage students to estimate numbers of slaves in the American South and North, numbers of successful escapes, numbers of stations on the Underground Railroad, and numbers of slaves owned by U.S. Presidents. Work in small groups to create the lists and then compile them in a class list. Suggest that they categorize the items in various ways: "We Know, We Think We Know" or "No Argument, Arguments," for instance. Go back to these "facts" throughout the theme study to correct, discard, or affirm them.

Play recordings of songs from slavery: "Many Thousand Gone," "No More Auction Block for Me," "Go Down, Moses."

Make the next step a picture book one as well. There are many outstanding picture books relevant to the study of slavery (see below), and they make fine learning experiences for middle school children. Hand out some to small groups of students for closer perusal. If students aren't used to cooperative learning or small group independent work, you may need to structure the group with assigned roles such as reader, recorder, and connector. Another possible structure is to have one student focus totally on illustration, another on text, and a third on making connections. For other groups, merely handing them the picture book will set them off to productive dialogue.

Bring the groups back together to compare and contrast their picture book reading and the information they gained from it. Put that information in chart form for the whole group's information. Correct any misconceptions or inconsistencies on the chart that their early research has uncovered.

FROM THE PICTURE BOOK READING:	
We know	We want to know
We think	Our first step in finding out

After explaining the book, read aloud selections from Julius Lester's **To Be A Slave** (see page 16) such as the following:

My new master, whose name I did not hear, took me that same day across the Patuxent, where I joined fifty-one other slaves whom he had bought in Maryland. Thirty-two of these were men, and nineteen were women. The women were merely tied together with a rope, about the size of a bed cord, which was tied like a halter round the neck of each; but the men, of whom I was the stoutest and strongest, were very differently caparisoned. A strong iron collar was closely fitted by means of a padlock round each of our necks. A chain of iron about a hundred feet in length was passed through the hasp of each padlock, except at the two ends, where the hasps of the padlocks passed through a link of the chain. In addition to this, we were handcuffed in pairs, with iron staples and bolts, with a short chain about a foot long uniting the handcuffs and their wearers in pairs. In this manner, we were chained alternately by the right and left hand; and the poor man to whom I was thus ironed wept like an infant when the blacksmith with his heavy hammer fastened the ends of the bolts that kept the staples from slipping from our arms. For my own part, I felt indifferent to my fate. It appeared to me that the worst had come, and that no change of fortune could harm me.

It may be time for you to start reading a slavery novel aloud. **Nightjohn,** by Gary Paulsen, is a good choice because it immediately engages the emotions of the listener (Doubleday, 1993 ISBN 0 385 30838 8). This is not difficult to read academically, but it's certainly difficult to read emotionally. Paulsen's attack is on two widely held false notions about slavery: that most slaves were happy and that most slaves could, if they wanted to, escape fairly easily. Sarny, a 12-year-old slave, is our view to the horror and brutality of the time and to the institution of slavery.

A good nonfictional read-aloud on the subject of slavery is **Many Thousand Gone** (listed below). Sharing a book together by having the teacher read it aloud gives students a basis of comparison with the information or books they are reading on their own.

A good nonfictional source for groups to share at this point might be **The Underground Railroad** by Raymond Bial (Houghton, 1995 ISBN 0 395 69937 1). This is a short, factual account in which clear and telling colored photographs dominate. It makes a nice stepping stone between the previous picture books and further research.

Before some of the students tackle that further research, they may need some preparation work. Looking at photographs and nonfictional pictorial information may be their next step. Discussing these in small groups may elicit further information known and ready to be researched. If you have the cooperation of the social studies teachers on this unit, the next step for some groups may be to read the section in the U.S. history text on slavery. This information is apt to be short and, for some students, challenging reading. Buddy reading, in which one student reads a short

selection aloud and the other student summarizes the information gained, might solve the problem. The roles can be retained or switched for the next section.

While that group is doing the guided reading outlined in the above paragraph, other children could be doing some research in nonfictional materials about slavery. Bring out all the resources, including the Internet, and let kids investigate any of the areas that interest them so far. The eventual goal is to publish their findings, and they can do so on a database on the computer or on bulletin boards or news sheets, perhaps labeled "Did You Know?" Expect that research will continue throughout the theme and will get better as information piles up.

After groups have concluded this phase of their research and discussion, call the entire class together to report to each other the results of their studies. Add their relevant information to the chart.

As soon as possible, let the students decide the directions of the discussion and further research. Participate yourself, as much as possible, as an equal learner, not as arbitrator or dispenser of knowledge. Read one book that you haven't read before and share your reactions to it as you read. If this is an early or first opportunity for such work, you may have to do more of the leading. The theme could stick to the time of Harriet Tubman or range into slavery past and present, the Civil War, civil rights, labor, and/or racism.

Bring in fiction and nonfiction on a wide variety of ability levels on the subject. Students should now be ready for the book talks you'll be doing on some or all of the following lengthier books that deal with various aspects of slavery. They should be given the opportunity to choose one of them for their own reading.

Offer students magazine articles as choices of reading material whenever possible. They are often vastly different than textbooks, and the articles are usually short, appealing to some students who are threatened by more formal material. **Cobblestone**, a history magazine for young readers, has many issues on the subject of slavery, and back issues are available from the publisher as well as in many libraries. The February 1981 issue was devoted to Harriet Tubman and contains several articles, maps, drawings, and photographs about her.

If you have multiple copies of some of these titles, students can read them in small groups or individually. See page 4 for ideas on group sharing of books. Because the level of sophistication necessary to appreciate these books varies widely, students should be able to find one that interests them that falls within their ability levels. However, the choice of material should be theirs and the way in which they read it should be up to them.

As you can see by the list of books below, there is no shortage of material on slavery, and students should be encouraged to read widely or intensely, depending on preference, and make journal entries as they do so. Ask them to name a time and date when enough material will have been absorbed so that a group, however large or small, may be able to discuss what they have read and learned.

You can confine the study to one classroom or let it become a building-wide investigation. Students can chose their own ways to react to this study. Poems, position papers, fictional writing, and nonfictional reports are just a few of the ways.

The artist of the original book we used here, Jacob Lawrence, has created many works of poster art, and his work can be further explored. Many other artists have portrayed various aspects of slavery, and photographs of sculpture and two-dimensional works have information to give our researchers.

Music can be confined to the above-mentioned slave songs or become an avenue of interpretation for students.

Find out where your community stood on the slavery issue. Find and read local newspapers of the 1850s and '60s. How many people kept slaves? How many slaves? Were there any known abolitionists in your area? Was anyone in your community on the Underground Railroad?

Find out about your own family and slavery. Were any of your ancestors slaves? Slave owners? Abolitionists? Conductors on the railroad?

At some point, look back with the students at the list of knowledges you made after reading **Harriet and the Promised Land**. Add to and amend that list or merely talk about newer learnings and understandings.

BOOK LIST

▶ Picture Books

★ ★ Chbosky, Stacy **Who Owns the Sun?** Landmark, 1988 ISBN 0 933 84914 1

This is particularly useful in a middle school classroom because the author/illustrator was 15 when it was published. It starts out sounding like a typical picture book for the very young in which a child keeps asking his father who owns the things he sees: the sun, the stars, the wind, and the flowers. Each time the father replies that no one can own that thing—it is too special to be owned by any one person. Then comes the awful question, "Who owns us?", and the answer is the man in the big house.

★ ★ ★ ★ Erickson, Paul **Daily Life on a Southern Plantation 1853** Lodestar, 1998 ISBN 525 67547 7

Like **Christmas in the Big House** (listed below), this book makes slavery seem even more ghastly as it depicts the very human, ordinary lives that surrounded the institution. Here we follow a day in the life of the plantation owners and their family, their white overseer, and their head slave and his family.

★ ★ ★ ★ Hopkinson, Deborah **Sweet Clara and the Freedom Quilt** Random, 1995 ISBN 0 679 874472 0, illustrated by James Ransome

Another slave teaches Sweet Clara how to quilt when she is sold away from her mother. Although Clara came as a field hand, Aunt Rachel is able to get her assigned to the big house. Clara learns about the land surrounding the plantation and, as she does so, she puts that information into a quilt map. When she finally makes her bid for freedom, Clara leaves the quilt behind hoping it will show other slaves the way.

★ ★ Johnson, Dolores **Now Let Me Fly: The Story of a Slave Family** Atheneum, 1992 ISBN 0 02 747699 5

This looks at a different phase of slavery as, through vivid illustration and text, we watch Minna go from her life in Africa before her capture and transport by slave ship to the plantation of Amadi. There she marries and has a family, but her husband and son are sold away to another plantation.

★ ★ ★ McKissack, Patricia and Frederick **Christmas in the Big House, Christmas in the Quarters** Scholastic, 1994 ISBN 0 590 43027 0, illustrated by John Thompson

This depiction of the holiday as celebrated on a Virginia plantation in 1859 is very close to nonfiction. The contrast between the two celebrations is very effectively done.

★ ★ ★ Ringgold, Faith **Aunt Harriet's Underground Railroad in the Sky** Crown, 1994 ISBN 0 517 58768 8

This is an interesting, impressionistic portrayal of the Underground Railroad. The "train" is presented as a literal train; the slaves fly free; the times vary from then and now. All of these factors could be confusing, but they make for a fascinating presentation.

★ ★ ★ ★ Turner, Ann **Nettie's Trip South** & Schuster, 1987 ISBN 0 02 789240 9, illustrated by Ronald Himler

Written as a letter to a friend, the book describes Nettie's reactions to slavery on her first trip to Richmond, Virginia.

★ ★ ★ Winter, Jeanette **Follow the Drinking Gourd** Knopf, 1992 ISBN 0 679 81997 5

The folk song "Follow the Drinking Gourd" is used as a message for flight by Peg Leg Joe as he moves from plantation to plantation.

▶ **Fiction**

★ ★ ★ Armstrong, Jennifer **Steal Away** Scholastic, 1993 ISBN 0 590 46921 5

Susannah, a white girl from the North who is forced to live in pre-Civil War Virginia, forms an alliance with Bethlehem, a slave assigned to her. Together they run north—Bethlehem to Canada, and Susannah back to Vermont.

★ ★ ★ Avi **Something Upstairs** Flare, 1990 ISBN 0 380 708531

This is a ghost/time-travel story in which Caleb, a 16-year-old slave, haunts the house where he is supposed to have killed himself. Kenny, now 16 himself, is drawn into the past by Caleb to find his murderer and clear his name.

★ ★ ★ Fox, Paula **Slave Dancer** Laurelleaf, 1997 ISBN 0 440 22739 9

Thirteen-year-old Jessie, a White boy, is kidnapped because of his ability to play the fife and forced to play his fife on a slave ship. Because the slaves must be exercised, Jessie is to play the music to which they must dance. The ship is wrecked, and the only two survivors are Jessie and Ras, a young slave. An old man helps Ras escape north and Jessie, who is greatly affected by what he has seen and experienced, get back to New Orleans.

★ ★ ★ ★ Fritz, Jean **Brady** Viking, 1987 ISBN 0 140 32258 2

Brady has always had trouble keeping secrets. Now he not only must keep the secret that his father is hiding a runaway slave, he must act for his father in the Underground Railroad.

★ ★ ★ Gaeddert, Louann **Breaking Free** Atheneum, 1992 ISBN 0 689 31882 9

This novel is about northern slavery, something seldom dealt with in children's fiction. Here we see it through the eyes of Richard, a 12-year-old orphan in Upstate New York in 1800, who secretly helps a slave learn to read and then to escape to Canada.

★ ★ Humence, Belinda **A Girl Called Boy** Clarion, 1982 ISBN 0 395 55698 8

This is a time-travel book that, like many of this genre, informs about both time periods. Boy's real name is Blanch Yancey, and she has frequently expressed her annoyance in her father's tales about his slave ancestors. Suddenly transported to the South in 1853, Blanch learns about families in slave time and in the present.

★ ★ ★ Lyons, Mary E. **Letters from a Slave Girl: The Story of Harriet Jacobs** Atheneum, 1992 ISBN 0 684 19446 5

This is a fictionalized account of the life of a real slave. Written as a series of letters from Harriet to various "dear ones" she has lost, the book tells of her heart-breaking existence, hiding for years within earshot of her children, but unable to be with them.

Paulsen, Gary **Nightjohn**
See above.

★ ★ ★ Paulsen, Gary **Sarny: A Life Remembered** Bantam, 1997 ISBN 0 385 32195 3

This sequel to *Nightjohn* zeroes in on Sarny's life after Emancipation. Her search for her children brings her to New Orleans, where she is befriended by Miss Laura, a black woman passing as white, who runs a "fancy house in New Orleans where men came and went." There's a stretch of coincidences here, but the brief novel makes compelling reading.

★ ★ ★ ★ Rinaldi, Ann **Hang a Thousand Trees with Ribbons: The Story of Phillis Wheatley** Harcourt, 1996 ISBN 0 15 200876 4

This challenging book deals with northern slavery, and is based upon the life of America's first black poet, Phillis Wheatley. We learn of her capture in Africa, the middle passage on the slave ship, and her sale to the Wheatley family. The author deals extensively with Phillis's feeling of being caught between two cultures and of her longing to be free.

★ ★ ★ ★ Rinaldi, Ann **Wolf by the Ears** Scholastic, 1991 ISBN 0 590 43413 6

This fine novel deals with Thomas Jefferson and his daughter/slave. It has long been rumored that Thomas Jefferson fathered some of his own slaves. This book accepts that as true and tells of the dilemma of one of his daughters who has led a privileged albeit shadow existence at Monticello. Now she must decide whether to escape and live as a free black woman or attempt to pass as a white woman.

▶ **Nonfiction**

★ ★ ★ ★ Bial, Raymond **Underground Railroad** Houghton, 1995 ISBN 0 395 69937 1

This photo essay is very effective. Bial uses objects and places to recreate the story of escapes—rivers crossed, plantations slaves ran from, and homes they ran to. He also includes drawings and prints from the time.

★ ★ ★ Fritz, Jean **Harriet Beecher Stowe and the Beecher Preachers** Putnam, 1994 ISBN 0 399 22666 4

This is one of Fritz's excellent biographies, and in telling us about the life and times of the author of *Uncle Tom's Cabin*, she deals with the alliance of women's rights advocates and abolitionists in New England.

★ ★ ★ Hamilton, Virginia **Many Thousand Gone: African Americans from Slavery to Freedom** Knopf, 1993 ISBN 0 394 82873 9, illustrated by Leo & Diane Dillon

This story is only 152 pages, but it's packed with grouped tales of slaves based on strict historical accounts. It goes well with Lester's **To Be a Slave** (see below). This is nonfictional writing at its most powerful, and the illustrations are superb.

★ ★ ★ ★ Lester, Julius **To Be a Slave** Scholastic, 1968 ISBN 0 590 42460 2

These are firsthand statements and narratives taken from writings and interviews of former slaves, and is divided into sections chronicling the processes of capture, transportation, enslavement, escape, emancipation, and reconstruction.

★ ★ Marston, Hope **Isaac Johnson: From Slave to Stonecutter** Cobblehill, 1995 ISBN 0 525 65165 9

This biography of a slave is taken from a pamphlet self-published by Johnson. His eventual escape from slavery and his service in the Union Army is interesting, but even more fascinating is his eventual discovery that his own white father had sold him and the rest of his family.

★ ★ McMullan, Kate **The Story of Harriet Tubman, Conductor of the Underground Railroad** Dell, 1991 ISBN 0 440 40400 2

The reading is not difficult, but the reader gets a picture of Tubman as more than the Moses figure in Lawrence's book.

Going West

COMMENTS

One strong connection between literature and history can be made through the books that deal with the cross-country journeys made by people in covered wagons and the frontier settlements they founded as the United States expanded its boundaries. Actually, the theme almost immediately breaks in two as it becomes apparent that the study of the settlement of the plains differs from the study of those who went on to Oregon and California. Even then, the theme can stop there or continue to a theme on Native Americans, the Old West, or the Gold Rush. Depending on how detailed and far-ranging a teacher chooses to make the subject, this can be a year-long theme or one of shorter duration. It will involve extensive map study as trails, nations, and settlements of the time are compared with modern maps of the area. Students should be encouraged to find a strand that interests them and pursue it. Science becomes involved as the conditions of climate and environment are studied.

The settlement of the plains, which spelled adventure and new lands for the European cultures, was genocide for the region's previous residents, and no study of that time should ignore the price paid by the American Indians. Students need to understand the politics of the time, particularly the concept of Manifest Destiny, in order to know why the free land was offered. The attitude of that time toward Native Americans and the various political and military leaders who set about annihilating them is essential background. Some students might like to discover the differences between the way Canada and the United States developed their respective territories.

Students should be encouraged to read appropriate sections of at least one of the nonfiction sources before, during, and/or after reading from fiction, comparing the information gained from each. Some motifs that are identifiable in the literature of the westward movement are: definition of home, search for adventure, prices paid for progress, group and individual survival, villainy and heroism.

PICTURE BOOK STARTERS

Although it's not historical, **If You're Not from the Prairie** . . ., by David Bouchard with illustrations by Henry Ripplinger (see below), may give students who are unfamiliar with the vast plains area some sense of the prairie. Students may want to use this format to write about their own areas in this way before launching into the historical study.

Use a different picture book to bring them back to the journey across those plains:

Mississippi Mud: Three Prairie Journals, by Ann Turner with illustrations by Robert J. Blake, is a picture book that offers three different perspectives of the same events. The three older children in the family keep journals as the family moves by covered wagon from Kentucky to Oregon.

▶ ACTIVITIES

I'm leaving because. . . . Students compose as many statements starting with that phrase as possible to accompany drawings of what the people were leaving behind.

Look at a map to find cities and towns on the Plains and in the West that were named for the cities and towns back East: Salem, Oregon, and Springfield, Illinois, for example.

Encourage students to start reading a historical novel set in the 1800s that deals with the westward migration. Many possibilities are listed below. As they read, they should meet frequently in small groups to discuss their reading. Frequently, events in the fiction should be checked against nonfiction sources for accuracy.

Use the history textbook and such books as Joy Hakim's **The New Nation** (Oxford, 1994 ISBN 0 19 507752 0), which is a historical survey covering the 50 years after Washington's inauguration, to get an overview of the time and to check historical facts against their fiction reading. Some selections should be taped for less able readers.

Find out about the Homestead Act. The document is on the Internet at **http://boserup. qal.berkeley.edu/~gene/145/documents/ homestead.htm**

What did you have to do to claim the land? How long could you take? Could single people file claims or only married couples? What was the reasoning behind the act?

What effect on westward migration did the discovery of gold in California have? There's some interesting information and pho-

tographs at **http://www.mindscape.com/ reference/california/gold.html** on the Web.

How did people in the East find out about the discovery of gold in California? How long would it take today?

A series of "what if" statements might make a good brainstorming activity for this study: "What if the United States had honored its treaties with the Native Americans?" "What if gold had been discovered in Illinois instead of California?" "What if the railroads had not been developed at this time?" "What if there had been no Homestead Act?"

Students should be encouraged to speculate on these statements and to add others. As the theme study continues, students may want to change these "what if" statements to a series of "because" statements, adding the information they have gathered.

Time lines almost always add to the understanding of a period in history. Post a long strip of paper that is marked off in 10-year periods starting with 1840 and going to 1920 along a hallway or other long expanse. Place a marker at 1862 and a sign indicating the passage of the Homestead Act. Add beginning and end markers for the Civil War. Let students add other information as they find it. Encourage them to add illustrations, newspaper accounts, and other sources of information.

Find out about the villains and heroes of the time as well as the people who made money in unforeseen ways, such as Levi Strauss.

Another possible activity to be carried on throughout the theme is a "Whatever Happened To . . ." in which various Indian nations, individual heroes and villains, boom town communities, and early settlements are followed through to the present day with maps showing their movement or progress.

http://indy4.fdl.cc.mn.us/~isk/maps/ mapmenu.html is a Web site which shows maps of Indian nations in the United States before contact with settlers. Make a list of those that still exist and the areas they now occupy.

As with any historical study, students should have a chance to see what was going on in other parts of the world during the expansion era of the United States. Names of prominent shakers and movers of the time can be added to a bulletin board together with illustrations and various newspaper articles, real and imaginary.

To personalize the experience and bring it into their present-day world, students might like to measure out the size of a covered wagon and then decide which of their own personal belongings would be worth taking, considering these space constraints.

Provide students with a list of the supplies necessary for wagon train travel: flour, cornmeal, sugar, rice, peas and beans, preserves, honey, vinegar, salt, ham, beef, smoked fish, water containers, blankets, mattresses, cooking utensils, axes, hatchets, sickles, spades, saws, nails, whetstones, tacks, needles, thread, scissors, wax, needles, twine, hammers, rope, chains, beeswax and tallow, rosin, guns, bullet molds, bars of lead, and medical supplies. Deciding how much of each would be enough without resulting in an unnecessary overload should be the next step. Students can form groups to make up rules for joining their wagon train and outline various jobs necessary for its progress across the Plains then and now.

Imagine the future possibility of establishing a colony on Europa (one of Jupiter's moons on which water has been discovered). Students could decide which of their belongings would be of the most use in that colony, and the group rules activity described above can be carried out for this possible journey as well.

➤ BOOK LIST

▶ Picture Books

Bouchard, David **If You're Not from the Prairie** Aladdin. 1998 ISBN 0 689 82035 6. illustrated by by Henry Ripplinger
See above.

★ ★ ★ ★ Goble, Paul **Death of the Iron Horse** Bradbury, 1987 ISBN 0 02 737830 6
The story is told from the point of view of the Indians and is based on an actual incident in 1867, when the Cheyenne Indians wrecked a Union Pacific freight train. As always with Goble's books, the illustrations are stunning and contain many of the patterns and rhythms of Native American design. The coming of the train fulfilled the dire prophecy of a Cheyenne prophet named Sweet Medicine and, through the brief account, you get some feeling for the threat the railroad represented to the people who lived on the Plains.

★ ★ ★ Harvey, Brett **Cassie's Journey: Going West in the 1860s** Holiday House, 1988 ISBN 0 8234 0684 9, illustrated by Deborah Kogan Ray
This is based on old diaries and gives a realistic, picture-book view of the reasons why some families went to California at the time, and of the hazards on the trail.

★ ★ ★ ★ Howard, Ellen **The Log Cabin Quilt** Holiday House, 1996 ISBN 0 8234 1247 4
This is a beautiful story of a motherless family that leaves Carolina and heads for Michigan. The grandmother throws onto the wagon a bag full of quilting pieces in spite of the father's baleful glance, declaring that she "aims to sit on them." Even after the log cabin is built, it doesn't seem like home, and it's not—until, after the father has been away hunting and the cold and storm eats at the chinks between the logs, the quilt pieces are used to stuff the cracks. This warms the cabin physically and visually. The illustrations are particularly informative and effective.

★ ★ ★ Pryor, Bonnie **Lottie's Dream** Simon & Schuster, 1992 ISBN 0 671 74774 6, illustrated by Mark Graham

Lottie, a little girl living in Kentucky, yearns to see the ocean, only to find that her family is planning to move even farther away, to the prairies of Kansas. They travel there by covered wagon, sharing the work of the trip and the work on the farm they build there. Lottie sees the ocean with her young husband, Ben, and wants to stay there, but they move on. Many years later, widowed, with children grown, Lottie buys a run-down cottage on the shore of Maine where her grandchildren come to vacation with her. This picture book shows the sweep of time, among other things.

★ ★ ★ Turner, Ann **Mississippi Mud** HarperCollins, 1997 ISBN 0 06 024432 1, illustrated by Robert J. Blake
See above.

★ ★ Van Leeuwen, Jean **Going West** Dial, 1992 ISBN 0 8037 1028 3, with illustrations by Thomas B. Allen

The illustrator uses striking charcoal and pastels to tell of the journey by covered wagon and arrival on the lonely prairie from the point of view of Hannah, a seven-year-old girl.

★ ★ Williams, David **Grandma Essie's Covered Wagon** Knopf, 1993 ISBN 0 679 80253 3, with illustrations by Wiktor Sadowski

This picture book is based on the memories of the author's grandmother. It tells of several journeys by covered wagon, from Missouri to Kansas, from Kansas to Oklahoma, and finally, from Oklahoma back to Missouri. The time setting for these travels, the early part of the twentieth century, is later than in some of the other books.

▶ **Novels**

★ ★ ★ ★ Conrad, Pam **Prairie Songs** HarperCollins, 1987 ISBN 0 06 440206 1

This is a very good and nonromantic vision of the life on the prairie for early settlers. Louisa loves the prairie and so does her father. Her mother seems at least to have adjusted to it. When the Doctor and Mrs. Berryman arrive to set up a home nearby, they are welcomed, but Mrs. Berryman faints when she sees the sod hut she will live in. Louisa tries to get her to see the beauty of the prairie, but Emmeline Berryman misses the city and its refinements. The life of the pioneers in Nebraska Territory proves to be too much for the physically and emotionally fragile woman. This book goes hand in hand with the author's nonfiction work **Prairie Visions** (see below).

★ ★ Holland, Isabelle **The Journey Home** Scholastic, 1990 ISBN 0 590 43110 2

This is an orphan train story. Maggie and her sister are adopted by a Kansas couple, but Maggie has a hard time facing the rigors of farm life, and the anti-Catholicism of her new home and neighbors. Gradually, she comes to love the prairie despite all its hardship. This book goes deeper and is stronger than many of the "orphan train" books.

★ ★ ★ Howard, Ellen **The Chickenhouse House** Atheneum, 1991 ISBN 0 689 31695 X

The story is based on one told by the author's aunt. Alena, whose family moves into the chicken house while waiting for their prairie home to be completed, is vexed by the lack of space and convenience until they move into their completed home. Suddenly, the closeness of the chicken house seems warmer and less lonely than the new one.

★ ★ ★ Lasky, Kathryn **Beyond the Divide** Aladdin, 1983 ISBN 0 689 80163 7

This is a much lengthier and more complicated novel than many on this list. Meribah Simon leaves her Amish family and community at the same time that her father does to seek a life beyond those confines. The descriptions of becoming members of a wagon train heading to California as part of the gold rush contains copious detail and information. Departing from St. Joseph, Meribah's father has desirable skills and earns much respect from their fellow travelers. Meribah, regarded as quaint and innocent, also gains a measure of respect until another teenager is raped by two men of the group and is shunned by the others. Meribah and her father befriend her, but it's not enough to avert another tragedy. When her father is injured, the wagon train goes on without them and they become victims of cruelty. Villains and heroes merge and exchange roles as the thirst for gold takes over. After the death of her father, Meribah learns to survive alone during a harsh winter in the Sierras, and is befriended at last by a young woman whose nation will also be eliminated eventually.

★ ★ Magorian, Jim **Keeper of Fire** Council for Indian Education, 1984 ISBN 0 9992 088 8

This gives a Native American point of view of the aftermath of the Battle of Little Bighorn. The Indians are fleeing west and north to Canada, hoping to escape the white man's wrath, which they know will be considerable after such a defeat. Shanni, a young hunter who is in training as a spiritual counselor of the nation, has lost his father in the battle, and he himself has been wounded and separated from his people in a later skirmish. Now, using his considerable survival and tracking skills, Shanni is trying to evade white soldiers and find his ever-moving nation.

Paulsen, Gary
★ ★ ★ **Call Me Francis Tucket** Delacorte, 1995 ISBN 0 385 32116 3
★ ★ ★ **Mr. Tucket** Bantam, 1995 ISBN 0 440 42233 5
★ ★ ★ **Tucket's Ride** Delacorte, 1997 ISBN 0 385 32199 6

Paulsen has written a series of short, somewhat humorous books about Francis Tucket, a young boy who gets separated from his wagon train on the trip west. While these books are not heavy in facts, they are pleasant reading and their accessibility to less able readers makes them valuable additions to the theme.

★ ★ ★ ★ Woodruff, Elvira **Dear Levi: Letters from the Overland Trail** Knopf, 1994 ISBN 0 679 84641 7

Taken from the diaries of people who actually made the journey, this book has more factual information than the "Tucket" books. However, the characterization is strong and the conflicts are well-presented.

Poetry
★ ★ ★ ★ Turner, Ann **Grass Songs** Harcourt, 1993 ISBN 0 15 136788 4

Ann Turner has used excerpts from diaries of women who traveled west by covered wagon as the basis of 17 poems in this book. The women she depicts have different feelings about the arduous life on the Plains. One or two revel in the freedom it gives, but most detail the heartbreak and hardships. This poetic look at the time and the women may give students a more intimate look at the time and events.

▶ Nonfiction

★ ★ ★ Axelrod, Alan **Songs of the Wild West** Metropolitan Museum of Art, Simon & Schuster, 1991 ISBN 0-671-74775-4

Axelrod uses paintings and statues from the museum and the words and music of popular songs from cowboys, outlaws, prospectors, gunfighters, railroad workers, and sodbusters. This book is a valuable source of information about the days of the old West, and a treasure of activities.

★ ★ ★ ★ Conrad, Pam **Prairie Visions: The Life and Times of Solomon Butcher** HarperCollins, 1991 ISBN 0 06 021373 6

This book provides factual background for her novel *Prairie Songs* (see above). Solomon Butcher was an itinerant photographer and sometime con-man in the late 1800s. He traveled the prairie in Nebraska Territory, taking photographs of pioneer families outside their sod homes. Many of his photographs are here, together with Pam Conrad's comments about what can be seen in them, and they add reality to the faces of the people on the prairie.

Fisher, Leonard Everett
★ **The Oregon Trail** Holiday House, 1990 ISBN 0 8234 0833 7
★ **The Railroads** Holiday House, 1979 ISBN 0 8234 0352 1

These two books give ample illustration and vivid accounts of the history of the time.

★ ★ ★ Freedman, Russell **Cowboys of the Wild West** Clarion, 1985 ISBN 0 395 54800 4

The book is amply illustrated with black-and-white photographs. It attempts to dispel some of the myths about cowboys while giving us information about their lives, tools, and work. Concentrating on a 30-year period, from right after the Civil War to the invention of barbed wire, which changed the work and life of cowboys forever, the author points out that many of the cowboys were black (freed slaves) and Hispanic workers.

★ ★ ★ Freedman, Russell **The Life and Death of Crazy Horse** Holiday House, 1996 ISBN 0 8234 1219 9

Here is the well-told story of the solitary Oglala Sioux whose vision and wisdom combined with his military prowess to make him a figure of great renown. Freedman uses black-and-white Sioux drawings to illustrate this careful and balanced account.

★ Katz, William **The Westward Movement & Abolitionism** Raintree/Steck-Vaughn, 1993 ISBN 0 8114 6276 5

This is more challenging and centers around the American idea of manifest destiny.

★ ★ ★ Lavender, David **Snowbound: The Tragic Story of the Donner Party** Holiday House, 1996 ISBN 0 8234 1231 8

This book brings to life the tragic story of the group who tried to take the shortcut to California. Emphasis is given to the fact that the leaders were naively following the explicit and wrong directions in a guidebook in spite of advice from other travelers. The cannibalism which the survivors resorted to is treated matter-of-factly, and the account is the fullest one I've seen in children's literature.

★ ★ Levine, Ellen **If You Traveled West in a Covered Wagon** Scholastic, 1986 ISBN 0 590 42229 4

This uses simple text and follows a question-and-answer format. More than the other books in this section, the focus is on the day-to-day aspects of travel. It should prove a valuable source of information for role-playing as well as other research.

Rounds, Glen
★ ★ **The Prairie Schooners** Holiday, 1968 ISBN 0 8234 1086 2
★ ★ ★ ★ **Sod Houses on the Great Plains** Holiday House, 1995 ISBN 0 8234 1162 1

These two light but very informative picture books offer easily accessible information on the subjects.

★ Shellenberger, Robert **Wagons West: Trail Tales 1848** Heritage West, 1991 ISBN 0 9623048 3 2

This book helps to personalize the events as it uses short stories and anecdotes taken from diaries and journals.

★ Smith-Baranzini, Marlene, and Howard Egger-Bovet Brown Paper School **U.S. Kids History: Book of the New American Nation** Little Brown, 1995 ISBN 0 316 22206 2

This book covers the time period in a conversational tone with effective sidebar information.

★ Steele, Phillip **Little Bighorn** Simon, 1992 ISBN 0 02 786885 0

Steele concentrates on the battle, but gives the background of treaties broken, and folly on the part of Custer.

★ Stein, Conrad R. **The Story of the Homestead Act** Childrens, 1978 ISBN 0 516 046160

This will provide readers with the details and provisions of the act that, more than any other, caused the push westward.

★ Toynton, Evelyn **Growing Up in America: 1830 to 1860** Millbrook, 1995 ISBN 1 56294 453 3

This photo essay centers on the children growing up in various venues during this time period. The section on Sioux children is particularly useful.

CHAPTER 3

Native Americans

➤ COMMENTS

The depiction of Native Americans in children's literature has varied widely in quality and accuracy. A study of the way in which that literature has reflected the changes in non-native views of Native Americans is one way in which history and literature can work together. A soon to be reissued book that is a very good source for information about the treatment of Native Americans in children's literature is **Books Without Bias: Through Indian Eyes** by Beverly Slapin and Doris Seale.

A Native American theme can also take the form of using the good literature by and about Indians, and can also take a more conventional approach.

Perhaps a word of caution belongs here before we immerse ourselves in this theme. The subject of Native American oppression is and should be a very emotional one to investigate. Students and teachers alike may need help handling some of the information that such an investigation turns up. It's important that teachers be aware of this and provide opportunities for students to talk and write about the experiences, or even to receive counseling if the need arises. Offering students a variety of ways in which to express their feelings is very important with this theme. Suggest writing, music, and art activities as possible

ways to deal with the subject. The Internet is a good source for ways in which this has been done by others.

➤ PICTURE BOOK STARTER

James Whetung and Paul Morin's picture book, **The Vision Seeker** (Stoddart, 1997 ISBN 0 7737 2966 6), is a good one to start this theme because it deals with the values of one people, the Anishinaabe Indians. The young boy who goes on a vision quest does so during a time when inter-tribal warfare has brought the Anishinaabe to a terrible state. He is given four grains of corn by his parents and told to go to the high place to seek a vision to help his people. There, after going without food and water for several days, he sees a lodge, inside of which are seven grandfathers each wearing his white hair in a different style. Each rubs the child with water from a sacred bowl and gives him a special gift: knowledge, love, honesty, strength, bravery, respect, or humility. The boy returns to his people to share his vision, each part of which is now incorporated into the sweat lodge ceremony.

This picture book is useful for our purposes because it addresses a specific Indian nation instead of being a generic story. The idea that Indians made war upon each other may be one worth discussing here, and the vision quest so described has parallels in many religions.

◢ ACTIVITIES

After sharing this book, questions such as, "What did you notice here?" and "What new information did you find?" may help to get some sense of inquiry started.

In our schools, we have often made the mistake of teaching about the Native Americans as if they were all one culture instead of investigating the diversity among nations. We have also left the impression with some students that Native American cultures have ceased to exist. To begin to chip away at this misinformation, start a list of Native American nations as you encounter them in the reading and research of this theme. Under each, list information about that specific group of people: location before and after the Europeans came, customs, beliefs, famous leaders, etc.

Many books about Indians written for children and young adults have been criticized for various reasons. For instance, Susan Jeffers' **Brother Eagle, Sister Sky** (Dial, 1991 ISBN 0 8037 0963 3), a picture book which purports to be the words of Chief Seattle, is often criticized by Native Americans and others. Find out what the controversy is and decide what you think should be done about the book. Look at other picture books such as those about Indian Two Feet and Little Runner. How do you think such books influence our perceptions of Native Americans?

Look at the Disney movie **Pocahontas**. If you knew nothing else about Native Americans and about Pocahontas, what would you know or think you knew after seeing this movie? Look at other movies with the same questions in mind.

Have a formal debate over the question of traitorous behavior on the part of Pocahontas,

Squanto, or Sacajewea, given that they all helped the European settlers. Did they therefore betray their various Indian nations?

In several of the novels listed below, young adults are asked to choose between an adopted Indian culture and their native white culture, or vice versa. Compare these books as to their depiction of both cultures. Do they do it fairly? Is there a conscious or unconscious attempt on the part of the author to paint one culture as more desirable than the other? What effect does this have on your perception of that culture?

Role-play some of the characters from the novels listed below, both Indian and non-Indian, telling what a relationship with the other culture did to their lives.

Students might like to investigate Native American authors. Who are they? Why are there so few of them? What are Native American nations attempting to do about this?

Bring in and read some of the Native American folktales and make a list of the values they seem to be stressing. Compare them to some European folktales.

Suggest that students form small groups to investigate one Native American nation's customs, folklore, and history, and then find an interesting way to transmit that information to the rest of the class.

Find out how many Native Americans were thought to be living in North America before 1620. Compare that figure with the most recent statistics.

Find a map showing the Indian tribal locations before the European conquest and trace their removal to other lands.

Find and read as many treaties made between Native Americans and the United States government as possible. Keep a list of promises made, broken, and kept. Speculate on what might have happened in American history if those promises had been kept.

Find quotes by various Native Americans that hold some meaning for you. Find a way to use art and calligraphy to present those quotes to the rest of the class.

Find out what the Bureau of Indian Affairs schools did and are doing to the Native American cultures.

Find out about the contributions of Native Americans in the wars since their conquest.

Find and read about Native Americans in a history textbook from the 1800s. Compare it with a modern history book's treatment of the same subject. What caused the changes?

Correspond with one or more of the Native American nations. Find out as much as you can about their current projects and problems. Set up an e-mail or snail mail correspondence with students living on various reservations.

What has gambling done to or for Native American nations today? Do you approve? Why or why not?

BOOK LIST

▶ Picture Books

★ ★ De Coteau Orie, Sandra **Did You Hear Wind Sing Your Name? An Oneida Song of Spring** Walker, 1995 ISBN 0 8027 8350 3, illustrated by Christopher Canyon

This is a beautiful book which poetically shouts the joy of nature.

★ ★ ★ ★ Goble, Paul **Beyond the Ridge** Simon & Schuster, 1992 ISBN 0 02 736581 6

The theme in this picture book is the Plains Indian view of death. An old woman is dying, and her unseen spirit leaves her body and begins a journey up to the ridge where voices from the next world call to her.

★ ★ ★ Goble, Paul **Buffalo Woman** Simon & schuster, 1981 ISBN 0 02 737720 2

In this story from the Plains Indians, a young hunter sees a buffalo transformed into a beautiful woman. They marry and have a son, Calf Boy, but her husband's people mistreat the woman, so she runs away with her son. Twice, on her journey back to her own people, her husband catches up with her, but both the son and wife warn him to stay back. He pursues them and must fight with an old bull in order to be taken into the Buffalo nation with his wife and child.

★ ★ ★ Martin, Rafe **The Rough-Face Girl** Putnam, 1989 ISBN 0 399 21859 9 illustrated by David Shannon

This is an Algonquin Cinderella story in which the "prince" is an invisible being who will only marry a woman who can see him. The abused youngest daughter of a poor man sees and describes him after her proud older sisters fail.

★ ★ Stroud, Virginia A. **Doesn't Fall Off His Horse** Dial, 1991 ISBN 0 8037 1634 6

Grandfather tells a child the story of how he earned his Indian name. In the course of the telling, we learn of counting coup, the ethics of the Kiowa people, and men's and women's roles in that society.

★ ★ Van Laan, Nancy **In a Circle Long Ago** Apple Soup, 1992 ISBN 0 679 85807 5

There is no shortage of Native American folktale books, but this collection of tales from several Native American cultures is particularly useful and well done. They represent many cultures, and are told simply and interestingly.

★ ★ ★ Whetung, James **The Vision Seeker** Stoddart, 1997 ISBN 0 7737 2966 6, illustrated by Paul Morin See above.

Novels

★ ★ Byars, Betsy **Trouble River** Viking, 1970 ISBN 0 670 73257 5

In this historical novel, the Indians are the enemy and the attackers. Twelve-year-old Dewey Martin has been left at the family's remote cabin on the prairie with his cranky grandmother while his parents go to a town to get better care when the new baby is born. The Indians attack, and Dewey's only hope is that the raft he built for fun will carry him and his grandmother down Trouble River to safety. The river presents one challenge and Grandma presents another as, perched in the middle of the raft on her rocking chair, no less, she complains and commands.

★ ★ ★ ★ DeFelice, Cynthia **Weasel** Simon & Schuster, 1991 ISBN 0 02 726457 2

This book explores the concepts of evil, guilt, and the need for revenge as carried out in frontier Ohio. Nathan Fowler and his sister are alone in the cabin when Ezra, a mute Indian, arrives and beckons them to follow him into the wilderness at night. With trepidation, they follow him and find their wounded father. Nathan is brought face to face with evil in the person of Weasel, an ex-Indian fighter. It is Weasel who cut out Ezra's tongue, although they had once been, if not friends, at least allies. Later, when Nathan has a chance and even a cause to kill Weasel, he does not, and this choice returns to haunt him.

★ ★ ★ Dorris, Michael **Guests** Hyperion, 1996 ISBN 0 7868 0047 X

Moss is angry with his father's invitation for the strangers to share their harvest feast and so runs into the forest, pretending to himself that it is his "Away Time," part of the manhood rites in his culture. After encountering another runaway, Trouble, Moss decides to begin his "Away Time" in reality, surviving alone in the forest. He's away only for a day, but believes he may have received advice from a porcupine, and when Trouble reappears, she helps him find his way home in time for the feast where strangers are behaving badly. They are obviously the new white settlers whose presence make Moss's difficulties more poignant. The story Moss's father tells at the feast is quite beautiful.

★ ★ ★ ★ Dorris, Michael **Morning Girl** Hyperion, 1991 ISBN 1 56282 284 5

Morning Girl, a Taino Indian, wakes early every morning. Star Boy, her younger brother, is up late into the night exploring the island and gazing at the stars. She feels her life would be blissful tranquility if only it weren't for her brother's loud and obnoxious ways. Then, when their mother miscarries, Morning Girl sees her brother's pain and fear, and discovers how close they really are. A dangerous storm and Star Boy's humiliation for his misbehaviour in front of the other islanders brings out the protectiveness in Morning Girl, and she receives a new name from her brother: The One Who Stands Beside. Always looming throughout this gentle book is the reader's knowledge that Christopher Columbus is coming, and the children's lives are about to change.

★ ★ ★ ★ Dorris, Michael **Sees Behind Trees** Hyperion, 1996 ISBN 0 7868 0224 3
This is a focus book (see page 163).

★ ★ ★ Finley, Mary **Peace Soaring Eagle** Simon & Schuster, 1991 ISBN 0 671 5598 6

Julio accompanies his Mexican adopted father to Bent's Fort, Colorado, in 1845. When his father is killed by Apache, the injured Julio is taken in by Cheyennes. Although he was raised as a Catholic, a vision quest helps him recall and recapture his early life, but he cannot fully accept the Cheyenne Way, either. The book divulges much information about the time and the Cheyenne culture.

★ ★ ★ Gardiner, John R. **Stone Fox** HarperCollins, 1979 ISBN 0 690 03983 2

Many readers will have encountered this book earlier, but for those who have not, it is an easily read, short, and exciting book. We get a dog race between two main contestants, and the reader really wants each of them to win. Little Willy wants the prize money to save his grandfather's farm. Stone Fox wants the prize money to buy back the land that has been taken away from his people. Searchlight, Willy's dog, races so hard his heart gives out, and Stone Fox becomes a hero rather than a rival for Little Willy in this touching story.

★ ★ George, Jean Craighead **The Talking Earth** HarperCollins, 1981 ISBN 0 06 440212 6

Billie has rejected her Seminole heritage and is attending school at the Kennedy Space Center. Sentenced by the elders to spend time alone in the Everglades, Billie begins to understand her people's reverence for life as she adopts an otter, a baby panther, and a turtle. From them, as well as from the other animals and the plants that she must now depend on for survival, Billie learns about the pollution of the Everglades and, indeed, of the entire earth.

★ ★ ★ ★ Hill, Kirkpatrick **Toughboy & Sister** McElderry, 1983 ISBN 0 689 59595 x

An Athabascan Indian brother and sister are forced to cope, alone, with the unforgiving environment of an isolated spot on the Yukon River, accompanied only by the memories from past years of watching their mother and father at work in the same fishing spot. The pot latch after their mother's death, the role of the women in that culture in deciding many big issues, the taciturn way of communicating feelings, and many of the foods and tools used in the story provide some solid information about the culture.

★ ★ ★ ★ Hudson, Jan **Sweetgrass** Philomel, 1984 ISBN 0 399 21721 5

Sweetgrass is a Blackfoot girl who is now 15, which is old to be single in her culture. Her father will not let her marry the man she loves because, he says, she is not yet mature enough. When smallpox strikes the people, it is Sweetgrass who becomes the strong one in the family. The story takes place in 1837, before the extensive use of guns and horses by the Blackfoot nation.

★ ★ ★ Keehn, Sally M. **I Am Regina** Philomel, 1991 ISBN 0 399 21797 5

This absorbing novel is set in 1755 as the French and Indian War begins. Ten-year-old Regina is taken by Indians from her family's home in central Pennsylvania. Her father and her brother, Christian, are killed and scalped in the attack. Regina and her older sister, Barbara, are captured but taken to different groups. Regina struggles to hold on to memories of her earlier life as she grows up under the name of Tskinak and starts to become an Indian herself.

★ ★ Magorian, James **Keeper of Fire** Council for Indian Affairs, 1984 ISBN 0 89992 088 8

The events that occurred after Custer's Last Stand are recounted from the Native American point of view. Shanni, a young hunter, is training to become the spiritual head of the nation and has been wounded in the battle. He seeks to find his people as they retreat to Canada to escape the soldiers who pursue them.

★ ★ ★ O'Dell, Scott **Sing Down to the Moon** Laurel Leaf, 1989 ISBN 0 440 40673

Bright Morning and her friend, Running Bird, are first captured by slave traders. When they escape their captors and return to their village, they find it being destroyed by the white men. Their whole nation is taken on a forced march to Fort Sumter, where they are held as prisoners for two years. With her friend Tall Boy, Bright Morning escapes these captors to return to her tribal canyon lands.

★ ★ ★ Richter, Conrad **The Light in the Forest** Fawcett, 1994 ISBN 0 440 70437 8

John Butler was taken from his family by a group of Lenape Indians when he was four years old. Adopted into the tribe by the great warrior Cuyloga, he was renamed True Son. After living his life with his adopted people, True Son learns of a treaty which has decreed that all white captives be returned to their own people. Who are his?

★ ★ ★ Rinaldi, Ann **Broken Days** Scholastic, 1997 ISBN 0 590 46053 6

This is the second in Rinaldi's Quilt Trilogy novels and is set in the days just prior to the War of 1812. Walking Breeze is the child of a Shawnee man and Thankful Chelmsford. Prior to age 14, she grew up in the Shawnee village of her father's people, but when her mother dies, she is relocated to Salem and her mother's relations. There, she must deal with the conflict of cultures, but she must also deal with her cousin's charge that she is not her mother's daughter.

★ ★ ★ Rinaldi, Ann **The Second Bend in the River** Scholastic, 1997 ISBN 0 590 74258 2

Tecumseh, the great Indian educator and linguist, has been a friend of Rebecca Galloway's Ohio family for years, and she is in love with him. When she is old enough to make the choice of the man and the culture she wants to spend her life with, it breaks at least two hearts.

★ ★ ★ Speare, Elizabeth George **The Sign of the Beaver** Dell, 1983 ISBN 0 440 47900 2

Set in 1768 in what was to become the state of Maine, we find Matt Hallowell, who has been left behind by his father in their new wilderness home while his father goes back to Massachusetts to get the rest of the family. Soon Matt gets into such difficulties that his survival is doubtful. Rescued by an Indian chief, Matt is asked to teach the chief's unwilling grandson, Attean, how to read.

★ ★ ★ Wunderli, Stephen **The Blue Between the Clouds** Holt, 1996 ISBN 0 8050 4819 7

Matt and Two Moons are best friends, and this book is a celebration of their friendship. Two Moon's parents are dead, and his sister wants him to live with her in Bozeman, Montana, but his grandfather, who lives on the reservation, has decreed that Two Moons can stay with Matt and his family for a while. Perhaps because both boys know their living arrangement is temporary, they thoroughly enjoy and understand each other. Both are determined to fly, and manage to do so, amazingly, with the help of a disturbed World War I veteran.

Nonfiction

★ ★ Arnold, Caroline **The Ancient Cliff Dwellers of Mesa Verde** Clarion, 1990 ISBN 0 395 56241 4

This is a good source for information on the Anasazi Indians who inhabited the mesas and cliffs of southwestern Colorado and northern Nevada. The illustrations are photographs of the Mesa Verde National Park and include interiors and exteriors of the pueblos. The text, which creates life in the early 12th century, is scrupulously accurate.

★ ★ ★ Ashabranner, Brent **A Strange & Distant Shore** Penguin, 1988 ISBN 0 525 65201 9

This account of the relocation of 75 Indians from their home in Oklahoma to an army fort at St. Augustine, Florida, gives us both a hero and a villain in a tale of hardship and cruelty. The relocation was ordered by General Philip Henry Sheridan, a man who believed the Indians were in the way of the development of Oklahoma. The man who was ordered to supervise the train trip and the relocation, Captain Richard Pratt, was a man of more compassion. Helpless to prevent most of the misery, he gave the Indians art supplies and encouraged them to paint out their rage. The resulting art work is part of the book's illustration.

★ ★ ★ Bruchac, Joseph **Lasting Echoes** Harcourt, 1998 ISBN 0 15 201327 X, illustrated by Paul Morin

In a style similar to that of Lester's To Be a Slave (see page 12), Bruchac intersperses direct quotes with narrative in order to tell the Native American's view of U.S. history. He covers seven generations of Native Americans, after citing the traditional view that we are in the middle of seven generations and so can know personally the three generations before us and the three generations after us. This is a valuable look at events we have usually seen from a different side.

★ ★ Freedman, Russell **Buffalo Hunt** Holiday House, 1983 ISBN 0 8234 0702

Freedman uses paintings and photographs liberally in his exploration and explanation of the role of the buffalo in the life of the Plains Indians prior to the settlers' annihilation of the herds. The rhythm of the herds became the rhythm of the Indians' lives, and they used every bit of the buffalo carcass in some way. Freedman shows the preparations, both physical and spiritual, for the hunt, as well as the celebrations and utilization of parts after the hunt.

★ ★ ★ Freedman, Russell **Indian Chiefs** Holiday House, 1993 ISBN 0 8234 0625

Freedman has selected six chiefs, each from a different nation, to show how these leaders reacted to the coming of the settlers. As always with a Freedman book, we get ample photographs, paintings, and maps. An introductory chapter gives an overview of the conflicting cultures of the 19th century, especially concerning the concept of ownership of land and other values.

★ ★ ★ Freedman, Russell **An Indian Winter** Holiday House, 1985 ISBN 0 8234 0930 9 with paintings by Karl Bodmer

The text and illustrations in this book are largely from a study that was made in 1833 by the German Prince Maximilian of Wied and the artist Karl Bodmer. Spending the winter with the Mandan Indians in what is now North Dakota, Maximilian took copious notes in his journals and later produced a book on the subject. Freedman uses Bodmer's paintings and self-portraits by Mandans of the time to explore the experience shared by Maximilian, Bodmer, and the Mandans with a clear narrative.

★ ★ ★ Freedman, Russell **The Life and Death of Crazy Horse** Holiday House, 1985 ISBN 0 8234 1219 9, illustrated by Amos Bad Heart Bull

In this biography, Freedman uses the work of one Native American artist for all the illustrations instead of his usual use of photographs and paintings. He tells us of Crazy Horse's life and death as well as the actions and reactions of many Native American chiefs as the white civilization moved inexorably westward.

★ ★ ★ Fritz, Jean **The Double Life of Pocahontas** Puffin, 1987 ISBN 0 14 032257 4

The controversial figure of Pocahontas is the subject of this biography. Fritz has been accused of using too much unsubstantiated information in this book. The story of Powhatan's daughter, who was caught between two cultures, is a fascinating one, however.

★ ★ ★ Goble, Paul **Death of the Iron Horse** Bradbury, 1971 ISBN 0 02 737830 6

In 1867, a small group of Cheyennes attacked and raided a Union Pacific train, spurred on by a prophet's dream that the plundering of the earth would follow the arrival of the white man. This sole incident in U.S. history in which Native Americans attacked and robbed a train is told from the Cheyenne point of view.

★ ★ Greenberg, Judith E. **A Pioneer Woman's Memoir** Watts, 1990 ISBN 0 531 11211 X

Edited by her children and grandchildren, this is the journal of Arabella Clemens, who traveled to Oregon in 1864 with her family. The immediacy of the account makes it compelling reading, but be aware that it reflects the perspective of a woman whose views on slavery and on Native Americans will need to be talked about with the readers.

★ ★ ★ Marrin, Albert **Cowboys, Indians & Gunfighters**
Simon & Schuster, 1992 ISBN 0 689 31774 3

Marrin spares the reader little violence as he depicts the development of the Plains with an accent on the cattle business. The massacres and atrocities committed by settlers and Indians are detailed, as is the slaughter of the buffalo. The work and habits of the cowboys are described, as are the lives of some of the more notorious cowboys.

★ ★ Philip, Neil **Earth Always Endures: Native American Poems** Viking, 1996 ISBN 0 670 86873 6

First of all, there are the photographs–beautiful portraits, for the most part, which speak clearly about dignity and heritage. The poems, taken from the traditions of many nations, are well chosen and are arranged to cover a full day, from dawn to dawn.

★ ★ ★ Philip, Neil **In a Sacred Manner I Live** Clarion, 1996 ISBN 0 395 84981

This is a beautiful book of black-and-white photographs and moving speeches by many great Native Americans. The first quote is Bear Eagle's title quote from 1907. The last is the prayer of Frank Fools Crow, the first Native American to offer the opening prayer for the United States Senate in 1975. In between we get quotes by the famous, Chief Joseph, Geronimo, Black Elk, and Sitting Bull among many others, and the relatively unknown, such as Torlino and Young Bull. Most of the time the photograph is of the speaker, and the faces tell as much as the words do. The words, of course, are masterful and full of beauty as well as wisdom. This is a book to cherish.

★ ★ ★ Sewall, Marcia **People of the Breaking Day**
Atheneum, 1979 ISBN 0 689 31407 8

In this beautiful picture book, the Wampanoags, who lived in the Plymouth area before the arrival of the Pilgrims, are the focus. A member of the nation tells us of the ceremonies and customs that mark the passages of life from birth to death of these people who lived in harmony with nature under the guidance and wisdom of Massasoit, just before the coming clash of cultures.

★ ★ ★ Sewall, Marcia **Thunder from the Clear Sky**
Atheneum, 1995 ISBN 0 689 31775 1

This picture book deals with the outbreak of hostility between the first settlers in Plymouth and the Native Americans there.

Sneve, Virginia Driving Hawk
★ ★ ★ ★ **The Apaches** ISBN 0 8234 1287 3
★ ★ ★ ★ **The Cherokees** ISBN 0 8234 1214 8
★ ★ ★ ★ **The Cheyennes** ISBN 0 823 41250 4
★ ★ ★ ★ **The Hopis** ISBN 0 8234 1194 X
★ ★ ★ ★ **The Iroquois** ISBN 0 8234 1163 X
★ ★ ★ ★ **The Navajos** ISBN 0 823 41039 0
★ ★ ★ ★ **The Nez Perce** ISBN 0 8234 1090 0
★ ★ ★ ★ **The Seminoles** ISBN 0 823 41112 5
★ ★ ★ ★ **The Sioux** ISBN 0 823 41017

This is an excellent series of books all illustrated by Ronald Himler and published by Holiday House. Each picture book gives a short creation story taken from that culture, and gives information about the nation's customs and beliefs then and now.

★ ★ ★ ★ Ziner, Feenie **Squanto** Linnet, 1989 ISBN 0 208 02274 0

This book is based mostly on historical fact with conversations supplied, and with some sketchy details filled in, by the author's imagination. It supplies much background information on this amazing man and on the people with whom he came in contact. Ziner succeeds in creating people of substance for whom we care deeply. Twice captured through treachery and transported to Europe, once to England and later as a slave to Spain, four times crossing an ocean that few in his time had ever crossed, Squanto led a life that would have broken most people. His role in the Pilgrims' survival occupies little space in this book, most of which is devoted to his life before coming to the Pilgrims. This book provides one rationale for the reasons why he helped the Pilgrims and introduces the concept of destiny.

Internet Connections
Visit these Web sites for further information about Indian captives:

http://www.rootsweb.com/~indian/index.htm is a searchable index of people taken prisoner by Indians during the Colonial years. The stories of their capture and their lives after that are included for many.

http://ps.superb.net/malec/homepage.htm contains stories about the capture, release, or escape of many people taken prisoner by Native Americans during the French and Indian Wars. There are also links to related sites.

http://www.nativeweb.org/ is a good general site on Native Americans, offering many links to other informational materials.

CHAPTER 4

The Holocaust

> COMMENTS

A study of the Holocaust makes a good theme for middle school students because of its obvious connection to history, because much good material on the Holocaust is available for students in the middle grades, and because, of course, we must never forget. In some states, it is a required part of the curriculum. It is also a subject wherein most of the reading is in nonfiction material. Indeed, that genre often outstrips the available fiction in drama and emotion. This enables discussion about primary and secondary sources, as well as a contrast between fiction and nonfiction.

Many schools have used **The Diary of Anne Frank** as a central book for this theme, and it makes a good one. First, Anne's age makes her an accessible contact for young readers, and the well-written diary allows us to slowly become immersed in her world and to witness the horror of her story.

Again, a word of caution belongs here before we immerse ourselves in this theme. The subject of the Holocaust is and should be a very emotional one to investigate. Students and teachers alike may need help handling some of the information that such an investigation turns up. It's important that teachers be aware of this and provide opportunities for students to talk and write about the experiences,

or even to receive counseling if the need arises. Offering students a variety of ways in which to express their feelings is very important with this theme. Suggest writing, music, and art activities as possible ways to deal with the subject. The Internet is a good source for ways in which this has been done by others.

A study of the Holocaust can take many directions, and students should be allowed as much choice as possible in the directions they take. The larger picture can be gained by looking at the causes and effects of World War II. We can gain a similarly larger perspective by looking at anti-Semitism historically. Students can read and compare individual accounts of the Holocaust survivors, or look at the statistics and the results of the master plan of genocide. The attempted genocide of the Jews can be compared with that of the American Indian and with the more current wars in Bosnia.

If individual divergence becomes difficult to keep track of, students can submit research and reading plans to the class, and group decisions can be made as to how their material can best be shared.

> PICTURE BOOK STARTER

Rose Blanche, by Christopher Gallaz and Roberto Innocenti (Harcourt, 1985 ISBN 0 15 200917 5), is a very affecting book. Beautifully illustrated, it tells the story of Rose Blanche, a young girl in a small town in Germany, who is relatively untouched by the presence of Nazis, their trucks, guns, and tanks, except to watch them curiously. One day she sees a little boy jump from the back of one of those trucks and attempt to run away, only to be turned over by the mayor of the town, who wears a Nazi armband, to the soldiers who thank him and drive away with the boy. Unnoticed, Rose Blanche follows the tracks of the truck to the outskirts of town where she discovers children behind electrified barbed wire. She gives them the only food she has—a bit of bread. After that, Rose Blanche grows thinner—in fact only Mayor remains fat—because she carries as much food as she can to the children behind the wires. Then, one day the people and soldiers flee the city and Rose Blanche walks alone in the fog to the camp only to find it empty. The last shot from a fleeing soldier kills Rose Blanche. This is a tragic story, and the translated text makes the words seem flat and, strangely, more effective.

▷ ACTIVITIES

In Ruth Sender's book **The Cage**, reference is made to the secret library of the Lodz Ghetto which the family hid in their home. Students might like to consider the reasons why the Nazis were burning books and controlling access to them in the light of censorship issues of today.

Go from there to other things censored by the Nazis: music and art.

Work with the numbers. Find population figures for the numbers of Jews in various European countries before and after the Holocaust.

How did the Nazis build that much hate? Investigate the propaganda methods used at the time.

What did the Nazis think they were going to accomplish by getting rid of all the Jews? Could they have accomplished it?

Read Lois Lowry's **The Giver** (see page 180), in which the importance of a society's memories of the past are key. Use it in a discussion about the importance of the phrase "Never forget" as applied to the Holocaust.

What's the difference between Holocaust and Pogrom? Is this the only Holocaust?

Compare the Holocaust to current genocide attempts in the world not only as to method, but as to the reaction of other countries then and now.

How did the survivors stay sane, and how was sanity maintained even among the inmates who did not survive?

Compare the propaganda of the Holocaust to that of the McCarthy era in the United States. Also compare the people who protested both events.

Find out what the criteria were for Jewishness in Nazi Germany.

Make a series of cause and effect graphs about the Holocaust. For instance:

CAUSE	EFFECT
Because of the Treaty of Versailles, Germany had to pay reparations for damages to civilians in World War I,	Germany was impoverished in the 1930s.
Because Germans were impoverished in the 1930s,	They were looking for a scapegoat.
Because they were looking for a scapegoat...	

Students could begin to locate Holocaust survivors in their communities to interview and to ask them to share some of their memories with the class.

Since interviewing is not a skill with which many students feel comfortable, some advance preparation will be necessary. Students can practice interviewing each other, perhaps using a technique described by Linda Rief in her book **Seeking Diversity**. In effect, she asks students to choose a person in class about whom you know the least and, before approaching them, write down five questions to ask that person in order to get to know them better. Ask the questions and record the answers. Then retreat to look over the answers to see what appeared that you didn't expect or that you find interesting and want to know more about. Write five more questions based on that one thing from the earlier interview. Ask the questions and record the answers, this time trying to note direct quotes and significant words that show that person's unique qualities. Note body language and tone as well as spoken words. I've found it useful to ask students to retreat once more to compose and ask one follow-up question before writing about the interview.

Other possible avenues of investigation of the Holocaust include finding out about the various ghettos. What did people outside the ghettos know of what was going on in there? Students can investigate the role of the Jewish resistance and the role of teenagers in it. The Holocaust produced many villains and at least as many heroes. Mengele, Eichmann, and Hitler himself only begin the list of villains. Hero lists may start with Schindler or Korczak. The work of Nazi hunters may interest some students.

View together some of the following films: **Schindler's List** (1993), **The Diary of Anne Frank** (1959), **Holocaust** (1978), **Korczak** (1990), **Playing for Time** (1980), **Wallenberg: A Hero's Story** (1985). Compare your reactions to the film with those of various written accounts.

The Internet holds a host of material about the Holocaust, and researching there may be the direction some of the students will want to take next. Some good starting addresses are:

http://www.annefrank.com/, which is the home page for Anne Frank Online. There you can find out where the traveling exhibit is now and where it's going. There's a brief biography of Anne and some good material on what happened to the diary after her death.

http://www.annefrank.com/anne/story/story01.html is a page of photographs and captions on the life of Anne Frank. A site that provides links to many more Holocaust sites can be found at **http://remember.org/**.

An alphabet of Auschwitz concentration camp can be found at **http://www.spectacle.org/695/ausch.html**. Each letter of the alphabet provides a link to more information about the Holocaust in general and the camp in particular. This way of dispensing information on the Holocaust may give some students ideas as to how to present their own discoveries and reactions. Washington, D.C., is not the only site for a Holocaust museum, and **http://www.yahoo.com/Arts/Humanities/History/20th_Century/Holocaust__The/Holocaust_Memorials/** gives information about museums and memorials around the world. **ftp://rtfm.mit.edu/pub/usenet/news.answers/holocaust/** is a site where many documents on the Holocaust are archived.

➤ BOOK LIST

▶ Picture Books

Hoestlandt, Jo, and Johanna Kang **Star of Fear, Star of Hope** Walker, 1995 ISBN 0 8027 8374 0

    This picture book, set in wartime France, allows us to watch with a gentile child, Helen, the persecution of her Jewish friend, Lydia. She notices first the yellow star Lydia must wear and the fear she exhibits. Then Lydia disappears. The illustrations show the children playing together quietly and then long columns of suitcase-carrying people being marched away.

★ ★ ★ Wild, Margret, and Julie Vivas **Let the Celebrations Begin!** Watts, 1991 ISBN 0 531 08537 9

    A young woman prisoner at Bergen Belsen concentration camp tells how, upon hearing of the liberation to come, some of the women there used scraps of material—often torn from their own clothing—to make toys for the surviving children to celebrate their freedom. This is a tribute to the survival of hope under obscene circumstances, but has been criticized as being unrealistic.

▶ Novels

Dillon, James **The Children of Bach** Simon & Schuster, 1992 ISBN 0 684 19440 6

    Dillon tells the story of a music-loving family torn apart by the Nazis. When the children arrive home to find the rest of their family gone, they maintain their sanity by playing the music they all shared. Later, a priest and Peter play Bach's *Double Concerto for Violin* to celebrate their coming escape and to honor the people who were to have played it in concert, Peter's father and mother.

★ ★ ★ ★ Laird, Christa **Shadow of the Wall** Greenwillow, 1990 ISBN 0 688 09336 1

    In this outstanding novel, Misha is living in an orphanage with his sister, Rachel, and their baby sister, Elena. They have been relocated to the Warsaw Ghetto, walled off from the rest of the city. The head of the orphanage is the real-life character Dr. Korczak. Soon Misha learns of the plan devised by Dr. Korczak and Misha's mother to smuggle two-year-old Elena out of the ghetto. Misha is the one who takes her to the back of a building where he places her, with her bag of belongings, into a trough in which she is quickly pulled up to a second-floor opening and disappears. Then the word goes out that Dr. Korczak and all the children of the orphanage are being marched out to the trains. Misha sees them, including his sister Rachel, going to what he now knows is certain death. He hears that Dr. Korczak chose to go with the children rather than accept a deal from the Nazis for his personal survival. With the departure of everyone he has ever known, his resolve strengthens for the resistance. He faces his fear of being underground in a skillfully described passage in which he goes through the muck of the sewer system, clinging desperately to the shirt of the boy who is in front of him. We leave the story with Misha making his first contact with his connection on the "outside."

★ ★ ★ ★ Levoy, Myron **Alan and Naomi** HarperCollins, 1977 ISBN 0 06 440209 6
This is a focus book (see page 178).

★ ★ ★ ★ Lowry, Lois **Number the Stars** Houghton, 1989 ISBN 0 395 51060 0

    This Newbery Award winner is very accessible and tells a story of Danish resistance to the Holocaust. By 1944, the Nazis had been in control of Denmark for several years and had been harassing Danish Jews since the occupation began. Now, however, the harassment turns uglier, and they are preparing to "relocate" all of Denmark's Jews to concentration camps or worse. Here is the heroism exhibited by citizens of occupied Denmark to smuggle their Jews to Sweden before this can happen. We see their underground battle through the eyes of 10-year-old Annemarie Johansen, whose friend, Ellen Rosen, and her family are in grave danger. The solution seems to lie in pretending that Ellen is a member of the Johansen family in order to fool the Nazis. The courage of the Rosen family and their fellow Jews is shared by those of the Johansen family and friends. The facts that Annemarie is a real person and that this is the slightly fictionalized account of her story makes the impact of this book even greater.

★ ★ Sichnur, Steven **The Shadow Children** Morrow, 1994 ISBN 0 688 13281 2

    This is a combination ghost story and historical novel. Etienne spends his summers on his grandfather's farm in rural France after World War II. He learns that thousands of Jewish children hid there during the Holocaust, but when the Nazis came, the villagers, including his grandparents, abandoned the children. Etienne himself begins to see shadow children in the woods. It seems that only he can see them and hear their sobbing. Etienne's attempt to reconcile his kind and loving grandfather with the man who betrayed the children is a heart-breaking one.

★ Treseder, Terry Walton **Hear O Israel: A Story of the Warsaw Ghetto** Simon & Schuster, 1990 ISBN 0 689 31456 6

Another Holocaust novel for slightly younger readers is this brief novel told in the voice of Isaac, living with his family in the ghetto. In spite of increasing deprivation, Isaac's religious family tries to celebrate his brother's bar mitzvah, and even a seder using a stone, a stick, and a handful of dirt to represent the traditional egg, shank of meat, and bitter herbs. Even the depressing life in the ghetto is better than their life in Treblinka, however.

★ ★ Vos, Ida **Anna Is Still Here** Houghton, 1993 ISBN 0 395 65368

Ida Vos deals with the lingering horror of the Holocaust. Thirteen-year-old Anna Markus is living in Holland after the war, during which she hid in an attic. Reunited now with her surviving family, Anna tries for normalcy, but can't raise her voice above a whisper. Her parents refuse to talk about their wartime horrors. Contrary to the hopes of many, anti-Semitism is still present. Anna's German friend, Mrs. Neumann, won't leave her home in case her child should come home, and won't change her dress for fear that if the child does come, she won't recognize her mother. This is not an action-packed story, but a quiet, thoughtful one.

★ ★ ★ Williams, Laura **Behind the Bedroom Wall** Milkweed Editions, 1996 ISBN 1 57131 606 X

This story is interesting because it shows a German family's heroism during the Holocaust. At the beginning of the story, Korinna is a loyal German child. She adores the Fuhrer and listens raptly to his radio speeches. She's an active member of the Jungmadel, the Nazi youth group. Her parents encourage her participation and seem loyal Germans themselves. Then Korinna discovers that the sounds she has been hearing in her bedroom wall were not caused by mice, as she had been told, but by hated Jews—a woman and her five-year-old daughter. They've been hiding in a tiny space behind her wardrobe. Korinna is appalled at her traitorous parents' behavior. She knows she must turn them in to the authorities. The transformation of Korinna from naive loyal Hitler-follower to responsible and clever rebel is believable. There is some suspense, and the ending leaves Korinna and her mother and father, having helped the Jews to escape, escaping themselves.

★ ★ ★ Yolen, Jane **The Devil's Arithmetic** Puffin, 1990 ISBN 0 14 034535 3

This is a time-travel book. Hannah is a modern child who resents her family's and her religion's traditions, finding them meaningless and annoying, and feeling no connection with them. At a seder at her grandparents' house in the Bronx, Hannah opens the door for the prophet Elijah and is transported back to the time of the Holocaust. She is now her aunt's childhood friend, Chaya, for whom she was named, and experiences life in a concentration camp together with her aunt, the child Rivka. When she is one of four girls allowed to escape the ovens, she substitutes herself for Rivka. Yolen is a master storyteller, and her novel of the Holocaust brings the present to the past.

▶ Nonfiction

★ ★ Abells, Chana Byers **The Children We Remember** Greenwillow, 1986 ISBN 0 688 06371 3

This is a book in which short phrases and photographs combine to tell the story with great depth of emotion. The life of these children before the Holocaust helps to humanize them, making the lines and photographs of the story after the rise of the Nazis even more powerful. The line "sometimes they put children to death" stands beside a picture showing a mother shielding her toddler while both are shot.

★ ★ Adler, David, and Karen Ritz **Child of the Warsaw Ghetto** Holiday House, 1995 ISBN 0 8234 1160 5

This is a picture book biography, telling the story of Froim Baum, a Holocaust survivor. Through the story of this one boy's life, using cunning and courage to survive, Adler tells the story of Hitler's rise, the invasion of Poland, and the death camps.

★ ★ Adler, David A. **Hilde and Eli: Children of the Holocaust** Holiday House, 1994 ISBN 0 8234 1091 9

This is the tragic tale of two children who did not escape the Holocaust. Hilde Rosenzweig's childhood was interrupted when her family tried to escape before the Nazi noose tightened around them. Her eldest brother got to America and fought in the United States army during the latter part of the war. Hilde and her mother were gassed on a train when Hilde was 18. Eli Lax was younger than Hilde when the Nazis took power, and his eldest sister had made it to America, but he and his father and brother died at Auschwitz.

★ ★ Auerbacher, Inge **I Am a Star: Child of the Holocaust** Puffin, 1993 ISBN 0 14 036401 3

The author was one of 13 out of 1,200 in her transport to Terezin who survived, along with two other family members. The idea that an inmate's survival in the camps, or even whether or not he or she would be sent to a camp, was often dependent on a Nazi's flick of a finger, is one of the most powerful presentations in the book. We get examples of Auerbacher's poetry as well as her narrative, which includes some of the history of anti-Semitism.

★ Ayer, Eleanor **The United States Holocaust Memorial Museum: America Keeps the Memory Alive** Silver Burdett, 1995 ISBN 0 87518 649 1

If a field trip to the Holocaust Museum in Washington, D.C., is not possible, this book will at least make students aware of its existence. We go through the building with Ayer and witness the testimony present in those exhibits.

★ ★ ★ Bernstein, Sara Tuvel **The Seamstress: A Memoir of Survival** Putnam, 1997 ISBN 0 399 14322 X

Sara was feisty from the beginning. Growing up in rural Romania, she accepted a scholarship to a school in Bucharest much against her father's wishes. When a priest's anti-Semitism there became apparent, she threw an inkwell at him. Expelled for that, she found work as a seamstress in Bucharest, where her blond hair and blue eyes helped her escape, for awhile, the increasing hardships placed upon the Jews by the fascist Iron Guard. Eventually, she ended up in Ravensbruck concentration camp, where 19 out of every 20 women died. Sara's skill, determination, and brains helped her survive. She weighed only 44 pounds when rescue came in the person of a young soldier who wept as he carried her to freedom.

Chaikin, Miriam **A Nightmare in History: The Holocaust** Clarion, 1987 ISBN 0 89919 461 3

This is simply and movingly written. Unlike most of the other books for young people on the Holocaust, this one talks about Hitler himself and examines the way he rose to power. Chaikin also makes the clear point that the Holocaust was not just racial hatred gone wild, but a careful plan by the Nazis to exterminate the Jews.

★ ★ Finkelstein, Norman H. **Remember Not to Forget: A Memory of the Holocaust** Watts, 1985 ISBN 0 531 04892 6

In this emotional but carefully researched book, Finkelstein starts way back in the first century to tell how the Jews were scattered after Jerusalem was destroyed. She brings us rapidly to the rise of the Third Reich, lingers there to describe its horrors, and then goes on to the establishment of the Jewish state of Israel.

★ ★ ★ Friedman, Ina **The Other Victims: First Person Stories of Non-Jews Persecuted by the Nazis** Houghton, 1990 ISBN 0 395 50212 8

Friedman tells us that in addition to the six million Jews killed in the Holocaust, five million others were killed by the Nazis. She has collected 11 accounts from those who survived, prefacing each with well researched historical information and a haunting quote from Hitler or another Nazi official about the policies regarding these people. Each account stands on its own. These are stories of the gypsies, the homosexuals, the Christian clergy, the Jehovah's Witnesses, the deaf, those intermarried with Jews, the blacks, the artists, the political dissidents, the Czechs, the Poles, the Dutch, and the French who were murdered by the Nazis. The accounts bear witness to the killings, the arrests, the forced labor, the starvation, and the gassings. We get an increasingly clear picture of the devastation caused by the Nazi party in Europe, the inhuman conditions, the deliberate genocide, and the mad dash for power and superiority.

★ ★ ★ Greenfield, Howard **The Hidden Children** Ticknor & Fields, 1993 ISBN 0 395 66074 2

Greenfield tells the stories of 15 children who survived the Holocaust by being hidden, and later by immigrating to the United States. These interviews of those former children are arranged chronologically, rather like Julius Lester's *To Be a Slave* (see page 34), starting with their lives before the war, the events that drove them into hiding, their experiences while hiding, and their later liberation. Individual stories blend together here giving us an overall picture.

★ ★ ★ Landau, Elaine **We Survived the Holocaust** Watts, 1991 ISBN 0 531 11115 6

Walls presents 16 first-person accounts of Jews who survived the Holocaust. Done with sensitivity and thoroughness, these are portraits of courage and survival amidst incredible persecution. This is rich material through which to find out about the lives of individuals, and for getting a broad picture of the place and time.

★ ★ Meltzer, Milton **Never to Forget: the Jews of the Holocaust** HarperCollins, 1976 ISBN 0 06 024175 6

Meltzer uses documents such as letters, diaries, poems, and songs from the Jews in ghettos and concentration camps to tell their moving stories.

★ ★ Meltzer, Milton **Rescue: The Story of How Gentiles Saved Jews in the Holocaust** HarperCollins, 1988 ISBN 0 06 024209 4

Here Meltzer tells the stories of the people who helped when governments would not. This book makes a good introduction to the film *Schindler's List* because it includes a section on Oskar Schindler.

★ Resnick, Abraham **The Holocaust** Kycebtm, 1991 ISBN 1 56006 124 3 1

The book combines a general account of the Holocaust with more personal ones and adds many photographs and, like **Smoke and Ashes** (see below), puts the tragedy into a larger historical perspective. Of particular interest might be the chapter on the resistance movement of the Righteous Gentiles in all the countries of Europe.

★ ★ ★ Rochman, Hazel, and Darlene McCampbell **Bearing Witness: Stories of the Holocaust** Orchard, 1995 ISBN 0 531 08788 3

This is an anthology of writings by 16 authors on the Holocaust and contains both fiction and nonfictional work, as well as poetry. One short story, "The Shawl," is particularly effective, and you may wish to read it aloud to the class.

★ ★ ★ Rogasky, Barbara **Smoke and Ashes: The Story of the Holocaust** Holiday House, 1988 ISBN 0 8234 0697 0

This photo essay begins with information about the history of anti-Semitism from the 1600s on. Much of its information on the Holocaust itself comes from the Nazis' own records. We see the deportations, the forced labor, the Warsaw Ghetto, Auschwitz, and the heaps of bodies and skeletal survivors found by the liberators. Particularly haunting is the photograph of a bin containing thousands of the victims' wedding bands kept by the Nazi's for profit. That picture, like the one of the storeroom filled with their shoes, help to make real the ghastly numbers.

★ ★ Rosenberg, Maxine B. **Hiding to Survive: Stories of Jewish Children Rescued from the Holocaust** Clarion, 1994 ISBN 0 395 65014 3

Fourteen first-person accounts combine to tell the stories of these 50- and 60-year-olds looking back on their childhood in Europe. Photos accompany each oral history. The relationships between the children and the people who hid them are interesting to explore. After all, these people went to great lengths converting space to hide the children, some of whom they had never before met, yet they risked their lives for them. The ache of these children, living with strangers and longing for their parents and their freedom, tears at your heart.

★ ★ Rossel, Seymour **The Holocaust: The World and the Jews** Behrman House, 1992 ISBN 0 87441 526 8

This book offers an extremely accessible overview of the Holocaust in a straightforward text replete with primary sources and arranged by chapters which include the Nazi rise, the ghettos, the resistance, the death camps, and the Nuremberg trials.

★ ★ ★ ★ Sender, Ruth Minsky **The Cage** Simon & Schuster, 1986 ISBN 0 02 781830 6

This is one of several Holocaust books by Ruth Minsky Sender. Although the book focuses on the life of the author at age 16, there is much in the narrative here about the price paid by six million Jews. As the net tightens around the Jews in Poland, Riva and her brothers are subjected first to the torments of their Christian neighbors, people who were once their friends. Later, they are forcibly moved into the ghetto at Warsaw and still later to Auschwitz. There, because of Riva's ability to write poetry, which helps her fellow prisoners bear the cruelty and indignities visited upon them by the Nazis, she is treasured by them and by one of the camp wardens. Wisely, she lets the events carry their own emotional weight, and it's a heavy one.

★ ★ Sender, Ruth Minsky **The Holocaust Lady** Simon & Schuster, 1992 ISBN 0 02 781832 2

This volume relates events in the author's life after her removal to the United States, where she finally got to tell her story.

★ ★ ★ Siegal, Aranka **Upon the Head of a Goat: A Childhood in Hungary 1939-1944** Farrar, 1981 ISBN 0 374 38059 7

Siegal's first book starts with Piri's visit to her grandmother in the Ukraine, which was intended to be a short one, but she is prevented from returning home to Hungary by the onslaught of World War II. This memoir details the destruction of Piri's family as the noose tightens around her people. The inexorable pace at which the events occurred and the helplessness of the innocent are the focuses of this book.

★ ★ Siegal, Aranka **Grace in the Wilderness: After the Liberation** Farrar, 1985 ISBN 0 374 32760 2

Siegal's second book takes up where **Upon the Head of a Goat** leaves off. After surviving the death camp, guilt overcomes Piri and her sister, Iboya, as they are sent to Sweden to try to resume a normal life. Iboya works on a farm while Piri works in the city before they emigrate to America. The decisions they make and the ghastly memories they carry typify those of many other Holocaust survivors.

★ ★ ★ ★ Van der Rol, Ruud, and Rian Verhoeven **Anne Frank: Beyond the Diary** Viking, 1993 ISBN 0 670 84932 4

The authors bring family photographs and other biographical material on Anne Frank and the others who lived in the "secret annex." The authors work at the Anne Frank House in Amsterdam, and the book uncovers much material which enlightens and strengthens the original diary.

★ ★ ★ Wiesel, Elie **Night** Bantam, 1982 ISBN 0 553 27253 5

Although this is technically a novel, it is usually treated as an autobiography. Wiesel attempts to deal with the meaning of the horror of the Holocaust and poses the unanswerable question of how God could have allowed this terrible thing to happen.

▶ **Film**

Better than the book if an actual visit to the Holocaust Memorial Museum is impossible, is the film **For The Living** (WETA PBS Video ISBN 0 7936 1045 1). Ed Asner narrates the video, explaining the planning, design, and construction of the museum. We are party to interviews with the architect, designers, and curators of the building, as well as the testimony of some of the survivors.

▶ **The Internet**

http://www.historyplace.com/fworldwar2/holocaust/timeline.html is a Holocaust time line offering year-by-year coverage.

Immigration

COMMENTS

The study of immigration is one way to personalize history because it offers the opportunity to study one's own roots. In fact, it may be a way to get to know one's grandparents. On a larger level, it becomes a study of world history as the various reasons for immigration to the United States necessitate a look at the history of the territories from which immigrants came. The life these immigrants led once they entered the United States depended on how and why they were absorbed into the cultures and work force.

PICTURE BOOK STARTER

In America, by Marissa Moss (Dutton, 1994 ISBN 0 525 45152 8), contrasts the two worlds of the immigrant experience both visually and in text. As Grandfather and Walter walk to the post office, the old man tells his grandson about coming to America from Lithuania when he was 10. The images of life in Europe are blurred, while those of the present-day scene are crisp and clear.

ACTIVITIES

Some students can find out about their first family immigration to America. For some students, finding the first immigrants in their family is simply a matter of looking at an already existing family history or simply asking a parent about the experience. For others, the task is more complicated, but it almost always produces some interesting results. Students might like to investigate such things as: the reasons why their ancestors came to the United States, whether or not they were part of a large number of immigrants at the time, the conditions they left behind, the work they did when they got here, the areas they settled, the living conditions there, and some of the major events occurring at that time. A word of warning, however: take cognizance of the fact that many students do not know and perhaps cannot know about their family trees. Care must be taken to give alternative searches for these students without embarrassing them.

An investigation of immigration laws and how they have changed over the years, the quota system and how and why it was implemented, and proposed changes in the law today are all possible avenues for further study. Students might like to investigate how one would go about immigrating to or from the United States today. Other questions for investigation: What's the difference between an immigrant and a refugee, as well as the differences between economic and political refugees? Which refugees are offered asylum here?

Contact a church that is engaged in helping immigrants and refugees, legal or otherwise. Find out how they go about it and how much cooperation they get from the governments of various countries.

The Internet offers a good deal of information on immigration. The American Immigration Home Page: **www.bergen.org/ AAST/Projects/ Immigration/** is the address of a site designed and maintained by a 10th-grade history class. It contains historical information about four major waves of immigration in the United States. American Immigration Sources on the Net **http://www. wave.net/upg/immigration/resource.html** offers information and links on current immigration laws and conditions.

As with any theme study, a bulletin board on which students are encouraged to post notices about information found and sources of further information is useful.

Look at your own community for signs of past and present immigration. Often ethnic groups settled in one area of town. Look at the history of the various churches and social clubs to get some sense of this. Many festivals and parades commemorate immigrant customs and festivals.

Find folk dances and folk songs from some of the cultures within your city.

Find out which local landmarks, buildings, railroads, canals, and the like were built with immigrant labor. Compare the wages of those laborers with current purchasing power of labor wages in your community.

What's your community doing to help new immigrants? What can you do to help those organizations?

Conduct a debate about some community efforts to curtail benefits (welfare, education, health) of current immigrants.

You may want to suggest that students select a work of fiction (see book list below) and then research the country from which those particular immigrants came, the statistics on when and how many immigrants came here from that country, the jobs available here for them, etc.

➤ BOOK LIST

▶ Picture Books

★ ★ ★ Bunting, Eve **How Many Days to America: A Thanksgiving Story**, Clarion, 1988 ISBN 0 89919 521 0, illustrated by Beth Peck

This is a picture book in which the action and feelings of modern immigrants echoes that of the original Pilgrims.

★ ★ ★ Garland, Sherry **The Lotus Seed** Harcourt, 1993 ISBN 0 15 249465 0, with illustrations by Tatsuro Kiuchi

This subdued but touching story is accompanied by formal, subdued illustrations. It tells of a young Vietnamese woman who sees the emperor weep as he gives up the throne of his country in 1945. Determined to keep a small piece of the vanished beauty of the palace, she snatches a seed from a lotus pod there. As the years go by, the seed holds hope for her. When she and her family flee Vietnam, the seed goes with them to America. There, one of her grandchildren, much to everyone's dismay, plants the seed and forgets where he had planted it. The seed, even after all those years, takes root and blossoms. All of the grandchildren take seeds and will hand them down to future generations.

★ ★ Greenberg, Melanie Hope **Aunt Lilly's Laundromat** Dutton, 1994 ISBN 0 525 45211 7

Greenberg portrays a Haitian woman who came to this country as a young girl and now lives in Brooklyn, where she runs a Laundromat. As she goes about her work there, she recalls details from her life in Haiti and adorns the walls of the Laundromat with pictures of those memories.

★ Howlett, Bud **I'm New Here** Houghton, 1993 ISBN 0 395 64049 0

Photographs tell the story of a present-day immigrant from El Salvador and focuses on the first day of school for the fifth grader.

★ ★ Leighton, Marianne, and Dennis Nolan **An Ellis Island Christmas** Viking, 1992 ISBN 0 670 83182 4

This is set at the turn of the century. Krysia describes her journey from Poland with her mother and brothers to join her father on Ellis Island on Christmas Eve. Her thrill at arrival is tempered by the fear that the immigration officials may send her back to Poland.

★ ★ ★ Levinson, Riki **Watch the Stars Come Out** Dutton, 1985 ISBN 0 525 44205 7, illustrated by Diane Goode

This book portrays Great-grandmother's immigration to America as related when a grandmother and granddaughter share a family photograph album. The illustrations detail the immigrant experience in New York's Lower East Side.

★ ★ ★ Levitin, Sonia **A Piece of Home** Dial, 1996 ISBN 0 8037 1626 5, illustrated by Juan Wijngaard

Gregor and his family are emigrating from Russia to join relatives in the United States. When told he can take only one treasure, much to his parents' dismay, Gregor elects to take the small, faded quilt his great-grandmother made. On the long trip, Gregor is both warmed and comforted by the quilt. When they are in his relatives' home, he finds his young cousin Elie has one just like it.

★ ★ ★ Say, Allen **Grandfather's Journey** Houghton, 1993 ISBN 0 395 57035 2

Allen Say won the Caldecott Award for this book, which is taken from his grandfather's own story of being caught between two worlds: those of his native Japan and of California. The sense of belonging in neither place is beautifully portrayed.

★ ★ ★ Turner, Ann Turner **Through Moon and Stars and Night Skies** HarperCollins, 1990 ISBN 0 06 026190 0, illustrated by James G. Hale

This tells of an increasingly common immigrant experience: that of a child coming to a new family in America. The story is told by the child, and we know it is not the first time he has told it. The child, who is Asian, travels many miles to join an adoptive family in the United States. He has a picture of the people who are to be his new parents and the house where he is to live. He clutches these during the long, sleepless trip. The family strives to make the child feel wanted and loved, and to make the unfamiliar setting as familiar as possible.

★ ★ Watson, Mary **The Butterfly Seeds** Morrow, 1995 ISBN 0 688 14132 3

Jake must leave his grandfather behind as he and his family emigrate to America at the turn of the century. Grandfather gives him "butterfly seeds" to plant in the new country. The picture book details the immigration experience, including the settlement in a city tenement where Jake plants the seeds in a window box.

▶ **Novels**

★ ★ ★ Buss, Fran Leeper **Journey of the Sparrows** Dutton, 1991 ISBN 0 525 67362 8

Here we see the immigrant experience through the eyes of an illegal alien family from El Salvador. Using newspaper articles and headlines, we watch 15-year-old Maria take the long and terrifying journey to America with her six-year-old brother, Oscar, and her pregnant sister, Julia. For most of the journey, they travel in a crate. They fear not only the immigration services, but the Guardias, who killed their father and may well wreak further harm on the family. Even after their arrival in Chicago, their troubles are not over, as they share crowded quarters with other illegals and Maria must work in a sweat shop to support them.

Gross, Virginia **It's Only Goodbye** Viking, 1990 ISBN 0 670 83289 8

This is a short, easily accessible novel about a young immigrant from France who comes with his father to America. On the journey here, the father is arrested for theft, and the experience becomes even more arduous.

★ ★ ★ Hesse, Karen **Letters from Rifka** Holt, 1992 ISBN 0 8050 1964 2

This is a very strong but brief novel which is based on the memories of the author's aunt. Presented as a series of letters never sent from Rifka to her cousin, whom she left behind in Russia, it portrays the suffering endured by Rifka's family during the times of upheaval in Russia: not only are they poor peasants, they are Jews. Her two older brothers have already emigrated to America, and now, the remainder of the family is forced to flee or suffer further hardships. During the trip to America, Rifka contracts ringworm and has to remain behind in Belgium while the family goes on to New York. Cleared to come to America at last, she is nearly killed during a storm at sea. Even when she arrives at Ellis Island, her troubles are not over. There, too, she is retained because of what they fear is uncured ringworm and because her hair has not grown in. On Ellis Island, she becomes a substitute mother for a frightened Russian peasant boy and a little baby. Reunited with her own family at last, the book ends with their new beginning.

★ ★ ★ Levitin, Sonia **Journey to America**
Simon & Schuster, 1987 ISBN 0 689 71130 1

Levitin has written three novels about a Jewish family, the Platts, who emigrate from Nazi Germany just before the war. Lisa, older sister Ruth, younger sister Annie, and Mother and Father Platt try to cope with life in Nazi Germany in 1938. As this becomes increasingly impossible, Father flees to America, and the rest of the family go to Switzerland to wait for their father to send enough money for them to go to America. The family endures fears, separations, and poverty until Father earns enough money and sends the proper forms.

★ ★ ★ Levitin, Sonia **Silver Days** Simon & Schuster, 1989 ISBN 0 689 31563 5

The Platt family, now in America, has only memories of the once prosperous life they left behind when they fled Nazi Germany. They struggle in a tenement in New York City until Papa decides to move to California. Here, life is better for them: Lisa is able to dance again; Ruth finds love; and Annie has a Japanese friend who is later interned in a camp.

★ ★ ★ Levitin, Sonia **Annie's Promise** Atheneum, 1993 ISBN 0 689 31752 2

This book follows **Silver Days** and is set in the final days of World War II. Now in Los Angeles, Annie tries to escape the net of overprotectiveness cast by her Jewish immigrant parents. Going away to camp helps in her quest, and Annie, who resents her parents "jabber" in German, learns to understand their need for it and to respect their struggle. She also must face their racist attitude toward her black friend and her own less-than-perfect character.

Nixon, Joan Lowry
★ ★ **Land of Dreams** Delacorte, 1994 ISBN 0 385 31170 2
★ ★ **Land of Hope** Laurel Leaf, 1993 ISBN 0 440 21597 8
★ ★ **Land of Promise** Bantam, 1993 ISBN 0 553 08111 X

This series of novels portrays the various lives led by three young girls who arrive at Ellis Island together.

★ ★ ★ Paulsen, Gary **The Crossing** Orchard, 1987 ISBN 0 531 08309 8

Paulsen also deals with illegal immigrants. This short, brutal novel gives us Manny Bustos, who is 14 but small for his age, a street kid in Juarez, Mexico, who lies and steals for survival. He tries to steal the wallet of a veteran of the Vietnam war, Robert Locke, who is deeply disturbed, but who tries to help Manny cross to El Paso, Texas, and a new life there.

★ ★ ★ Whelan, Gloria **Goodbye, Vietnam** Knopf, 1992 ISBN 0 679 82263 1

Whelan tells about a more recent immigration and describes many of the current dangers facing immigrants. It starts in Vietnam, where the police are coming to take Mai's grandmother away because she is a healer and because she practices the old religion, which is now illegal. Mai's father was taken away for a year, and the family fears he will be taken away again. Their village must give most of the rice they raise to the government, and so they come closer and closer to starvation each year. Mai's mother and father decide to attempt to escape to America. The journey is long and arduous. They must spend all their money to get supplies from people whose business it is to rip-off refugees. The boat they must take is old and not seaworthy, it is crowded with as many people as could possibly squeeze onto it, and the sea is full of pirates.

Nonfiction
★ Andryszewski, Tricia **Immigration: Newcomers and Their Impact on the U.S.** Millbrook, 1995

This is more scholarly than most of the rest of the books on this list. The impact of immigration then and now is covered, as are the various reasons for immigration, and there are extensive surveys and interviews of immigrants. The second half of the book concentrates on modern immigration.

★ ★ Ashabranner, Brent **Our Beckoning Borders: Illegal Immigration to America** Cobblehill/Dutton, 1996 ISBN 0 525 65223 X

Ashabranner looks at a complex social issue that is sure to spark discussion and debate. The personal stories and black-and-white photos—particularly those which show the juxtaposition of the poverty of a Mexican village and the modern U.S. city just across the border—explain what compels people to continue trying to "cross over," regardless of the risks. At the same time, he also addresses the often-mixed response of the American people and government.

★ Bender, David **Immigration: Opposing Viewpoints** Greenhaven, 1990 ISBN 0 89908 485 0

This is a more difficult book than the other nonfiction listed here. It carefully delineates the factors for debate about the current state of immigration, both legal and illegal, in the United States.

★ ★ ★ Freedman, Russell **Immigrant Kids** Puffin, 0 14 037594 5

Early 20th-century New York City is brought to life by period photographs and first-person accounts of immigrant kids of the time. Like everything else Freedman has done, this book is superb. The photographs and captions alone immerse you in life at the turn of the century. He covers the passage and Ellis Island in the first chapter, then turns to the schools, the streets, and the jobs. His chapter on tenement life is particularly well done.

★ ★ Jacobs, William Jay **Ellis Island: New Hope in a New Land** Scribner, 1990 ISBN 0 684 19171 7

Jacobs gives an intimate, you-are-there approach to the feelings, sights, and smells of arrival at Ellis Island. The book is liberally illustrated with photographs and contains information on the current state of immigration to America, as well as the historic coverage.

★ ★ Ketchum, Liza **The Gold Rush** Little, 1996 ISBN 0 316 49047 4

This is a very approachable but quite comprehensive book that gives a well-rounded look at the effects of the discovery of gold at Sutter's Mill. Besides portraying gold fever and the disruption it caused in the lives of many, as well as the riches gained by a few, the book talks about its effect on immigration, the racism and prejudice which followed, and the Manifest Destiny it encouraged.

★ Koral, April **An Album of the Great Wave of Immigration** Watts, 1992 ISBN 0 531 11123 7

This documentary covers the years from 1890 to 1924 and concentrates on Southern and Eastern Europeans. The author details much of the experience: the reasons for leaving the mother country, the conditions in transit, the entry points, and the difficulties faced by new arrivals.

★ ★ Kroll, Steven **Ellis Island** Holiday, 1995 ISBN 0 8234 1192 3

Kroll uses black-and-white illustrations and occasional watercolor images which echo early portraits and photographs of the people who came through Ellis Island from 1892 to 1924. The text is factual narrative delivered in an unemotional but clear tone.

★ Reimers, David **The Immigrant Experience** Chelsea, 1989 ISBN 0 87754 881 1

This book gives fairly detailed information on the causes and effects of four major waves of immigration to America, including the one after World War II.

★ Sandler, Martin **Immigrants** HarperCollins, 1995 ISBN 0 06 024507 7

Sandler gives a nice overview with a collection of photographs and interviews that focus on the period from 18470 to 1920.

Protest and Rebellion

☞ COMMENTS

Adolescence is often a time of reassessing one's role in life and seizing control where possible. Thus, it makes sense that students of that age might be interested in a theme that deals with similar struggles on personal and larger stages of protest and rebellion. Historically, the theme can cover civil rights and anti-war protests as well as protests against tyranny and revolution, if that's the direction your curriculum suggests. The theme should include many biographies of such people as Martin Luther King Jr., Cesar Chavez, Daniel Shay, John Brown, and other leaders of revolt.

☞ PICTURE BOOK STARTER

One excellent picture book that deals with protest and the courage involved in it is **Rebel** by Allan Baillie, with illustrations by Di Wu (Ticknor & Fields, 1994 ISBN 0 395 69250 4). In this book, a general marches his troops into a Burmese village, declaring that he is now in control of all their lives. Suddenly, from amidst the crowd, a child's sandal is thrown at him. All of the children are brought before him, and he orders his troops to search for the person wearing only one sandal. However, he turns to find that all the villagers—adults as well as children—have thrown their sandals into a pile and they all stand barefooted. Amidst their derision, the general and his troops depart. An author's note states that the story is based on truth.

☞ ACTIVITIES

While cynics among us would agree that a more likely outcome of the act of defiance in **Rebel** would be a massacre rather than the departure of a humiliated general, apparently in this instance it was not. Students might like to discuss the reasons why it succeeded, the speed with which the villagers perceived the problem and thought of a solution, and whether or not it was foolhardy for the first shoe to be thrown. A possible next step would be to find out about the real-life situation which inspired the book and to find similar real-life instances of such group action to protect a single member.

Think of an injustice you perceive either in your school or locality. What can you do about it? How far are you willing to go to protest that injustice? How much support will you need to be effective? How could you go about getting that support?

Look beyond your local area for an injustice you feel strongly about. What can you do about it? Do it. Is there an organized protest against it? Organize a letter-writing or telephone campaign to raise money for an existing organization.

Find out about the principles of peaceable protest. How did Gandhi and King use those principles? Where did they learn them?

Find out about the effect Gandhi had on the British rule of India.

Research areas for this theme would likely include resistance movements during World War II and other conflicts, as well as acts of civil disobedience throughout history. The women's suffrage movement, the anti-war and animal rights movements, abortion protests and demonstrations, labor strikes, the student protests in China and elsewhere, and environmental advocacy have all produced acts of defiance and protest. Students should be encouraged to find one such area and investigate it as thoroughly as possible, and then find a way to convey their information to the rest of the class. Encourage them to go beneath the surface, deciding who benefited, who suffered, who organized, who financed, and what the result was of each protest.

Often, music is a strong motivator in protest movements. Find and sing some of the songs that have been effective throughout our history.

Read aloud some of the poems from **Beat Voices: An Anthology of Beat Poetry**.

Having read books and accounts of protest, students need to look at the events in order to summarize them. Which protests succeeded? Was the success immediate or long-range? Did numbers of protesters matter? Did the methods of protest matter? Did it effect one area more than another? How long had the perceived abuses gone on before an organized protest beganHow wide was the support?

▶ BOOK LIST

▶ Picture Books

★ ★ ★ Coleman, Evelyn, and Tyrone Geter **White Socks Only** Whitman, 1996 ISBN 0 8075 8955 1

A grandmother tells of an incident when she was young. She didn't get to town often, and this day when she strolled there, she was wearing her good clothes, including clean white socks. When she saw a sign on a drinking fountain labeled "Whites Only," she didn't hesitate to take a drink, for that's what she was wearing. A white man then began to beat her with his belt. Other black people took a drink and shared the beating.

★ ★ ★ Swope, Sam **The Araboolies of Liberty Street** Potter, 1989 ISBN 0 517 57411 X

Absolute conformity is demanded in a small town. The rules are those of General Pinch and his wife, who have totally intimidated the populace. Then the Araboolies move in next door to the Pinches. They don't understand the language and don't care. Their carefree existence starts a protest.

▶ Novels

★ ★ ★ Barron, T.A. **The Ancient One** Putnam, 1992 ISBN 0 399 21899 8

Barron gives us a time-travel book in which Kate becomes involved in protest in the present and magic in the past as she fights for the preservation of a virgin stand of redwood trees. Saving them, in this fantasy, means that Kate must also solve an ancient riddle.

★ ★ ★ Byars, Betsy **The Two-Thousand Pound Goldfish** HarperCollins, 1982 ISBN 1 557 36131 2

This is a novel about the effects of protest on innocents. The children's mother goes underground when a death results from her participation in a political action. They are living with their grandmother, who has disowned their mother, to whom they remain fiercely loyal. When their grandmother dies, they are sure that their mother will come back for them.

★ ★ ★ Collier, James and Christopher **The Winter Hero** Scholastic, 1985 ISBN 0 590 42604 4

Shay's Rebellion, a conflict waged by the farmers of western Massachusetts against taxes, is seen through the eyes of Justin, a young man who was too young to fight in the Revolution, but ready to fight this time.

★ ★ ★ Gordon, Sheila **Middle of Somewhere: A Story of South Africa** Orchard, 1990 ISBN 0 531 05908 1

The scene here is a black township in South Africa during the time of Apartheid. Bulldozers are about to clear the village Rebecca has lived in all her life in order to make room for white homes. The resulting protest is picked up by the media, and her father is imprisoned, to be released later with Nelson Mandela. We see it all through the eyes of nine-year-old Rebecca.

★ ★ ★ Lasky, Kathryn **Memoirs of a Bookbat** Harcourt, 1994 ISBN 0 15 215727 1

Harper's family has reformed. Her mother and father no longer drink and fight; they have joined a religious group called F.A.C.E. (Family Action for Christian Education) and have now set off, via motor home, to participate in protests and to ban books that don't suit their values. Because Harper is an avid reader whose eclectic selections often fall afoul of her parents' wishes, she would be in trouble if they knew what she was reading. She hides her books behind false book covers while she is reading and in a secret compartment in their mobile home when she is not. They move frequently, but Harper always manages to locate the library first. Now, they have settled in a California community, and Harper has made a friend in Gray, the child of liberal parents. So far, her rebellion has been hidden, and confrontation with her parents has been minimal. Now, they are all to participate in a demonstration against abortion, and although Harper thinks she might well be against it, she cannot participate. This is a story about values and about the right of parents to control what their children read and the ideas to which they are exposed.

★ ★ Lowry, Lois **Taking Care of Terrific** Dell, 1984 ISBN 0 395 34070 5

Enid takes a job babysitting, and frequently takes the child to Boston Common. There she becomes friendly with a homeless woman and soon becomes involved in a protest by the homeless.

★ ★ ★ ★ Lutzeier, Elizabeth **The Wall** Holiday, 1991 ISBN 0 8234 0987 2
This is a focus book (see page 184).

★ ★ ★ McDonald, Joyce **Comfort Creek** Delacorte, 1997 ISBN 0 385 32232 1

Quinella's mother left her children to pursue a singing career. They've been living in a trailer in a trailer park. Quinella's father is out of work when the phosphate mine closes, and moves the trailer to a remote area of a cypress swamp. Even those primitive quarters may be lost if he can't find a job soon. It ought to be good news, then, that a new phosphate mine may open.

However, opening that mine would necessitate the destruction of a community, and Quinella joins their protest.

★ ★ ★ Paterson, Katherine **Lyddie** Lodestar, 1991 ISBN 0 525 67338 5

This novel also belongs in this theme, not so much because of Lyddie's protest, but because of Diana, a factory worker with whom Lyddie makes friends. Diana urges the other girls to sign a protest petition, asking for better working conditions. Lyddie does not sign the petition but is influenced by the more radical Diana. The novel may lead readers into an investigation of labor protests then and now. This is a focus book (see page 193).

★ ★ Qualey, Marsha **Come In from the Cold** Houghton, 1994 ISBN 0 395 68986 4

In 1969, Maud's sister Lucy was killed during a Vietnam War demonstration. Jeff's brother was killed in the Vietnam War. Jeff and Maud react differently to their family's loss, but are drawn together by their mutual pain and their need to believe that they can make a difference. Arguments on both sides of the issue get exposure and respect in this novel.

★ ★ ★ Reeder, Carolyn **Grandpa's Mountain** Camelot, 1993 ISBN 0 380 71914 2

Grandpa is having trouble getting the neighbors to join him in protesting the government's buying up of land in the area to form the new Shenandoah National Park. Many are quite willing to take the offered money and relocate. Carrie, staying with her grandparents for the summer, becomes drawn into the battle, standing up for her grandfather's position as he fights every step of the way.

★ ★ ★ ★ Spinelli, Jerry **Wringer** HarperCollins, 1997 ISBN 0 06 024913 7

The men of the town shoot pigeons in a yearly ritual. One boy rebels. This is a focus book (see page 204).

★ ★ ★ ★ Woodson, Jacqueline **The House You Pass on the Way** Delacorte, 1997 ISBN 0 385 32189 9

This is much more than a protest novel: we get beautiful, almost lyrical writing; insight into the sexuality and choices of two very different teenage girls; a look at the effects of interracial marriage; a loving family that dares to defy convention; a glimpse of heroism on the part of a long-dead couple; and the effects of anger, racism, and grief on them all. Yet, nothing very much happens.

Staggerlee, who lives outside a small, Southern town, is a loner, set apart from her classmates in many ways. They consider her stuck-up and attribute that to the fact that her grandmother and grandfather are town heroes. (Her grandparents were famous entertainers who lost their lives while lending their fame to a protest march.) Her mother is also a loner, perhaps because she is one of the few white women in the mostly black community. Staggerlee's father has been shunned by his family since he married a white woman, but he remains open and friendly. Dotti, Staggerlee's older sister, is also very popular in the community, but Staggerlee walks alone until she meets Trout, an adopted cousin who comes to stay with the family for a summer. Immediately, a bond is made between the two girls, and is made stronger because they are both gay. Suddenly, Staggerlee has someone to talk and walk with for one idyllic summer. Although they don't act on their sexuality, both know that, next summer, Trout will come back and the relationship will continue. However, a letter from Trout changes everything.

▶ Poetry

★ ★ Kherdian, David **Beat Voices: An Anthology of Beat Poetry** Holt, 1995 ISBN 0 805 03315 7

These are the noisy, outrageous, and sometimes outraged voices of the Beat Generation.

Nonfiction

★ Katz, William Loren **Breaking the Chains: African-American Slave Resistance** Simon & Schuster, 1990 ISBN 0 689 31493 0

Katz focuses on many acts of rebellion and protest by slaves, and the book can lead students in that direction.

★ Kroll, Steven **The Boston Tea Party** Holiday House, 1998 ISBN 0 8234 1316 0

Kroll traces the causes of the action and then the protest itself in a simple, straightforward manner.

★ ★ Kronenwetter, Michael **The Peace Commandos: Nonviolent Heroes in the Struggle Against War & Injustice** Silver Burdett, 1994 ISBN 0 02 751051 4

This book gives brief accounts of the actions of many protesters, with particular emphasis on wars of the 20th century. The author's sympathies with pacifism are apparent.

★ ★ ★ Kronenwetter, Michael **Protest!** Twenty First Century, 1996 ISBN 0 805 041036

The author discusses all kinds of protest: from a child refusing to go to bed to organized political actions and even wars. The scope is international, and the book is valuable for its comprehensiveness.

★ Lawson, Don, and Wendy Barish **The French Resistance** Simon & Schuster, 1984 ISBN 0 685 07808 6

This book deals with spy and espionage activities, as well as acts of defiance against the Nazis.

★ ★ Rappaport, Doreen **Tinker vs. Des Moines: Student Rights on Trial** HarperCollins, 1993 ISBN 0 06 025117 4

This is part of a series of books in which readers are given both sides of an issue and then asked to judge it for themselves. In this volume, the issue is a 1965 case in which students' civil liberties were at stake. Seven students wore black armbands to protest the Vietnam War. Suspended from school, three of them sued the school board.

★ ★ Terkel, Susan **People Power: A Look at Nonviolent Action and Defense** Lodestar, 1996 ISBN 0 525 67434 9

This book gives readers the chance to decide a court case that took place during the Vietnam era in which a group of high school students wore black armbands and were suspended from school. The background of the times is given, as are interviews with the participants many years after it was settled.

★ ★ ★ Tillage, Leon Walker **Leon's Story** Farrar, 1997 ISBN 0 374 34379 9

Leon's story is of sharecroppers, of African-American segregation, of protest marches, and of dignity. Leon Tillage is now a janitor in a school in Baltimore, Maryland, and the book is inspired by a yearly speech he gives there to the students. Although his parents were poor, they had dignity and pride. Leon, unlike his parents, took part in the civil rights marches and protests of the sixties. This is an insider's look at the time and events that changed America.

★ **Viva: Women and Popular Protest in Latin America** Routledge, 1993 ISBN 0 415 07312 X

This anthology is a collection of essays and accounts of women's issues in Latin American countries.

Biography

COMMENTS

The study of biography makes an excellent bridge between history and literature. Each life story is not only a history of the subject, but a depiction of a specific time period. Also, the field of expertise or accomplishment achieved by various subjects of biographies can link this theme to many others in various disciplines. On the other hand, a biography is a literary form or genre and, as such, can be studied in that way. Because of the vast array of biographies and autobiographies available now for young readers, students can choose to read a book about people whose work or area of expertise is of interest to them and/or one that is an outstanding piece of literature. There are many biographies, particularly those of sports figures or entertainers, which are not very well done but will be chosen because of their subject. Some of the activities we suggest in this genre study are designed to help students differentiate between better and lesser works.

PICTURE BOOK STARTER

Allen Say's **Grandfather's Journey** (Houghton, 1993 ISBN 0 395 57035 2) is, as the title suggests, the story of his grandfather, who emigrated to America from Japan. Although he loved his chosen home, California, he remained tied to Japan and spent most of his life longing for whichever place he had just left. The book accents the estrangement he felt in each culture, which accents a common motif in many biographies.

ACTIVITIES

Before setting about reading various, more lengthy biographies, students might like to make outlines of important persons in their own lives. Encouraging them to outline the biography rather than writing it out allows them to search out and organize their information without taking the time necessary to carry their writing to the final draft. It's also an opportunity to show students various kinds of outline forms and their uses in organizing materials. Some students may find webbing a more useful form than the traditional outline. Time lines also can become a form of outline.

Check newspapers and magazines for obituaries of famous people and not for the brief biography these articles offer. Compare them to the lengthier biographies for the things that are omitted.

Students can follow up this activity by outlining their own real or imaginary autobiographies.

The Arts and Entertainment Network on television broadcasts a nightly biography pro-

Name	Field of Success	Barriers	Helpers	Defining Moments

gram. Encourage the students to watch a few of these and to look for the ways in which the producers interest the viewers in the material. Later, they can compare these to the techniques used by print biographers.

When students are ready to locate and begin reading biographies and autobiographies, encourage them to browse through several before settling in on one. They need to be interested in the subject, of course, but should also look for a writing style that reaches them.

Bring students together frequently as they are reading their biographies for discussions in small and large groups. Searching for a defining moment or epiphany in the life of a person, and varying judgments of what that is, is one way to start a dialogue among readers of various biographies. Other areas for discus-

sion include: barriers between the protagonist and success; people who helped and hindered; contributions to society; and high points in that person's life.

As they gather that information, it may be helpful to record their observations in table format like the one above.

Another way of organizing different information is to list a series of events that took place during the subject's lifetime. Then find out what, if anything, the subject thought about those various events. For instance, the following graphic shows such information about James Madison. A few events from his lifetime are placed around his silhouette, with his opinions in comic strip bubbles:

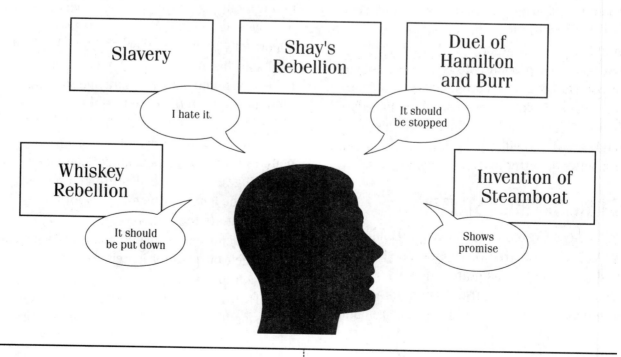

Check the Internet for information about their subject or about the time in which they live.

Students can make a web of their biographies and join them to other webs at one point or another.

Using newspaper and magazine articles about the subjects of their biographies should help students become aware of choices the writers made on what to include in their books. These sources will also help students define the era and area in which their subjects lived.

Each student can do a storyboard for a proposed movie or television show on the subject of her or his biography. Such things as opening scene, costumes, props, and possible casting should be noted.

A biography time line on which students enter specific events in their subjects' lives can be displayed. Such an activity helps students realize contemporaries of the biographee. Add important world events to the time line in order to see other factors that may have influenced their lives.

▶ BOOK LIST

▶ Picture Book Biographies

★ ★ ★ Cooney, Barbara **Eleanor** Viking, 1996 ISBN 0 670 86159 6

This is the story of the childhood and emerging adulthood of Eleanor Roosevelt. Cooney's illustrations capture the time, as well as the loneliness of the neglected child who became one of America's most beloved first ladies.

★ Cooper, Floyd **Coming Home: From the Life of Langston Hughes** Philomel, 1994 ISBN 0 399 22682 6

This shows the early years of the lonely child raised in Harlem by a grandmother who kept him isolated from others.

★ ★ Miller, William **Zora Hurston and the Chinaberry Tree** Lee & Low, 1994 ISBN 1 880000 14 8, illustrated by Ying-Hwa Hu

This picture book is about an author whose work may be unfamiliar to your students, but they may want to read some of her writings after reading this biography of a child who adored her mother and fought with her father, who tried to temper her spirit.

★ ★ ★ Miller, William **Frederick Douglass: The Last Day of Slavery** Lee & Low, 1992 ISBN 1 880000 17 2

Concentrating on the youth of Douglass, who became an eloquent orator, Miller shows us the child's feelings as his mother is sold to a different master.

★ ★ ★ ★ Sis, Peter **The Three Golden Keys** Doubleday, 1994 ISBN 0 385 47292 7

In an effort to tell his young daughter about himself, Peter Sis created this picture book. Knowing him means knowing the city of Prague and, in this intriguing and complicated picture book, Sis combines the sights, feelings, and legends of Prague with facts about his childhood there.

★ ★ ★ ★ Stanley, Diane **Cleopatra** Morrow, 1994 ISBN 0 688 10414 2

Illuminating illustrations depict the time beautifully. Cleopatra's use of power to beguile Caesar and others is the focus of this picture book.

▶ Lengthier Biographies

★ ★ ★ Bober, Natalie **Thomas Jefferson: Man on a Mountain** Atheneum, 1988 ISBN 0 689 31154 0

Natalie Bober is not as prolific as Jean Fritz, but she has created several worthwhile biographies for young adult readers. This book chronicles the events in the life of Jefferson but keeps him at arm's length—a distant but heroic figure.

★ ★ ★ Bober, Natalie **Abigail Adams: Witness to a Revolution** Atheneum, 1995 ISBN 0 689 31760 3

Bober's portrayal of Abigail Adams is more intimate and passionate. Bober uses letters to build a background of the life in the 18th century for the intelligent woman who challenged that time with her complex opinions and advice for her husband.

★ ★ ★ Bober, Natalie **A Restless Spirit** Holt, 1991 ISBN 0 8050 1672

Bober's biography of Robert Frost is a complex story befitting the man who became America's poet while wrestling with the anger and depression that haunted him. Frost's life, with an accent on his great love for his long-suffering wife, Elinor, is told clearly and sometimes lyrically, interweaving excerpts from his work and photographs of him, as well as those of friends and family. Something of the man's torment and guilt is related as well: the death and unhappiness of so many of those he loved or who loved him took its toll. The ever-changing houses and locales to which he led his family boggles the mind, but his restlessness and determination to succeed as a poet took precedence over everything else, and Elinor lent her will to his. Bober's portrait of the kindly, devoted father and teacher is at odds with some accounts, but she avoids the common error made by some biographers for young people of glossing over all unpleasantness and faults.

★ ★ ★ Bruchac, Joseph **Bowman's Store** Dial, 1997 ISBN 0 8037 1997 3

Author and storyteller Joseph Bruchac tells about growing up in a small town near Saratoga Springs, New York. Because of his abusive father, Bruchac was raised by his grandparents, Jesse and Marion Dunham Bowman. Jesse was Abenaki Indian, although he never admitted it, and Bruchac's life has centered around his search for his Native American roots. Bruchac tells his story with humor and with great respect toward his grandparents and the love and values they gave him. Almost every chapter begins with an Abenaki or Anishinaabe legend or myth. The biography is touching and gives an interesting look at the subtle racism in that time and place.

★ ★ ★ Byars, Betsy **The Moon and I** Morrow, 1996 ISBN 0 688 13704 0

Byars' brief memoir is downright hilarious. She tells about her methods of writing, several incidents from her childhood, and her passion to find out about things. It's an outstanding and very funny work, and many of the chapters make excellent read-aloud material. With a light and humorous touch, Ms. Byars tells of the way she writes her books. Throughout the account, she also tells of her relationship with a snake, Moon, which she found near her cabin. Her need to learn more about snakes in general and Moon in particular became an obsession that, for a brief time, dominated her existence. That obsession, the reasons for it, and the ways in which she conducted her research are so interesting and helpful that you want to read the brief book aloud at the outset of a research project.

★ ★ Cleary, Beverly **A Girl from Yamhill** Morrow, 1988 ISBN 0 688 07800 1

This autobiography of an author whose large volume of work many children have enjoyed covers the years from her earliest memory at age two to the day she leaves Oregon for a new life in Oregon. This is not the warm, joyful book that some readers of her novels will expect; at times this is a painful book about a mother whose love often overpowers and manipulates her daughter's life.

★ ★ Collier, James Lincoln **Louie Armstrong: An American Success Story** Simon & schuster, 1985 ISBN 0 02 722830 4

Collier has written several biographies of music greats. This biography of Louie Armstrong touches on the racism and exploitation that Armstrong had to deal with during his struggle to the top. Collier starts with the honky tonk music of New Orleans that inspired Armstrong's use of a mellophone in the "Colored Waif's Home" and ends with his lasting influence on American music.

★ ★ ★ ★ Freedman, Russell **Eleanor Roosevelt** Clarion, 1993 ISBN 0 89919 862 7

This is a good follow-up to the picture book by Barbara Cooney discussed earlier because it covers the same period of time in the life of Eleanor Roosevelt, as well as her later achievements. Freedman does not hesitate to put things in his biographies for young people that are usually restricted to adult biographies. Here, Franklin Roosevelt's affair with Lucy Mercer is dealt with, albeit delicately, as are the effects that it had on Eleanor's life. Although Freedman obviously respects his subjects, he does not hesitate to point out their flaws as well as their triumphs.

★ ★ ★ ★ Freedman, Russell **Franklin Delano Roosevelt** Clarion, 1990 ISBN 0 89919 379 X

Freedman's earlier book on her husband is equally successful. The book is scrupulously researched and, like Freedman's other work, is obviously not just an adult biography dumbed down. Using photographs, journals, and letters, Freedman provides a fascinating and intimate biography of the man whose life and deeds influenced millions.

★ ★ ★ ★ Freedman, Russell **Lincoln: A Photobiography** Clarion, 1987 ISBN 0 89919 379 X

This biography won the Newbery Award. Like the other biographies by this author, the fluent text and copious photographs and drawings make the book read like a novel. He does not oversimplify the life of Lincoln; complex issues such as his lifelong bout with depression, his wife's financial difficulties, and his sometimes contradictory stands on slavery are all discussed.

Fritz, Jean

Her biographies form two groups: shorter ones for younger readers, and more complex and lengthy ones for older, more adept readers. Into this first category go her Bicentennial series of biographies, which first appeared around 1976. These brief books, like her longer ones, bring the founding fathers to life, pointing out their foibles as well as their accomplishments. As is indicated by the title questions, the touch is light but the research is considerable. They are not fictionalized. Like the sports biographies by Carl Green, these brief biographies of historical figures provide accessibility to the genre for many who would be frightened away by lengthier books. They are:

★ ★ ★ **Why Don't You Get a Horse, Sam Adams** Putnam, 1974 ISBN 0 698 20292 9

★ ★ **Where Do You Think You're Going, Christopher Columbus** Putnam, 1981 ISBN 0 399 20734 1

★ ★ **Who's That Stepping on Plymouth Rock** Putnam, 1975 ISBN 0 698 20325 9

★ ★ **What's the Big Idea, Ben Franklin** Putnam, 1982 ISBN 0 698 20365 8

Where Was Patrick Henry on the 29th of May Putnam, 1982 ISBN 0 698 20307 0

★ ★ ★ **Will You Sign Here, John Hancock** Putnam, 1982 ISBN 0 698 20308 9

★ ★ ★ **And Then What Happened, Paul Revere** Putnam, 1973 ISBN 0 698 20541 3

★ ★ ★ **Can't You Make Them Behave, King George** Putnam, 1996 ISBN 0 698 11402 7

The second cluster of biographies by Fritz is longer works. Her unique ability to bring larger-than-life heroes and villains of history into human focus makes these outstanding works. They include:

★ ★ ★ **Stonewall** Putnam, 1979 ISBN 0 14 032937 4

The man who stood like a stone wall at the Battle of Manassas is Fritz's subject this time. Although "Stonewall" Jackson was a fine leader of men, he was a bizarre man. He insisted that his diet, for no particular reason, consist only of stale bread, lemons, and lean meat. He slept in a certain posture each night and had rules for every occasion.

★ ★ ★ **Traitor: The Case of Benedict Arnold** Puffin, 1989 ISBN 0 14 032940 4)

Fritz shows her skill in giving many sides of a character about which most of us have learned only one. Although his name is probably among the most widely known of the people in the American Revolution, few Americans are quite sure just what it is that he did, knowing only that it was traitorous. As always, with Fritz's work, the book is carefully researched, and she invents and assumes nothing. If there is conversation, it is verified in historical research. Yet, she manages to imbue her history with life in a way that few historical writers for adults or for children can manage without lapsing into fiction. Here is his flamboyant life from his boyhood in Norwich, Connecticut, to his death, not in battle as he had hoped, but in bed in London. Here is his heroism in earlier times, his greed, and, at last, his incredible treachery.

★ ★ ★ **Make Way for Sam Houston** Putnam, 1986 ISBN 0 399 21303 1

Fritz brings the Texan hero into focus. She makes sure that we know about his self-education and his great achievements as hero of the War of 1812, the governor of two states, and president of the country of Texas. She also tells us about his marriage to an Indian woman while he was already legally married, and his considerable problem with alcohol.

★ ★ ★ **Bully for You, Teddy Roosevelt** Putnam, 1991 ISBN 0 399 21769 X

This biography gives us a well-rounded portrait of the exuberant first President Roosevelt. Fritz shows him swaggering through the streets of New York as the city's police commissioner in pink shirts and silk cummerbund. But she also shows his impact on government, conservation, and big business. Like much of Fritz's work, this is an affectionate portrait.

★ ★ ★ **Great Little Madison** Putnam, 1989 ISBN 0 399 21768 1

Fritz humanizes a man whose personality is often buried in history. Outshone by the more colorful and charismatic Jefferson and Washington, the focus of this book is Madison's passion to create the ideal government exemplified at the Constitutional Convention, during which the future of the country "lay in the hands of 55 unpredictable men."

★ ★ ★ **You Want Women to Vote, Lizzie Stanton?** Putnam, 1995 ISBN 0 399 22786 5

This book is halfway between Fritz's brief, question biographies and her longer ones, some of which are mentioned above. As always, she writes with liberal use of humorous details but sticks to the facts. Stanton's busy life was full of travel speeches and a lifelong commitment, not only to that of equal rights for women, but also to the abolition of slavery.

★ ★ ★ **Harriet Beecher Stowe and the Beecher Preachers** Putnam, 1994 ISBN 0 399 22666 4

This is a fascinating story of the woman born at a time when women could not be heard in public, who rose to become a preacher like her father, although with a different mission. The family founded by Lyman Beecher was a complex and intriguing one, and Fritz tells their story well. Lyman intended to have only sons and desired that each of them become a preacher like himself. He was disappointed when Harriet was born and when three more daughters followed. He did have seven sons, and they all became preachers, with varying degrees of success. Two of them committed suicide. Ironically, though several of his daughters became involved in public speaking in an age when this was prohibited, it was Harriet who became the greatest preacher of them all with the publication of her book *Uncle Tom's Cabin*. As always with a Fritz book, you get the facts, but in such a way as to make the character about whose life she tells spring to life from the page.

★ ★ ★ **The Double Life of Pocahontas** Putnam, 1983 ISBN 0 399 2106 4

Fritz manages to demystify the Indian princess and portray the brief life of a woman caught between two cultures.

★ ★ ★ Fritz, Jean **Homesick: My Own Story** Dell, 1984 ISBN 0 440 43683 4

Jean Fritz has penned numerous biographies, many of which are cited above, but she has also written two autobiographies. She has slightly fictionalized her own biography, something she never does in her other works. She does this in order to use recalled conversation in this book about her early life in Wuhan, China, where she is homesick for an America she has never seen.

★ ★ ★ ★ Fritz, Jean **China Homecoming** Putnam, 1985 ISBN 0 399 21182 9

This is the story of her return to her childhood home in China and all its memories. In her earlier book, *Homesick: My Own Story* (see above), she wrote about her birth and childhood in China. In this book, she tells of her recent trip to China to rediscover her roots there. As always, she writes compellingly, and the reader is drawn into the history of the country as she discovers it herself. Traveling as a "Friend of China" and with what she calls a rudimentary ability with the language, Fritz was able to make new friends, discover her "hometown," and come to grip with the changes, both for good and not so good, in modern China. Her respect for its past and for its culture and people was as apparent to those who came in contact with her there as it is for the reader. Although the intent of the book is not really to teach the reader about the history of China, it is a pleasant surprise to find that happening.

★ Gherman, Beverly **E. B. White: Some Writer!** Atheneum, 1992 ISBN 0 689 31672 0

This is a bit adulatory, but gives some insights into this shy, talented author of *Charlotte's Web, Stuart Little,* and *Trumpet of the Swan.*

Green, Carl

Green has written several short biographies of sports heroes on levels which are accessible to less able middle school readers without sacrificing content: **Babe Ruth** (Crestwood, 1992 ISBN 0 89686 741 2), **Jackie Robinson** (Crestwood, 1992 ISBN 0 89686 743 9), **Babe Didrikson Zaharias** (Silver Burdett, 1993 ISBN 0 89686 736 6), **Jackie Joyner-Kersee** (Crestwood, 1994 ISBN 0 89686 838 9), **Jesse Owens** (Crestwood, 1992 ISBN 0 89686 742 0), **Jim Thorpe** (Silver, 1992 ISBN 0 89686 740 4), **Joe DiMaggio** (Silver, 1993 ISBN 0 89686 738 2), **Kareem Abdul-Jabbar** (Silver, 1993 ISBN 0 89686 737 4), and **Muhammed Ali** (Silver, 1993 ISBN 0 89686 739 0). These cannot be called great literature, but they are all clearly written and liberally illustrated with photographs. They provide background information and highlights in the sports careers of their subjects. As such, they may allow access to this theme study to some students who might otherwise be uninterested.

★ Greenfield, Eloise **Childtimes: A Three-Generational Memoir** HarperTrophy, 1979 ISBN 0 690 03875, with illustrations by Jerry Pinkney

Photos and drawings illustrate this story of the big events in the African-American lives of the author, her mother, and her grandmother.

★ ★ ★ Hopkins, Lee Bennett **Been to Yesterdays: Poems of a Life** Boyds Mills Press, 1995 ISBN 1 56397 467 3

This autobiography of a children's poet and anthologist is a series of connected short poems covering one year—the 13th—in his life. During that year, his quarreling parents divorced and his beloved grandmother died, but there is more. The style is simple and very elegant. He starts with an overly bright look at his supposedly ideal family, and then, poem by poem, we get more of the story and more of the cracks in the ideal picture.

★ Lipsyte, Robert **Jim Thorpe: 20th Century Jock** HarperCollins, 1993 ISBN 0 06 022988 8

This biography is also quite accessible, but is a more involved work than Green's. The young Native American, who spent most of his childhood in a reservation boarding school, succeeded in a triumph over the prejudice and racism that dominated the time.

★ Little, Jean **Little by Little** Viking, 1988 ISBN 0 670 81649 3

Novelist Jean Little tells the story of the childhood and young adult years of the girl with severely limited vision who grew up to be a writer. Her Canadian childhood included taunts from other children about her handicap and her will to succeed.

★ ★ ★ Owens, Richard **Meet the Author** Richard Owen Publishers

We can't leave this subset of author biographies and autobiographies without mentioning a series of books published by Richard Owen Publishers called **Meet the Author**. This ever-expanding series deals with children's authors and illustrators. Written by the authors with a text accessible by third-grade readers and up, these autobiographies contain many color photographs of the subject going about his or her life. They are an excellent resource.

★ ★ ★ ★ Peck, Richard **Anonymously Yours** Morrow, 1991 ISBN 0 688 13702 4

Again, we have the autobiography of an author who is often a favorite among young adult readers. The book is part autobiography and part advice book. Peck's blend of humor and sincerity makes his undisguised sermons quite palatable.

★ ★ ★ Peet, Bill **Bill Peet's Autobiography** Houghton, 1989 ISBN 0 395 50932 7

This is one of the most interesting of the author biographies. Many students will remember reading some of his picture books. Peet tells about his childhood, of course, but some of the most interesting passages describe his work at the Disney studios. Peet's liberal use of his own sketches help to enlighten and brighten the work.

CHAPTER 8

The River

COMMENTS

Depending on your purpose, the River Theme can be slanted toward science or social studies or kept as a predominately literary one. If it's science you're aiming for, you'll get into environmental issues connected with rivers and water, the physical properties of water and water treatment areas, or weather and the water cycle.

If social studies is the discipline you wish to combine with literature, you can do an exploration of the world's rivers and the cultures that have grown up around them.

In literature, the river can be more than a setting—it can appear as a symbol, a motif, or sometimes even as a character. The river is an excellent topic for study in the middle school because its familiarity offers common ground to a diverse group of students. Some students will be able to grasp the symbolism of rivers, find it in many works of literature, and go on to find other symbols in books. Other students can see the river, and work with it only when it is more obviously the subject or scene of action, but they can find the variations in its literal use in many works.

Dealing with the river first in its simplest form—that of the setting for or scene of action—we come up with several outstanding works of fiction and nonfiction. It is possible to use this topic to aim the students toward **Huckleberry Finn** as the major culminating work. Researching rivers as a subject, starting with a local river, is one possible approach to the theme. We can explore its plants and animals, determine how it affects people, and investigate how people have changed rivers, currently and historically. We can look historically at the uses of waterpower from the rivers. We can expand our focus by investigating major rivers worldwide, finding out how they have affected life near them. Consider letting the students loose to follow the connections that make sense to them, bringing them together periodically to reveal their discoveries.

When we look at concrete objects (such as a river) as standing for abstract ideas, we are using symbolism—a powerful literary tool. In recognizing that such an object can be more than its literal self, we are opening a work of literature to the many layers of meaning beyond the literal. This is not only fun for middle school students to play with, it is a necessary stage in their reading development. See page 132 for other books with strong or interesting symbols.

PICTURE BOOK STARTER

Lynn Cherry's wonderful **A River Ran Wild** (Gulliver, 1992 ISBN 0 15 200542 0) is a good starting place. In this book, the focus is on the Nashua River in New Hampshire, and it becomes a microcosm for the history of humans in that area. There is also the underlying concept of the river of time. The book is full of information and inspiration.

◢ ACTIVITIES

A River Ran Wild's most direct application is to the environment, and that may be the direction you and your students decide to take. It should be a short step from the Nashua River to a river in your area. Cherry's book starts with the past, but you may get more students involved by starting with the present for your research project. You'll need current and detailed maps. First of all, where does your river begin and end? What rivers and brooks feed it, and what does it, in turn, feed? Get the students to list the towns and cities on the river. Can they find out how each place affects the river? What does each place gain from the river? Is the river cleaner or dirtier after leaving that area? What about the students' own city? What does it do to the river? What has the river done to the cities? Are there organizations working to clean it up? How successful have they been? Can your students get involved? For starters, they can collect and evaluate water samples before and after flowing through a specific spot.

Now, we can look backward. Send students searching through newspaper files in the library to see if they can do a history of their own river, similar to Lynn Cherry's. A search of old maps at your town or city hall should show the development of towns and cities along the river. Who can tell you about local river wildlife? A field trip in order to make your own observations may hold answers. Books such as **Pond & River**, by Steve Parker, are great for showing the kinds of plants and animals students might find, and for initial classification of specimens.

Katherine Paterson's novel **Lyddie** (see page 193) would be a good book for some readers to tackle after *A River Ran Wild*. In 1843, Lyddie goes to work in the mills of Lowell, Massachusetts, which is on the Merrimac, the river into which the Nashua River flows. After reading *Lyddie*, students might like to do further research on mills and factories and their present and past effects on rivers, or they could sidestep into the use of child labor in those mills, finding out why it started and stopped—if, indeed, it has stopped.

Some students might like to look at a book about another river not far from the Nashua: Jane Yolen and Barbara Cooney's picture book **Letting Swift River Go**. In the 1930s, dams were built on the Swift River in central Massachusetts to create Quabbin Reservoir to serve as water supply for Boston, many miles to the east. To accomplish this, four Massachusetts towns were drowned. The story is movingly told from the point of view of one little girl who lived in one of those towns.

You can also look at rivers from the physical science point of view after reading *Letting Swift River Go*. The physical properties of water necessitate the various dams and levees in the book. The ways in which the water gets to Boston can lead to a study of water purification methods.

Walter Wick's amazing nonfictional picture book **A Drop of Water** (see below) holds the motivation for a whole study of water and its properties.

It's only a short step from that book to the water cycle and to weather-related books, just a few of which are listed below.

Letting Swift River Go can also lead to an investigation of how and why we've changed the course of many of our rivers and the results of those changes.

Letting Swift River Go might also lead to the novel **The Walking Stones.** This book is well within the reach of most fifth-grade readers. The Bodach, a mystical personage, and Donald Campbell, a human boy, combine efforts to stop the flooding of a peaceful and mythologically important valley. Students who are working with this book might like to go on to similar river stories, like those of the Colorado River, dammed to form Lake Mead, and the Columbia River, similarly harnessed.

Readers bring their previous ideas and experiences to the reading. Some writers use this facility in readers to communicate through symbols. The following exercises can help students discover their preconceived notions of "River," and to play with it as a symbol.

Ask the students to close their eyes and picture a word you are about to use, and then tell exactly what they see. The word, of course, is "river." After getting a few responses, prod them with such questions as, "Is it day or night?" "How big is the river?" "How do you feel being near the river?" "Are you alone?" "What's near or in the river?" Write a few words from their descriptions on the board or overhead.

When that source dries up, look together at the words for commonalties and differences. Choose adjectives to put in front of "river": deep, still, turbulent, clear, muddy. How do these words change the students' images?

Go on to river-related words: rapids, waterfalls, fish, turtles, frogs, mud, banks, rocks. Sounds of the river might include: babble, trickle, rush, roar, splash. Feelings brought to mind by the river might be: peace, fear, tranquillity, excitement. Go for synonyms and types of rivers: rivulet, brook, torrent, stream.

Stretch all these out as far as the students' minds will take them. Cover the area with river words. Then begin to put phrases together: "the deep, dark, tranquil river"; "the roaring, twisting torrent"; "the mysterious, beckoning, watery road." Ask students to think about how these river ideas could be used by a writer to convey a feeling or to be a symbol of something else.

Search **Bartlett's Quotations** and other references to find quotes about a river. This might be a good time to share your favorite poem or quotation about a river. Some of ours include:

"A river seems a magic thing. A magic, moving, living part of the very earth itself—for it is from the soil, both from its depth and from its surface, that a river has its beginning."
Photographer Laura Gilpin

"I was born upon thy bank, river,
My blood flows in thy stream,
And thou meanderest forever
At the bottom of my dream."
Henry David Thoreau

"You cannot step twice into the same river; for fresh waters are ever flowing in upon you."
Heraclitus

"I do not know much about the gods; but I think that the river is a strong brown god—sullen, untamed and untractable."
T.S. Eliot

And, because we may be aiming the whole theme toward *Huckleberry Finn*, here is a quotation from Mark Twain:

"The face of the water, in time, became a wonderful book—a book that was a dead language to the uneducated passenger, but which told its mind to me without reserve, delivering its most cherished secrets as clearly as if it uttered them with a voice. And it was not a book to be read once and thrown aside, for it had a new story to tell every day."

Post these or other river quotes and encourage students to add their own favorites as the theme progresses.

Some students will be able to see that, in the Gilpin quotation, the river is described by someone who sees it vividly, while some of the other writers use the river as a symbol. This could be a jumping off place for generating things the river could symbolize for each writer. Students may want to go in search of other quotes at this time. Suggest that they keep an eye out for such river symbolism as they read, or that they might want to use such symbols themselves in their own writing.

Mary Oliver's poem, "How I Went Truant from School to Visit a River," in Paul B. Janeczko's **Preposterous** (currently out of print but in many libraries), describes her day at a local river: its "bloodroot bloomed like alabaster verbs" and "the fine geometry/ Of blue and wet-legged herons. . . ."

Jim Simmerman's poem "Distance," in Janeczko's **Looking for Your Name** (see page 127), uses wading in a river as part of his exploration of time, space, and distance. You can find more poetry in **Snow Toward Evening: A Year in a River Valley**, a collection of poems by Wordsworth, Updike, Hughes, and others, illustrated with paintings of the Hudson River valley throughout the year (see page 126).

A river is used as a proving place in Marion Bauer's **On My Honor** (reviewed on page 57). In this short and very easily read novel, two boys dare each other to swim in a forbidden river. The result is the death of one boy and overwhelming guilt on the part of the other. What is it they are trying to prove? What does the river symbolize? What else could the author have used in place of the river and how would that have changed the book?

In any of the books listed here, look for descriptive passages of the river. How does the author use description to strengthen and define the symbolism? What, if anything, in the plot leads you to believe the river might be a symbol of something greater? Do the events that follow strengthen, broaden, or change the symbolism?

The river is frequently used as a symbol of a current of thoughts or events. Read Lois Lowry's Newbery Award speech for **The Giver** (*Horn Book Magazine*, July/August 1994) to see how she uses the symbolism of the river in describing her thoughts as she came to write the book.

It's almost impossible to use rivers, especially the Mississippi River, as a theme without bringing in Mark Twain's work. Indeed, his books have been the force behind the whole study. The **Adventures of Tom Sawyer** makes an excellent read aloud or read alone from about fifth grade and up. Episodic in nature, the book is a historical novel of a different sort than those students are usually accustomed to because, at the time it was written, the setting was almost current. Students can get from it some insight into small-town life and values at the turn of the century. Tom's hijinks and sense of fun and adventure should strike an accord with some of today's youth, and the cave and cemetery chapters are downright scary.

The depiction of Injun Joe may provide an opportunity for discussion about the treatment of Native Americans in real life and in the fiction of the time. The depiction of African Americans in *Tom Sawyer* is also worth investigating. Figuring out what Twain was trying to tell his readers about life, about the river, and about tolerance should lead to the deepest layer of meaning: theme.

On one level, *Huckleberry Finn* is also an adventure story, almost as episodic as *Tom Sawyer*, although with darker undertones. Twain speaks through Huck, and we view the incidents and adventures through his eyes. On another level, it's a story about the rite of passage to adulthood, although Huck himself changes little from beginning to end. Most of his conceptions about the evils of civilization are proven true by the behavior of the townspeople he encounters. The book can also be considered as a jab at the folly of human institutions, with slavery as its main target. The river provides beauty, simplicity, and adventure in *Huckleberry Finn*. Of course, the very fact that this book has been the focus of so many attempts at censorship from a variety of groups with varying agendas makes the book worth reading and evaluating.

BOOK LIST

▶ Picture Books

★ ★ Carlstrom, Nancy White **Raven & River** Little Brown, 1997 ISBN 0 316 12894 5
Striking illustrations show an icebound river and the animals that live around it.

★ ★ ★ Calhoun, Mary **Flood** Morrow, 1997 ISBN 0 688 13919 1, illustrated by Erick Ingraham
This is an insider's look at the great Midwestern flood of 1993, as a child watches his family cope with the rising waters.

★ ★ ★ ★ Cherry, Lynne **A River Ran Wild: An Environmental History** Gulliver, 1992 ISBN 0 15 200542 0
We see the Nashua River first in its pristine state and then watch as people move in and change the river until it becomes an unsightly, polluted mess. We then see the results of a campaign to clean it up.

★ ★ Locker, Thomas **Where the River Begins** Dial, 1984 ISBN 0 8037 0089 X
Boys who live beside the river are taken to its source by their grandfather.

★ ★ ★ London, Jonathan **Voices of the Wild** Crown, 1993 ISBN 0 517 59214 7
Each animal living in and around a river sees a man paddling a canoe, and we see that man from their visual and textual perspective. Each animal speaks and defines itself in relation to the man. The man says nothing until the end of the story. The effect is that of a human observing the wild without unduly disturbing it.

★ ★ ★ Lyon, George Ella **Come a Tide** Orchard, 1990 ISBN 0 531 05854 9, illustrated by Stephen Gammell
The river is rising with the heavy rain, and some folks in rural Kentucky know how to band together to face the challenge.

★ ★ ★ Yolen, Jane **Letting Swift River Go** Little, 1995 ISBN 0 316 96860 9
See above.

Novels

★ ★ Banks, Lynn Reid **One More River** Morrow, 1992 ISBN 0 688 10893 8
The river is a mark of division between two possible friends in this book. Fourteen-year-old Lesley Shelby's life has been ideal—wealthy parents and great friends, and she's considered attractive and popular. Then, her parents decide to emigrate to Israel to live on a kibbutz. Life in the kibbutz is difficult for the spoiled little rich girl. It isn't until her daring and foolhardy initiation into the kibbutz youth group, and her trials in the Six-Day War that Lesley comes to feel that she belongs. Her brother, Noah, enlists with the Israelis, and the family is reunited. Lesley, who had felt friendship for Mustapha, an Arab farm boy from the other side of the Jordan River, sees him in a conquered town after the war. She wedges a photograph of them, which had connected them as friends, into the Wall with a message in three languages: "Peace between us and between our peoples."

★ ★ Byars, Betsy **Trouble River** Viking, 1989 ISBN 0 140 34243 5
This is not a difficult book, but it is a good adventure story. There's a wonderfully obstinate grandmother who sits on a rocking chair in the middle of a rickety raft built by her grandson—their only hope for survival. She nags him constantly, even though she doesn't know anything about rafting or rivers; she can't help it—she's a nagger, born and bred. The river here is an escape from danger. Students who read this novel might like to talk about the image of Native Americans in this book.

★ ★ ★ DeFelice, Cynthia **Lostman's River** Camelot, 1995 ISBN 0 380 72396 4

Tyler has lived in the Everglades with his family since his father fled New York State, fearing he would be accused of murder. The family needs money, so Tyler signs on with a man who is engaged in "scientific work." This is a time when exotic birds were hunted for their plumage, and Strawbridge, the man who hires Tyler, wants to kill the birds for museum specimens before they become extinct.

★ ★ ★ Hamilton, Virginia **Cousins** Philomel, 1990 ISBN 0 399 22164 6

This is another book where the river proves fatal. Hamilton gives us an exuberant, delightful, and very believable heroine, Cammy. Cammy loves and hates with almost the same gusto. She loves her grandmother, who is in a nursing home and failing rapidly, and she loves her mother and her older brother. She hates her absolutely perfect cousin, Patty Ann, even while she envies her. She tolerates and alternately hates, pities, and loves her other cousin, Eloise. Then, at day camp, the gentle story explodes as Eloise gets swept away in the current of a river and is saved by Patty Ann, who drowns. Before it's over, everybody, but especially Cammy, has some hard lessons to learn.

★ ★ ★ Hunter, Mollie **The Walking Stones** Harcourt, 1996 ISBN 0 15 20095 7
See above.

★ ★ Paulsen, Gary **The River** Yearling, 1993 ISBN 0 440 40753 2

The river here is the means by which Brian is able to get an unconscious man to a trading post. In this sequel to **Hatchet,** Brian has been asked by government researchers to reenact his adventure in the wilderness. When the camp is struck by lightning, resulting in an unconscious researcher, Brian builds a raft and conquers the river.

Stevermer, Caroline **River Rats** Harcourt, 1992 ISBN 0 15 200895 0

The river here is the means of transportation and the means of survival. See also page 66.

Twain, Mark **Huckleberry Finn** (many editions)
See above.

Twain, Mark **Tom Sawyer** (many editions)
See above.

► Nonfiction

★ ★ Hiscock, Bruce **The Big Rivers: The Missouri, the Mississippi and the Ohio** Atheneum, 1997 ISBN 0 689 80871 2

This is more about the flooding created by the rivers than about the rivers themselves, but the information provided about the large tidal basin that they create is very useful.

★ ★ Kroll, Steven **Lewis and Clark: Explorers of the American West** Holiday House, 1994 ISBN 0 8234 1034 X

This picture book of history is well done. The illustrations are more than the static creations typical in such books. The text is clear and sufficiently detailed to pique interest.

★ Lewin, Ted **Sacred River** Clarion, 1995 ISBN 0 395 69846 4

The illustrations in this book about the Ganges are superb. The text is less successful, but it tells about the ceremonial role of the river.

★ ★ ★ Lourie, Peter **Everglades: Buffalo Tiger & the River of Grass** Boyds Mill, 1998 ISBN 1 563 97702 8

Buffalo Tiger is a Miccosukee Indian. He tells us some of the past history of the Everglades and takes us on a tour showing the encroachments and devastation of developers.

★ ★ Lourie, Peter **Hudson River: An Adventure from the Mountains to the Sea** Boyds Mill, 1998 ISBN 1 563 97703 6

We accompany the author/photographer on a 315-mile canoe trip from Lake Tear in the Adirondacks, where the Hudson River begins, to Battery Park at the tip of Manhattan, where it empties into the sea. On the way, we observe the Spier Falls Dam, the locks on the Champlain Canal, and various other landmarks.

★ ★ ★ Paulsen, Gary **Father Water, Mother Woods: Essays on Fishing and Hunting in the North Woods** Delacorte, 1994 ISBN 0 385 32053 1

These essays are replete with Paulsen's love for and knowledge of the outdoors. Many are set in and around rivers, but in his chapter called "Running the River," Paulsen talks about the river as the highway to all things. Within the context of boys, including himself, on a hilarious and aborted camping trip, he talks about the river, its dangers, and its mystery.

★ Powledge, Fred **Working River** Farrar, 1995 ISBN 0 374 38527 0

Maryland's Patuxent River is the focus of this book, and through the river we see the history of the area, the past uses of the river, and its current state.

★ ★ ★ Simon, Seymour **Weather** Morrow, 1993 ISBN 0 688 10546 7

Simon uses wonderful and dramatic color photos and a clear, exuberant text to explain some of the phenomena of weather.

★ ★ ★ ★ Wick, Walter **A Drop of Water** Scholastic, 1997 ISBN 0 590 22197 3

Amazing color photographs demonstrate the properties of water. A simple text explains the photographs, and at the end of the book, the author suggests a series of experiments for further exploration.

Survival

COMMENTS

The topic of survival is so open that almost any work of fiction and many biographies could be included within that term of reference. After all, in one sense or another, survival of a character or characters makes up most plots. As such, it makes a good starting point for literature groups in which everybody has read a different book. For the purposes of this discussion, let's deal with books in which survival is literally involved.

Such a study quickly takes on a scientific bent because the study of survival is, to one degree or another, the study of environment, as well as that of the skills and physical and emotional abilities necessary to survive in that environment.

There are, of course, classic stories of survival, such as **Robinson Crusoe**, **Swiss Family Robinson**, **Call of the Wild**, and **White Fang**. Some students may be ready to read these but should probably be discouraged from reading the cut-down and abridged versions. To do so is to eliminate some of the fine writing that has made such books endure.

There are many categories into which survival stories fit: physical and emotional survival; survival in the wilderness and in urban areas; animal and human survival stories; and stories in which animals and humans cooperate for survival. Another dichotomy may be survival made necessary by cataclysmic events, such as airplane crashes, floods, or storms, and those in which an individual or group of individuals have more or less deliberately put themselves at risk. Students can choose books in a given category or think of a book they have read in terms of which category would be most apropos.

PICTURE BOOK STARTER

A picture book with a slightly oblique form of survival—cultural and familial survival in a war—is Florence Parry Heide's **Sami and the Time of Troubles** (Clarion, 1992 ISBN 0 395 55964 2). Sami tells how, when the bombs are dropping and the fighting is active in his area, he and his family live in the basement of his uncle's house, where the adults try valiantly to keep the family feeling safe and loved. When the bombing temporarily stops, they can go to the market and even to the beach. They have brought their treasures with them into the dark basement: their carpets, a brass vase—anything to keep alive a memory of better times. When it is safe, they go outside, and Sami finds his friends again amidst the rubble. People shop, and even have a wedding, and life seems almost normal. Surprisingly, or maybe not so surprisingly, the children play at war.

➤ ACTIVITIES

Students should select and read a survival story and be prepared to work with it over a period of time. There are questions that may help students evaluate or discuss a book, such as: Whose survival was at risk in my book? Was physical or emotional survival at risk? What skills or implements were used in the quest for survival? What prior knowledge was useful? What new knowledge was acquired along the way? Who grew or changed as a result of the experience, and would it have happened anyway? How much of the journey or quest for survival was an internal battle? Who or what hindered or aided in the survival? Is future survival likely for this character after this adventure? Readers who bring to the discussion answers to any or all of those questions should be in good shape to talk about their books from the aspect of survival. The group should also be in a position wherein a comparison of the disparate plots, author's knowledge, and techniques and characterization is likely.

Some books, of course, have survival as a more specific element, and these can be viewed through the questions listed above, as well as through more direct questions. Because the topic of physical survival has intrigued many authors, we have a wide range of survival books on a variety of difficulty levels.

The topic of survival can lead to a research project that entails finding real people who survived against the odds. This may necessitate reading some of the aforementioned biographies, interviews, or newspaper and magazine coverage of such events. Twisting that periodical information only slightly, students can make it into a writing activity after deciding which of those real-life events could be the nucleus of a piece of fictional writing.

Another direction for writing or discussion might be deciding on a specific environment where survival could be challenging, deciding on a few minimum supplies and necessary skills, and posing the problem of a specific person in that environment. This leads the theme into areas of science and math as students research the reality of survival in a given area.

Students can speculate on the various survival situations in which their particular strengths would be useful, and might like to write a fictional or real-life situation of personal survival.

Reading and researching survival stories can lead to some community activities and involvement on the part of students, such as discovering local homeless people's attempts to survive. Doing this, and looking at historical events that threatened survival of large numbers of people, such as the Holocaust (see page 30) and various natural disasters, connect the survival theme with social studies and science.

Survival stories can be looked at critically. Could a human survive in that situation by the resources used in the book? Is it believable? In **Julie of the Wolves**, for instance, some people knowledgeable in the ways of wolves say that they would not have befriended Julie in such a way. Jean George, on the other hand, claims to have researched her book carefully and found evidence of similar behavior on the part of the wolves. Regardless of the science involved, students might like to consider how George and other survival authors made the situation believable. When or where in the reading of the story did they, as readers, make the leap of faith, or did they?

⊳ BOOK LIST

▶ Picture Books

★ ★ Kinsey-Warnock, Natalie **The Bear That Heard Crying** Cobblehill, 1993 ISBN 0 525 65103 9

This is based on a historical incident in 1783 in New Hampshire. A three-year-old child wanders into the woods and is missing for four days. When searchers find bear tracks beside those of the child, they are sure that she has been attacked and give up the search until a stranger claims to have seen her in a dream and leads them to the child. The child talks about a big black dog that kept her warm in the wilderness.

★ ★ Murphy, Jim **The Call of the Wolves** Scholastic, 1994 ISBN 0 590 41940 4

In this picture book, the reader gets an animal survival story. A wolf, wounded and separated from the pack, must survive long enough to rejoin the pack.

Novels

★ ★ Baillie, Allan **Adrift** Viking, 1992 ISBN 0 670 84474 8

This is a story, based on a real-life incident, set in Australia. Flynn, his younger sister, Sally, and her cat jump aboard a crate floating by the shore. When the crate drifts out to sea, Sally is unwilling to abandon her cat, so they move farther and farther from safety. Eventually, Flynn rigs his shirt as a sail and they reach land in time to be rescued by a passing ship. In the meantime, however, Flynn has had time to come to grips with his relationship with his father, whom he alternately resents and emulates.

★ ★ ★ ★ Burgess, Melvin **The Cry of the Wolf** Tambourine, 1990 ISBN 0 688 11744 9

This is a novel in which the survival is not that of a human, but of an animal. Here we start with an assumption that there are still a few wild wolves in England, and only a few people are aware of this. What if one of those people was an obsessive, half-mad, extremely able hunter who was determined to have the "honor" of killing the last wolf in England? This is one of the focus books that is more fully explored on page 153. For other tales of animal survival, see the animal theme on page 97.

★ ★ ★ ★ Byars, Betsy **The Pinballs** HarperCollins, 1977 ISBN 0 06 020917 8

Survival of a different sort, emotional survival, is the theme here. Byars gives us some unforgettable characters: Carlie, Harvey, and Thomas J., three foster children taken in by the Masons, who have cared for many other foster children in the past. It's Carlie who compares the children to pinballs—controlled by external forces, and at the mercy of fate. She has survived thus far by refusing to be vulnerable. The others have various mechanisms in place, but the Masons provide a supportive environment in which the children learn to care for each other and begin to experience love and trust.

★ ★ ★ Campbell, Eric **The Place of Lions** Harcourt, 1990 ISBN 0 15 21031 9

This is a very good survival story which has some wonderfully descriptive passages about Africa, in general, and lions, in particular. On a journey into Tanzania, where his father is to take a new job, the plane carrying Chris and his father crashes. The pilot is seriously injured and unconscious. His father has a broken leg, but Chris, though hurt, is ambulatory. This is fortunate, because the plane has crashed near a pride of lions, and Chris is witness to a battle between age and youth. The old male lion is challenged by a young one, and barely manages to maintain his supremacy after a fierce battle. Chris has, in the meantime, decided to go for help. Chris is followed across the plain by the old, dying lion, and a mysterious connection is made as both head for a hill—where the lion seeks to die, and Chris seeks help.

★ ★ Carter, Alden **Between a Rock and a Hard Place** Scholastic, 1995 ISBN 0 590 48684 5

This is an adventure that takes place in the wilderness of the Boundary Waters of northern Minnesota, where two cousins, Mark and Randy, are sent by their fathers on a traditional coming-of-age endeavor. Randy is diabetic and less athletic than Mark, but things go well until a bear gets into the food shortly before their canoe is destroyed in the rapids and their other supplies, including Randy's insulin, is lost. Randy falls into a diabetic coma, and Mark must go to get help. The language the boys use may offend some readers, but the story is exciting and believable.

★ ★ ★ ★ Cole, Brock **The Goats** Aerial Fiction, 1987 ISBN 0 374 32678 9

Harsher, and reminiscent of **Lord of the Flies**, this is a book for a slightly younger audience than *Flies*. Laura and Howie are the victims of a camp prank where a boy and a girl are stripped and left on an island in the lake. They are the Goats, chosen because of their inability to fit in. Laura and Howie decide to disappear, both for revenge and because they don't want to return to the cruelty of the kids at the camp. The story takes place as the kids go from place to place trying to avoid detection, periodically calling Laura's mother to ask her to come get them.

★ ★ ★ ★ George, Jean **Julie of the Wolves**
HarperCollins, 1972 ISBN 0 06 021943 2

In this Newbery Award winner, George gives us Julie (or Miyak), a young girl fleeing from a brutal, arranged marriage out onto the Alaskan tundra, where her survival depends on adoption by a wolf pack. Succeeding in this endeavor, she must save not only herself, but the wolf pack, from the encroaching civilization.

★ ★ ★ Hill, Kirkpatrick **Toughboy and Sister** McElderry, 1990 ISBN 0 689 59595 X

This is set in the culture of the Native Americans in Alaska. John and Annie Laurie, more commonly known as Toughboy and Sister, love the fish camp where they have spent every summer they can remember. They have watched their mother and father catch the salmon, set up the fish wheel, and cut and smoke the fish each year. Then their mother dies, and their father changes. He drinks too much and becomes irresponsible. When he dies after abandoning them at the fish camp, miles from their homes, the 11-year-old boy and his sister get through each day, including a bear attack, and draw closer together. Even more important, they survive until help finally comes.

★ ★ ★ ★ Hobbs, William **Far North** Morrow, 1996 ISBN 0 688 14192 7

Far North is set in the same general area as **Hatchet** (see below), but is a longer and somewhat more challenging book to read. Like many of the best survival stories, it concerns more than physical survival. Evident in this book is a respect for the Old Ways of the Dene people and for the animals, as well as a concern about their survival. Gabe and his Dene roommate, Raymond, together with Raymond's great-uncle Johnny Raven, crash-land in the remote area of the Nahanni River in the Northwest Territories in November. The bush pilot is killed shortly afterward. Johnny Raven imparts as much as he can of the myth and the skill of his people to the boys before he dies, and even after his death his spirit seems to guide them as the boys make their own way out. This is good, action-filled reading. The description of Gabe's encounter with a grizzly is a good, short piece to read aloud.

★ ★ ★ Houston, James **Frozen Fire** Atheneum, 1977 ISBN 0-689-70489-

When Matthew Morgan's mother died, his father, a prospecting geologist for whom luck is always waiting on the next expedition, sets out with Matthew for Frobisher Bay in the Canadian Arctic to live on Baffin Island. Once there, Mr. Morgan and Charlie (a daredevil Australian helicopter pilot) set off, in a storm, to find a lode of copper ore to make their fortunes. When they do

not return, Matt and his new Eskimo friend go after them, hoping to be able to find and save them. This is a real survival story based on the actual journey taken by an Eskimo boy in 1960. It also displays Eskimo life and values.

★ ★ ★ Kidd, Diana **Onion Tears** Orchard, 1991 ISBN 0 531 05870 0

A different culture is featured within this short novel. Nam has survived the war that tore apart her country and her family. Without knowing their fate, Nam has come to Australia, where she helps another refugee, Chu Minh, run a restaurant. Her tears for her family are unshed, and she stoically absorbs the taunts and jibes from her classmates in Miss Lily's class until Miss Lily, the only one who seems to understand and care about Nam, becomes ill. The tears shed for Miss Lily are Nam's first since her own tragedies. The story is short but well written and should promote much discussion.

★ ★ ★ Lasky, Kathryn **Beyond the Divide** Aladdin, 1983 ISBN 0 689 80163 7

In this survival tale set in the 19th century, Meribah Simon starts her journey as part of an Amish family in Pennsylvania. Already, there is discord, however, as her father, and even his family, is shunned by the community, because he attended the funeral of a non-Amish friend. Meribah leaves the family at the same time as her father to seek a life beyond those confines. The descriptions of their becoming members of a wagon train heading to California as part of the Gold Rush contains many details and much information. Departing from St. Joseph, Meribah's father has many skills and earns respect from their fellow travelers. Meribah, regarded as quaint and innocent, also gains a measure of respect. When her father is injured, however, the wagon train goes on without them and they become victims of much cruelty. Villains and heroes merge and exchange roles as the thirst for gold takes over. After the death of her father, Meribah learns to survive alone during a harsh winter in the Sierras, befriended at last by a young woman whose people will also be eliminated eventually. Meribah is a strong female character, and this survival tale, like the best of its kind, is as much about survival of the spirit as of the body. Its prologue foreshadows the events in this book, as does Lowry's in **Autumn Street**.

★ ★ Masterton, David **Get Out of My Face** Atheneum, 1991 ISBN 0 689 31675 5

This story is about Kate, who is trying to adjust to her new family when her father remarries, but her stepsister, Linda, and stepbrother, Joey, seem programmed to make her life miserable. On a family camping trip, the children's canoe is overturned, and their survival depends on luck and cooperation.

★ ★ Morey, Walt **Death Walk** Blue Heron, 1991 ISBN 0 936085 18 5

The dialogue in this survival story is often wooden, but the conflict it portrays is interesting. Joel Rogers's mother has died recently and, in their grief, the boy and his father have grown apart. Joel runs away and ends up in remote Alaska, alone and without skills. Fortunately, he is taken in by Mike Donovan, a man who is himself running away, but who has far more survival skills. He also has two untamed wolves to whom he relates. Joel has no choice but to stay with Mike, especially because two other men are after him. Joel and Mike learn from each other. This book is also about the necessity for physical fighting, though it draws back from taking human life. It would contrast well with more pacifistic books. Also, in this book the wolves are honored, but everybody runs a trap line and hunts for other beasts.

★ Myers, Edward **Climb or Die** Hyperion, 1994 ISBN 0 7868 0026 7

This is a novel that gives us a brother and sister, Danielle and Jake, who must scale a mountain to get help for their injured parents after their car careens off the highway, 20 miles from the nearest town. Danielle has more athletic ability than her brother, but his inventive and creative mind is equally necessary for their success.

★ ★ ★ Naylor, Phyllis Reynolds **The Fear Place** Atheneum, 1994 ISBN 0 689 31866 9

Naylor has given us a good, although not very deep, story of two teenage brothers—their misunderstandings and fights, and eventual peace. Mainly, however, it's about facing one's fears and overcoming them. The two brothers are alone in the Colorado wilderness when they part company after a fight. The elder, Gordon, goes through a difficult mountain trail to an even more remote area. At first, Doug is delighted that his tormentor is gone, especially when he makes friends with a mountain lion. Gradually, however, he becomes worried about Gordon, and takes the fearful trail (over which he once collapsed) to find that Gordon has broken his leg and is ill with fever. Now, he must travel the trail again—this time with his brother on his back.

★ ★ ★ ★ Paulsen, Gary **Hatchet** Penguin, 1988 ISBN 0 14 032724 X

This novel is a very popular survival story, and many of your students will have encountered it in elementary school. For those who have not, however, it's an exciting and very accessible adventure story. When the small plane bringing Brian to his father crashes in the Canadian wilderness, Brian must use the only tool he has, a hatchet, and his own instincts to survive for many months until help comes.

★ ★ ★ ★ Paulsen, Gary **The Haymeadow** Delacorte, 1992 ISBN 0 385 30621 0

The survival here is less traumatic than in some of these other selections. Help will come, and John knows it. John Baron has just turned 14 when he is sent by his stern, uncommunicative father to spend the summer in the haymeadow alone with 6,000 sheep, two horses, and four dogs. Fortunately, the dogs are trained sheepherders, because without them John could not have done it. John has always identified with and tried to emulate his grandfather, or at least the stories he heard about him. In the haymeadow, John comes to face his fears as well as his dreams. When his father comes to the haymeadow, he also faces him and finds out the truth about his grandfather, his father, and himself.

★ ★ ★ Paulsen, Gary **Call Me Francis Tucket** Delacorte, 1995 ISBN 0 385 32116 3

This is set in the same era as **Beyond the Divide**. This brief novel is lighter than most of Paulsen's survival stories, but it's well done. A sequel *to* **Mr. Tucket**, this story starts with Francis, alone, but with a rifle and a mare, trying to relocate his family's wagon train. Soon, a couple of nefarious men relieve him of the horse, rifle, clothing, and food, leaving him shirtless with his broken-down mule. The mule turns out to be a blessing in disguise as it helps Francis get back his mare, clothing, and gun. Soon Francis finds two children abandoned on the trail and becomes a family man in spite of himself.

★ ★ Peck, Robert Newton **Arly's Run** Walker, 1991 ISBN 0-8027-8120-

This is a sequel to **Arly**. It opens with Brother Smith rowing Arly to freedom across Lake Okeechobee. However, stormy waves swamp the boat, taking Brother Smith under. Arly is saved by clinging to an oar. His letter that will explain who he is to the family which has agreed to take him in at Moore Haven is kept carefully in his shirt pocket. Somehow he makes it to shore, only to be captured and held for profit by crew bosses who bus their workers from farm harvest to farm harvest under subhuman conditions. Arly is tattooed with a number and put on the work team. There is no sense of community among the abused workers, and an old drunk called Coo Coo is the only one who even speaks to Arly. They become close friends, looking out for each other. Meanwhile, there is a hurricane on its way from Africa. As with many other such books, survival here is as much emotional as it is physical.

★ ★ ★ ★ Rathe, Gustave **The Wreck of the Barque Stefano Off the North West Cape of Australia in 1875** Farrar, 1992 ISBN 0 374 38585 8

This is another good survival-after-a-disaster story. Although the titled wreck does indeed occur at the beginning of this story, based closely on fact, the main part of the book concerns the happenings after the wreck. The author's grandfather and a few others survived, due largely to the kindness and concern of several groups of aborigines and their own determination and inventiveness. The book, therefore, contains a great deal of information about the aborigines and their adaptation to the land and to a nomadic existence. The book reminds one of *Robinson Crusoe*, of course, and it is not easy reading—the print is fine and the language style fairly complicated. For readers who like the facts or something closely akin to them and who are intrigued by the challenges facing the shipwreck survivors, however, it is well worth the effort.

★ Regan, Dian Curtis **Game of Survival** Avon, 1989 ISBN 0 380 75585 8

Nicky's plan for romance during a high school camping trip is thwarted when he is paired off with Marta, an athletic but less appealing partner than he had in mind. However, the initial game turns into a battle for survival as they become lost in a snowstorm. Marta's skills become vital, and when they find an injured camper, there is an ethical dilemma as well as a physical one.

★ ★ ★ ★ Stevermer, Caroline **River Rats** Harcourt, 1992 ISBN 0 15 200895 0

The River Rats have survived since the Flash in a loosely structured society in which each of the six survivors has a skill necessary for the group. They have commandeered a paddle boat and are using it as their refuge, home, and means of travel. Some cities and towns still stand, and the River Rats visit these locations, deliver mail, play their music (powered by ingeniously constructed batteries), and receive food and goods as trade. When they somewhat grudgingly rescue a man from his determined pursuers, the Lesters, they become the target of not only the Lesters, but of the Wild Boys as well, because the man, King, has things stored in a secret

hideaway that are of immense value: guns. The book is better than similar books because it deals with the many ways people survive, and refuses to judge them as good or bad. It also has literary connections to Mark Twain and Pandora's box. It's exciting and should bring up some interesting thoughts and discussions.

★ ★ ★ Taylor, Theodore **The Cay** Doubleday, 1987 ISBN 0 385 07906 0

Here we find Philip and Timothy. Phillip is a privileged and racially prejudiced child who, after a German torpedo sinks their ship, is stranded with Timothy, an old black man. It is Timothy who teaches the now blinded Phillip to survive on an almost barren island, before dying from his wounds.

★ ★ ★ ★ Voigt, Cynthia **Homecoming** Simon & Schuster, 1981 ISBN 0 689 30833 7

Voigt deals with emotional and physical survival. **Homecoming**, as well as the other books in the Tillerman saga, is about the survival of a family after being deserted by their mentally ill mother in a parking lot in Connecticut. Dicey, as the eldest child, is responsible for keeping the family together and finding an eventual home for them with their estranged grandmother in Maryland.

★ ★ ★ Westall, Robert **The Kingdom by the Sea** Farrar, 1990 ISBN 0 374 44060 3

A later historical period, that of World War II, is the focus of this book. The air-raid siren goes off again in the middle of the night, and Harry, 13, and his family go through their well-practiced procedure. Harry gathers up necessities and runs to the shelter, but his parents and younger sister never arrive. After the bombing, his family is presumed dead. Harry sets out on his own. Down on the beach, he finds an overturned boat for shelter, and a dog to befriend. Together, they journey slowly along the coast, dodging the authorities and surviving several scrapes with danger. Harry learns to scavenge off the beach from a slightly crazy old man, stays in a trailer left open for wanderers, befriends a group of soldiers stationed along the coast, and finds a new home with a man whose son died in the war.

▶ **Nonfiction**

★ ★ ★ Krementz, Jill **How It Feels When a Parent Dies** Knopf, 1981 ISBN 0 394 51911 6

Krementz is dealing with emotional survival after tragedy. She gives us 18 young people, ages seven to 16, who tell of their experiences with losing a parent. Their words are well chosen, and photos by the author accompany the text. Their stories give us a wide range of personal experiences with death and reactions to it. The young people talk plainly of their feelings, the expected and the unexpected, the pain and the numbness, the confusion and the healing. We hear about their experiences with funerals, with the surviving parent, and with peers. This book is a wonderful one for issues of death, dying, and survival.

★ ★ ★ ★ Krementz, Jill **How it Feels to Fight For Your Life** Joy St, 1989 ISBN 0 316 50364 9

Fourteen children, ages seven to16, talk frankly of their experiences dealing with chronic illness, life-threatening diseases, or disability, and share with us their hopes for the future. There is no bathos here. The young people's stories are accompanied by insightful photos. Their experiences are rendered faithfully, and explore issues of coping methods and adaptation, courage, support of family and friends, reflection on the hard times, and optimism. Krementz is gifted in giving us an honest view into their lives.

★ ★ ★ Wilkes, Sybella **One Day We Had to Run!** Millbrook, 1994 ISBN 1 56294 844 X

This is an effective book that personalizes the plight of refugees from many parts of the world. We get a background in the country of origin, its plight, and the reason for flight. A specific refugee is shown, and he or she tells of his/her flight. Stories and paintings by each child, and others with similar backgrounds, are then included before we go on to the next refugee or displaced person.

10

Music

⊳ COMMENTS

With cutbacks in the arts programs in many communities, it is particularly important to reach into those areas through other disciplines. Music and literature are natural companions; every song is an example of that partnership. Music and science are also closely related. To study how music is made is to step into the science of sound. Music and social studies are a little less obvious as companions, but the study of folk songs, as well as classical music and the lives of composers, brings us to both history and geography.

Brainstorm with a music teacher on some ways to incorporate music appreciation activities into your theme.

See also page 191 for other ideas about music in connection with the focus book, **I Will Call It Georgie's Blues**.

⊳ PICTURE BOOK STARTER

Gabriella's Song, by Candace Fleming (see below), is a good picture book to begin the music theme because it starts with everyday rhythms and builds to a symphony. Gabriella, on her way home from the marketplace in Venice, hears the jingling of coins and the toll of a bell, and begins to hum a tune based on those rhythms. Stopping at the bakery, Gabriella hums, and the baker picks up her tune. He transfers it to a lonely widow, who is overheard humming it by a gondolier. Eventually, the tune reaches the ears of a composer, who finds it is just what he needs for part of his symphony.

⊳ ACTIVITIES

Start the way Gabriella did, by having one student tap out a rhythm, and let others improvise tunes based on that rhythm using voices, tone bells, harmonicas, or piano.

List as many kinds of music as possible. Keep the list growing as the theme develops.

Play a different kind of music each day as the students enter the classroom.

Look at the sheet music for as many of those selections as possible. Get the math teacher to help analyze them mathematically, and the music teacher to do the same musically.

Put a different student in charge of selecting the music and for posting any lyrics each morning on charts or on the overhead projector. Analyze the lyrics as to rhyme and rhythm schemes, as well as symbols and meaning.

Assemble as many kinds of musical instruments as possible. Figure out together how each instrument produces the sound.

Use a computer sound program to portray the sounds of the instruments on screen for further comparison and analysis.

Use the same computer sound program to analyze the voices of different students, both as they sing and as they talk.

Make a musical "Petting Zoo" for younger grade students. Have all students who play a musical instrument set up a display and demonstration for the younger students to view and listen to.

Suggest that students read one of the books of musical fiction listed below and prepare a multimedia interpretation of it, using appropriate music background.

Select favorite poems and find tunes that will work with them. See page 125 for more ideas on this activity.

Much information has appeared in the media recently regarding "The Mozart Effect" and its improvement of people's abilities to study and to concentrate. Have one or more students investigate the literature on the subject. One comprehensive source is **The Mozart Effect: Tapping the Power of Music to Heal the Body, Strengthen the Mind and Unlock the Creative Spirit,** by Don G. Campbell (Avon, 1997 ISBN 0 380 97418 5).

With the class, devise an experiment to prove or disprove the "Mozart Effect" on their thinking. Before doing so, have someone skilled in carrying out various experiments to advise students on various ways to do the study in order to make it most effective.

In some of the fiction listed below, music plays a central role. In others, it is more tangential to the plot. After students have read one or more of the books, conduct a dialogue on the subject and on the role of music in their lives.

BOOK LIST

▶ Picture Books

★ ★ ★ ★ Ackerman, Karen **Song and Dance Man** Knopf, 1988 ISBN 0 394 89330 1, illustrated by Stephen Gammell

Grandpa takes his grandchildren up to the attic where he opens his trunk and brings out his top hat and cane from his Vaudeville days. His soft-shoe and tap dance delights the children and himself.

★ ★ ★ Brett, Jan **Berlioz the Bear** Putnam, 1991 ISBN 0 399 22248 0

The plot of this picture book is obviously for the young, but the story of a bear bothered by a humming from his double bass brings in the instruments of the orchestra, and middle school students may enjoy the subplot in the frames.

★ ★ ★ Downing, Julie **Mozart Tonight** Simon & Schuster, 1991 ISBN 0 02 732881 3

This is a fictionalized biography as Mozart himself gets ready for the first performance of his opera *Don Giovanni*, and flashes back over his life.

★ ★ ★ Fleming, Candace **Gabriella's Song** Atheneum, 1997 ISBN 0 689 80973 5, with illustrations by Giselle Potter
See above.

★ Hofmeyr, Dianne **Do the Whales Still Sing?** Dial, 1995 ISBN 0 8037 1741 5

An old man, carving while leaning against an old ship, tells the boy about a sea captain who hunted whales until he heard them sing.

★ ★ Johnston, Tony **Grandpa's Song** Puffin, 1991 ISBN 0 14 055682 6

Grandpa loves to sing, and he does so with such gusto that it shakes the pictures on the walls. Then his memory begins to fade, and he forgets the song he loved. His relatives sing it to him with equal gusto.

▶ Novels

★ ★ Adler, Naomi **Play Me a Story: Nine Tales about Musical Instruments** Millbrook, 1998 ISBN 0 761 304010

These short stories range from myths such as "The Singer and the Dolphin" to a tale from modern Mongolia.

★ ★ ★ ★ Brooks, Bruce **Midnight Hour Encores** HarperCollins, 1986 ISBN 0 06 020710 8

Sib has been living alone with her father since shortly after her birth, when her mother walked out. They are close, and he encourages her talent with the cello. Now, she asks her father, whom she calls Taxi, to take her to California so that she can know her mother. On the trip across the country, Taxi and Sib learn much more about each other and about themselves.

★ Fenner, Carol **Yolanda's Genius** Simon & Schuster, 1995 ISBN 0 689 80001 0

Yolanda's genius is her younger brother, Andrew. She's convinced that he has amazing musical talent, even though he is a nonreader. Her mother is not convinced. Fortunately, she gets the attention and the ear of blues musician B.B. King.

★ ★ ★ Fox, Paula **Slave Dancer** Bantam, 1982 ISBN 0 02 735560 8

Jessie is kidnapped and pressed aboard a slave ship because of his ability to play the flute. He must play it to force the slaves to exercise. When the ship is wrecked, the only two survivors are Jesse and Ras a young slave. An old man helps Ras get to the North and Jesse get back to New Orleans.

★ ★ ★ ★ Hesse, Karen **Out of the Dust** Scholastic, 1997 ISBN 0 590 36080 9

In this historical novel written in blank verse, the music, played by Billie Jo and her mother, are important to the plot. **Out of the Dust** is a focus book. See page 173.

★ ★ ★ MacKinnon, Bernie **Song for a Shadow** Houghton, 1991 ISBN 0 395 55419 5

Aaron has had enough of living in the shadow of his father's stardom. His mother is in a mental health facility for her recurring problems of letting go of the sixties and her former relationship with Aaron's father. Aaron hitchhikes to Maine, where he is taken in by Jerry Ferguson and his family, who own the corner store in a small town. He works hard to build a new life for himself. He grows to love the small town and, most of all, to cherish his acceptance by the Ferguson family, which is so healthy compared to his own. He loves playing the guitar and becomes involved in a rock band with Doug. They work hard practicing and are excited about a battle of the bands coming in the summer. He begins a romantic relationship with Gail, who finds his secrecy frustrating. Aaron finds that even from afar, his father haunts him and that he must still resolve his feelings about him. This story is realistic in its portrayal of

teenage life and of the frustrations of someone growing up in the shadow of an absent father. It is rich in the experience of teenage rock bands and the work of a musician.

★ ★ ★ MacLachlan, Patricia **The Facts and Fictions of Minna Pratt** HarperCollins, 1988 ISBN 0 06 024114 4

The plot concerns Minna's search for vibrato. The book moves slowly, but the reader begins to care about a fellow who played his concerts on a street corner, and Minna's music teacher, Mr. Porch (called Old Back behind his back). Minna's mother, Mrs. Pratt, keeps house by moving piles about occasionally and keeping a basket of unmatched socks for years. Minna wants the vibrato that will move her from adequate to better than good cellist. She also wants a boyfriend—maybe Lucas— and a way to talk to her mother so that she will listen.

★ ★ ★ Namioka, Lensey **Yang the Youngest and His Terrible Ear** Little, 1992 ISBN 0 316 59701 5

In this short and tender novel we meet Yingtao, who considers himself a failure. To have a tin ear in a family of superb musicians is not easy. His only talent seems to be in baseball, but his father disparages the sport. Ying's best friend, Matthew, is in almost exactly the opposite situation: he's a talented musician and a lousy baseball player in a family that stresses athletics.

★ ★ ★ ★ Newton, Suzanne **I Will Call It Georgie's Blues** Puffin, 1990 ISBN 0 14 034536 1

Reverend Sloan's tyranny of his family puts them all in jeopardy, but it is Georgie, the youngest and most vulnerable, who suffers most. His older brother, Neal, escapes into his music, secretly taking the piano lessons his father forbids. This is a focus book (see page 191).

★ ★ ★ ★ Paterson, Katherine **Come Sing, Jimmy Jo** Dutton, 1985 ISBN 0 525 67267 6

Jimmy Jo's whole family is musical. His stepmother, father, and other relatives are on the road performing country music. He's staying with his grandmother, who is now considered too old to be with the others. It's she who encourages Jimmy Jo to develop his own singing talent, and when he does, he soon eclipses the others. There's a theme here about gifts and sharing those gifts.

★ ★ Thesman, Jean **Cattail Moon** Houghton, 1994 ISBN 0 395 67409 3

Julia's love of music and her musican friends puts her in conflict with her mother, so she goes to stay with her father. There, she makes contact with the ghost of a musician who left the man she loved in order to follow her musical career.

★ ★ ★ Voigt, Cynthia **Orfe** Atheneum, 1992 ISBN 0 689 31771 9

This is a modern version of the myth of Orpheus. See page 95.

★ ★ ★ Wolff, Virginia Euwer **The Mozart Season** Holt, 1991 ISBN 0 8050 1571 X

Allegra has been selected to compete in a musical competition, and she has selected a Mozart concerto as her concert piece. As the summer progresses, the events in Allegra's life become part of her interpretation of the concerto.

▶ Nonfiction

★ Gourse, Leslie **Blowing on the Changes: The Art of the Jazz Horn Players** Watts, 1997 ISBN 0 531 11357 4

This is one of a series of books, "The Art of Jazz." The text is informal but informative and interesting.

★ Hughes, Langston **The Book of Rhythms** Oxford, 1945 ISBN 0 19 509846 0

The great poet devotes his time and attention to an explanation of the pattern of rhythm in ordinary things.

★ ★ ★ Krull, Kathleen **Gonna Sing My Head Off! American Folk Songs for Children** Knopf, 1992 ISBN 0 679 87232 9

This is a good illustrated collection, with historical notes for each song.

★ ★ Les Chats Peles **Long Live Music!** Creative Editions, 1996 ISBN 0 15201310 5

This history of music, put together by an artists' collective, starts with Neolithic bone flutes and proceeds to the present day. Cartoon illustrations and delightfully accessible text keep us reading and learning from start to finish.

★ Monceaux, Morgan **Jazz: My Music, My People** Knopf, 1994 ISBN 0 679 05618 8

Brief bios of the jazz greats are illustrated with wonderful posters.

★ ★ ★ Raschka, Chris **Charlie Parker Played BeBop** Orchard, 1992 ISBN 0 531 08599 6

The text is rhythmic and the cadence is jazz in this picture-book look at jazz musician Charlie Parker.

★ Reisfeld, Randi **This Is the Sound: The Best of Alternative Rock** Aladdin, 1996 ISBN 0 689 80670 1

The author analyses the work of nine bands, as well as the personalities and emotions of the members.

★ ★ Sabbeth, Alex **Rubber-Band Banjos and a Java-Jive Bass: Projects and Activities on the Science of Music and Sound** John Wiley, 1997 ISBN 0 471 15675 2, illustrated by Laurel Aiello

This book clearly describes how to construct simple musical instruments, while explaining the science of sound that makes them work.

★ ★ ★ Schroeder, Alan **Satchmo's Blues** Doubleday, 1996 ISBN 0 385 32046 9, illustrated by Floyd Cooper

Cooper's impressionistic illustrations are just right for this picture book biography of Louis Armstrong.

★ Silverman, Jerry **African Roots: Traditional Black Music** Chelsea House, 1993 ISBN 0 791 01828 8

This book contains 28 songs from sub-Saharan Africa, both in their original language and in English. There are piano and guitar accompaniments for the songs, many of which will be familiar to most audiences

CHAPTER 11

Picture Books

Picture Books

▷ COMMENTS

The idea of using picture books in the middle schools is certainly not a new one. Even a casual browser of picture books in recent years readily concludes that many of these books are not aimed at the youngest members of the reading population. Look at Patricia Polacco's **Pink and Say** or Margaret Wild's and Julie Vivas's **Let the Celebrations Begin!**, for instance, and you know immediately that these books are designed for more sophisticated audiences, not the bedtime storybook crowd. Many teachers of older students have found picture books to be a pleasant, albeit challenging, avenue into many areas of study.

The advantages of using a picture book with middle school audiences are many. Within 10 minutes or so, a picture book can focus a classroom of students on a given problem, theme, or area of proposed study, something that cannot be done with a novel or even a film. Sharing George Ella Lyon and Peter Catalonado's wonderful picture book, **Cecil's Story**, can provide the impetus not only for a study of the Civil War, but because of its universal theme, it can start a discussion and an investigation into the effects of any war on the innocent. Looked at differently, the same book can be used to show students how an illustrator can add dimension to a text: *Cecil's Story* never mentions which war we are dealing with here; it's the illustrations that give us the Civil War setting. The literary technique of foreshadowing is also seen through the illustrations rather than the more commonly used text. (On the front cover, a boy is playing with toy soldiers, one of which is missing an arm. Later, the returning wounded father has only one arm.) Even grammar can be approached through picture books. The text uses the second person for the narrative and can be used as an illustration of that technique.

When you pick up a picture book and gather a group of students around you to view it, the attitude is usually one of pleasant, unthreatening expectation, something often missing when larger, more portentous volumes are opened. Less able readers can participate in the ensuing discussions with the same confidence and authority of their more skilled classmates.

These less able students provide a further rationale for using picture books with middle school classes and up. For them, plowing through a novel, even a short one, requires intense effort and concentration. Legitimizing picture books by sharing them as part of the class experience frees those readers and allows them the opportunity of using these books, as well as the more challenging ones, to extract story or information.

The artwork in many picture books is of very high caliber, making an obvious connection between literature and art. Illustrator studies can be as enlightening and useful as author studies and provide an opportunity for artistic students to shine. Various schools, media, and techniques of fine arts can be approached through the illustrative art in picture books.

▷ ACTIVITIES

As mentioned above, picture books can be shared by gathering students and carefully examining the book together. Another way of sharing a picture book is to read it aloud without showing the illustrations, letting students predict what they might be and then confirm or revise their predictions by examining the book.

Put out a large collection of the best of the picture books intended for older students and let students choose the ones they like best: the ones where illustrations are most interesting, or most intriguing, or have far-out plots.

Encourage students to examine the picture books, carefully noticing the decisions that had to be made: page layout, medium of illustration, style of illustration, length and style of text, number of pages, cover illustration and design. They should also make note of details that are in the text but not in the illustrations and vice versa, perhaps concluding that illustrations that only literally interpret the text are the least interesting.

Encourage students to take one illustrator whose work they particularly like and attempt to find every picture book that artist has done. Look at the books chronologically to see if and how the illustrator's work has changed.

Obtain multiple copies of **The Mysteries of Harris Burdick**, by Chris Van Allsburg, or the new enlarged portfolio edition (Houghton, 1996 ISBN 0 395 82784 1). Students need to see this work close-up if they are to appreciate it or to use it as inspiration for writing. Read the story, which is only one page of the book. It tells the reader/listener that a man named Harris Burdick once left this material at a publisher as samples of his work. The material included the title and one line from each of these stories he intended to write. Each was accompanied by an illustration from the story. Burdick then disappeared, never to be seen again. Now, the publisher is putting out this material with the plea that Harris Burdick return to tell him the rest of the stories. The book then goes on to show us these mysterious pictures and their intriguing titles and line from the text. One, for instance, shows a woman lying in bed quite obviously dead. An open book with a vine growing from it lies open beside her on the bed. The title of the story is "Mr. Linden's Library"; the line from the text reads: "He had warned her about the book. Now it was too late." Most of the "stories" are mysterious, but some are funny.

After reading the page and going over the rest of the book together (the class should be gathered around you so that some viewing is possible), suggest that they work in small groups on one picture, title, and line, brainstorming for the possible stories behind them. Each group should tell their story to another group before going on to do the same thing with another picture. After two or three pictures, each member of the group should pick one idea and go with it, writing down the story behind one of the pictures. Tell them to feel free to use any idea they heard, including their own, or to go off in a new direction. Besides serving as a good writing activity, this provides an entry to all of Van Allsburg's work, because so much of it is mysterious, and there is much of a typical Van Allsburg story which is only partly told.

Put out as many copies of as many of Van Allsburg's books as you can find and suggest that students find and bring in more. In each of his books, you can find all or part of the dog Fritz, first introduced in **The Garden of Abdul Gasazi**. Most people like this "Where's Waldo" kind of activity, and it will help students begin to look closely at his illustrations, which are intriguing. Van Allsburg has received the Caldecott Medal for two of his works: **Jumanji** and **The Polar Express**. Some students may be interested enough to find out who awards this prize and of what it consists.

In some of his books, particularly **Jumanji**, Van Allsburg manipulates perspective so that we appear to be at two different vantage points at the same time. We look down on the carpet while being able to see under a chair. Later in the book, we are beside a tree trunk while looking at other trees from several perspectives. In other books, **The Sweetest Fig**, for instance, some figures (look at the people in the restaurant) are inexplicably flattened while others are fully developed. In the same book, other images are distorted. Look at the knobs on the kitchen cabinets. Those doors shouldn't open. These and other distortions add to the feeling that we are in an impossible world. After pointing out one or two of these, ask students to find others. Encourage them to speculate on whether these warpings of perspective are intentional or inadvertent, as well as on the media Van Allsburg uses and why he chooses full color for some while doing others in one or two tones.

After delving into his illustrations as much as the group's interest allows, turn to the texts. Is there a common theme in his work? In many of the books, an adventure occurs which could be written off as a dream or a flight of fancy, except for the presence of a disturbing and very real remnant: the cap in **The Garden of Abdul Gasazi**, the bell in **Polar Express**, and the wrecked boat in **Wreck of the Zephyr**, for instance. The ending of **Jumanji** isn't much different, really, than the ending of **The Cat in the Hat** (Random, 1957 ISBN 0 394 89218 6). Can the students think of other novels or picture books that end that way?

Sometimes, particularly in **The Sweetest Fig**, **The Wretched Stone**, and **The Widow's Broom**, Van Allsburg appears to work in allegory, and students might like to speculate on his intent or on the moral in these. **The Stranger** must be an allegory, but the meaning is less clear. Who is the Stranger? These themes are present in other novels, as well as in picture books, and the search for others can be carried out and discussed.

Students might be interested to know that David Wiesner, author/illustrator of **Tuesday**, among other picture books, was a student of Van Allsburg. Can they see similarities in plot or illustration?

Another picture book artist whose work has multiple meanings and, therefore, may be of interest and use in the middle school program, is Maurice Sendak. He has referred collectively to three of his books as his "Trilogy of Childhood." Because his work has received much critical attention (as has Sendak himself), providing few easy answers to his work, middle school children should feel free to come to their own conclusions about the work of this enigmatic artist. At least two of these books will probably be familiar to many of the students from their own childhood.

The first of these, **Where the Wild Things Are,** is probably the one most familiar to students. Make copies of it available to students and suggest that they write down any observations they may have, from memories to criticism. Some may notice that the illustrations start small and increase in size to the climax of the book, then decrease, but never return to their original size. They may speculate on why this was done and what the size indicates. Others may notice the visual foreshadowing in the book as signs of the wild things appear in the room where Max is making his mischief: a wild thing puppet hanging from a clothesline, and a picture of a wild thing on the wall drawn by Max. Another bit of foreshadowing is the improvised tent and stool Max has created, which are very like the tent and stool Max uses as king of the wild things.

Other intriguing bits in the illustrations include the way in which the familiar world of Max's bedroom becomes the forest, the strange perspective of that same bedroom, and the phases of the moon. If no students notice these things, pointing out one or two of them may lead students to look more carefully.

The words, of course, have equal merit in this book in which illustrations and text are so closely intertwined. Students may like to speculate on the use of capitals. When Max and his unseen mother are battling, they speak to each other in full caps. Does that indicate volume, anger, or something else? Later, when Max is at the wild things and might well be shouting, there are no caps.

Other things to notice in the text include the way Sendak starts the story in such a way as to make us believe it—not with "Once upon a time" but with the declarative: "The night Max wore his wolf suit." Also, Sendak's use of language throughout this 32-page book is carefully chosen. An ocean "tumbled" by. Try using other words there and none of them seem to work as well as "tumble."

When *Where the Wild Things Are* was published, it caused much furor. It was the first picture book since Victorian times other than fairy tales in which monsters were shown. Adults were sure that it would frighten chil-

dren. Bruno Bettleheim, an eminent psychiatrist of the time, was less worried about the monsters than he was of the treatment of Max's anger and misbehavior, both of which were left unbridled or punished. He said that many children would be traumatized by the book. When it received the Caldecott Award, the clamor increased. Some librarians refused to buy it for their collections. Protest groups were organized by some conservative organizations. Learning about its history could lead to dialogues about censorship.

Getting back to the book itself, students should be encouraged not to write off Max's whole adventure as a dream. Does it have to be? Also, notice the amount of time in which the adventure must have taken place. In spite of the phases of the moon, it appears to be one evening's adventure. Time plays a big part in the other two books in the trilogy, as well.

After perusing and discussing *Where the Wild Things Are*, students might find it profitable to learn a little about the life of Sendak. Periodicals and critical works will provide much information about his early life in a Brooklyn tenement, where he was often ill and unable to play outside. His lifelong interest in Mickey Mouse and his collection of Mickey Mouse memorabilia have also influenced his work. Students can create a bulletin board of articles and information about Sendak and his work.

The second book in his trilogy, **In the Night Kitchen**, has its own perplexities and controversies. Students may be less familiar with this volume partly because its pictures of a nude little boy made some adults nervous. Some schools still keep it on special shelves or even paint diapers on Mickey. Give students ample opportunity to examine the book and make their own observations and conclusions.

Knowing about Sendak's fascination with Mickey Mouse may help students understand the book, and many will notice Mickey's resemblance to Max. They may be able to understand this book and the next one a little better by getting some information on the 1930s, the decade of Sendak's early childhood years. *In the Night Kitchen* has buildings made of food containers bearing brand names which might have been present in a pantry of that time. Sendak has said that a bread company's slogan, "Baked while you sleep," intrigued him as a child. For him, it signified all the things that went on in the adult world while the children were asleep. Surely it provides one key to the book. There are other mementos of his childhood in the book. For instance, it is dedicated to Sendak's parents, Sadie and Philip, and his birth date appears on one of the packages. His pet dog's name, Jenny, is the name of one of the streets.

Students may also note the very different art style in this book and, knowing that Sendak spent much of his youth reading comic books may provide some reason for the format. Notice also that none of the letters in the text is from printed fonts—each letter is carefully drawn by the artist. Deciding what Sendak is saying in the second book is anybody's guess, and the speculation is part of the fun.

The third book is the murkiest of the three. **Outside Over There** is done with full palette and a romantic style of illustration. Again, some background information is due the students. They should know that after the Lindbergh kidnapping in 1932, many parents, even very poor ones, became obsessed with the thought that their children were also in danger of being kidnapped. That the kidnapping of the Lindbergh baby occurred, apparently, when someone using a ladder climbed to the second story of the house and snatched the child from his crib, is also of interest here. Sendak's goblins use a ladder to snatch Ida's baby.

Other details are intriguing, as well. For

instance, what's wrong with the mother? She looks misshapen. Is she pregnant? The dog is perfectly drawn, but why is a dog, which is traditionally a watchdog, as passive as the mother? Notice the ship sinking. Is that Papa's ship? Is he dead? What's Mozart doing there? (Sendak loves the work of Mozart.) Watch the sunflowers. What about those sailors? Are they a statement like the one Brueghel makes in his painting *The Fall of Icarus* (see page 93)? Who are the goblins?

Notice also the sense of time within this book. On the first few pages of the book, Ida is helping her baby brother walk. He is just about to take a step. Notice the last illustration. He has just taken a step. Does Sendak mean that the entire story takes place in an instant? Is it a lightning fantasy on Ida's part? Does she resent her brother and the fact that he is often her responsibility?

Finally, let the students speculate on why Sendak calls these three books his "trilogy of childhood." Do they together represent what Sendak thinks childhood is? What do they say about childhood? about siblings? about parents? about women?

Find fine art prints that have some resemblance to the style of illustration in some of the books by other artists. For instance, Locker's work bears a strong resemblance to the Hudson River school of painting.

Look for art allusions in some of the picture books such as Peter Sis's **Three Golden Keys**, **Almost Famous Daisy**, and **How to Live Forever**.

Try a technique called "Split Images" as suggested in Johnson and Louis' **Bringing It All Together** (Heinemann, 1990 ISBN 0 435 08502 6). The activity encourages students to look carefully at a book and to listen to each other's observations attentively. Seat the students in two lines facing each other knee to knee. The rules are that they are not to turn around and that they may talk only to the person facing them. The leader then shows the cover of a picture book to the students facing her/him. Those students tell their partners what they see. The leader then shows the students facing the other way the first page of the book. The activity proceeds with each group of students alternately seeing every other page of the book and hearing what is on the alternative pages. Students should be encouraged to concentrate on the pictures rather than reading the text. Books chosen for "Split Images" should be unfamiliar to most of the children and should be short, boldly illustrated with a strong plot, and told with both text and pictures. A book that we've used very successfully with older students in this manner is David Wiesner's **Tuesday** (see below).

Activities after seeing the book in that manner can include: having individuals tell or write the story, letting partners work together to reconstruct it, having partners work together reconstructing one page from the book (one partner will have seen the page and the other only heard about it). Use those pictures to form a story wall, sequencing them on the wall, putting duplicate scenes in a vertical arrangement and then deciding which pages or incidents are missing and filling them in with other pictures or with summary paragraphs.

Sometimes it is advantageous to have a small group of students examine a new picture book with one student assigned to especially notice text, another to carefully observe illustrations, and another to articulate what each of them has missed. After a few such sessions, the roles merge naturally, with the usual result that students avoid flipping through a picture book quickly without observing subtleties of meaning and technique.

Look for hidden or subtle images in the work of Ed Young, particularly in **Sadako** and **Lon Po Po**. Also notice ways in which the Chinese American artist celebrates his heritage in his work.

After perusing many alphabet books, students can see that most are not merely a series of random objects and pictures beginning with each letter, but have a theme with the alphabet serving as a pattern of presentation. They can then decide on their own alphabet plot, means and media of illustration, and can design the pages and construct an alphabet book.

▷ BOOK LIST

(There are picture books listed for each theme in this book. See also pages 11, 17, 23, 30, 38, 43, 47, 54, 61, 68, 72, 80, 83, 97, 103, 110, 116, 122.)

★ ★ ★ Agee, Jon **The Incredible Painting of Felix Clousseau** Farrar, 1988 ISBN 0 374 33633 4

People ridicule Clousseau's simplistic paintings until he makes them come to life, but the abuses of his skill prove too much for the painter.

★ ★ ★ ★ Altman, Linda Jacobs **Amelia's Road** Lee & Low, 1993 ISBN 1 880000 04 0, illustrated by Enrique O. Sanchez

A migrant child's need to have a place to call her own is eloquently and simply told.

★ ★ ★ ★ Bang, Molly **The Grey Lady and the Strawberry Snatcher** Simon & Schuster, 1980 ISBN 0 02 29224

This wordless book uses figure/ground play to tell the story, making it an ideal art connection.

★ ★ ★ ★ Bang, Molly **The Paper Crane** Greenwillow, 1985 ISBN 0 688 04109 4

Origami is used in the illustration of this legend about hospitality and generosity.

★ ★ ★ ★ Banyai, Istvan **Zoom** Viking, 1995 ISBN 0 670 85804 8

This wordless book plays with perspective as it pulls the viewer back farther and farther from the original scene.

★ ★ ★ Baylor, Byrd **I'm in Charge of Celebrations** Scribner, 1986 ISBN 0 684 18579 2, illustrated by Peter Parnall

A child who loves the desert celebrates the natural phenomena she observes there.

★ ★ ★ Baylor, Byrd **The Table Where Rich People Sit** Simon & Schuster, 1994 ISBN 0 684 19653 0, illustrated by Peter Parnall

A discussion which starts out with monetary values soon expands into a look at one family's contributions and needs.

★ ★ ★ Bouchard, Dave **The Elders Are Watching** Vickers Fulcrum, 1993 ISBN 9 781555 911584, illustrated by Roy Henry

Northwest Indian images are accompanied by four-line stanzas in which the author, quoting the ancients, pleads for a change in the way humans treat the earth.

★ ★ ★ Bouchard, David **If You're Not from the Prairie** Atheneum, 1995 ISBN 0 689 80103 3

The book extolls the elements as experienced by a person who loves and thrives on the prairie.

★ ★ ★ Bunting, Eve **Train to Somewhere** Clarion, 1996 ISBN 0 395 71325 0, illustrated by Ronald Himler

The orphan trains carried unwanted children to farms in the Midwest. This book tells of the experience from one train-borne child's point of view.

★ ★ ★ Bunting, Eve **The Wall** Clarion, 1990 ISBN 0 395 51588 2, illustrated by Ronald Himler

A boy and his grandfather visit the Vietnam Memorial.

★ ★ ★ Chaucer, Geoffrey **Canterbury Tales** Hyman Lothrop, 1988 ISBN 0 688 062016, illustrated by Trina Schart

A few of the tales are included, and Hyman's illustrations bring their narrators to life.

★ ★ ★ Christelow, Eileen **What Do Authors Do?** Clarion, 1995 ISBN 0 395 71124 X

This is a delightful vehicle showing how two books by two different authors were inspired by the same incident.

★ ★ ★ Climo, Shirley **Egyptian Cinderella** Crowell, 1989 ISBN 0 690 04824 6

This variant of *Cinderella* brings much of the culture of the time and place into focus.

★ ★ ★ Coerr, Eleanor **Sadako** Paper Star, 1997 ISBN 0 698 11588 0, illustrated by Ed Young

This picture book version of the story, taken from a short novel, tells how a young victim of the bombing of Hiroshima received support and hope.

★ ★ Curry, Barbara **Sweet Words So Brave** Zino, 1996 ISBN 1 55933 179 8

Striking posters and collages combine with brief biographical sketches within a narrative to trace the history of African-American writing.

★ ★ De Coteau Orie, Sandra **Did You Hear the Wind Sing Your Name?** (Walker, 1995 ISBN 0 8027 8350 3)

Startlingly vivid illustrations and one-line questions about them exuberantly reveal the joy one may take in nature and the seasons.

★ ★ ★ Hamanaka, Sheila **The Journey** Orchard, 1990 ISBN 0 531 07060 3

Taken from a mural created by the author/illustrator, the images in this book are so strong that they provide continuity and depth to the chronology of the Japanese-American people during World War II.

★ ★ ★ Heide, Florence Parry **Sami and the Time of Troubles** Clarion, 1992 ISBN 0 395 55964 2

A family in Beirut, Lebanon, huddles together, amidst their most precious belongings, during a bombing, then emerges to function with amazing normality.

★ ★ ★ Houston, Gloria **My Great Aunt Arizona** HarperCollins, 1991 ISBN 0 06 022606 4

Arizona hoped to travel widely, but circumstances prevented it. However, she inspires her students to learn and to travel widely.

★ ★ ★ Johnston, Tony **The Ghost of Nicholas Greebe** Dial, 1996 ISBN 0 8037 1649 4

Early Massachusetts is the setting for this ghost story, which is not too spooky, and actually kind of fun.

★ ★ ★ Jonas, Ann **Reflections** Greenwillow, 1987 ISBN 0 688 06141 9

These images read one way through the first half of the story and then are turned upside down to finish it.

★ ★ ★ Lyon, George Ella **Cecil's Story** Orchard, 1991 ISBN 0 531 085120
See above.

★ ★ ★ Macaulay, David **Black and White** Houghton, 1990 ISBN 0 395 52151 3

This is a mind stretcher as four stories merge visually.

★ ★ ★ Macaulay, David **Rome Antics** Houghton, 1997 ISBN 0 395 82279 3

This almost wordless book is a pigeon's-eye view of Rome. A pigeon carries a message through modern Rome to the garret of an artist. In the process, we get wonderful vantage points for viewing the architecture and people of the city.

★ ★ ★ Polacco, Patricia **Pink & Say** Putnam, 1994 ISBN 0 399 22671 0

This heart-wrenching story tells of the friendship and fate of two Civil War soldiers (see above).

★ ★ ★ Say, Allen **Grandfather's Journey** Houghton, 1993 ISBN 0 395 57035 2

This is the story of the conflict one immigrant feels between the two cultures that are part of him.

★ ★ ★ Scieszka, Jon **The Stinky Cheese Man and Other Fairly Stupid Tales** Viking, 1992 ISBN 0 670 84487 X

Fairy tales are subjected to wild and very funny interpretations here.

★ ★ Sendak, Maurice **In the Night Kitchen** HarperCollins, 1970 ISBN 0 06 025489 0
See above.

★ ★ Sendak, Maurice **Outside Over There** HarperCollins, 1981 ISBN 0 06 025524 2
See above.

★ ★ ★ Sendak, Maurice **Where the Wild Things Are** HarperCollins, 1963 ISBN 0 06 443178 9
See above.

Siebert, Diane **Sierra** HarperCollins, 1991 ISBN 0 06 021639 5, illustrated by Wendell Minor

Geography and geology are set to poetry in this visual and lyrical exploration of one area.

★ ★ ★ Van Allsburg, Chris **Bad Day at Riverbend** Houghton, 1995 ISBN 0 395 67347 X
A mysterious substance falls from the sky and threatens this town in the Wild West.

★ ★ ★ Van Allsburg, Chris **The Garden of Abdul Gasazi** Houghton, 1979 ISBN 0 395 27804 X

Alan allows his friend's dog, Fritz, to wander into a magician's house, and he reappears as a duck.

★ ★ ★ Van Allsburg, Chris **Jumanji** Houghton, 1979 ISBN 0 395 30448 2

Children play a board game and find that every square they land on comes alive.

★ ★ ★ Van Allsburg, Chris **The Mysteries of Harris Burdick** Houghton, 1984 ISBN 0 395 35393 9
See above.

★ ★ Van Allsburg, Chris **Polar Express** Houghton, 1985 0 395 38949 6

A boy takes a magical midnight train to the North Pole.

★ ★ ★ Van Allsburg, Chris **The Stranger** Houghton, 1986 0 395 42331 7

A mysterious mute stranger is taken into a home and, while he's there, the seasons stop changing.

★ Van Allsburg, Chris **The Sweetest Fig** Houghton, 1993 ISBN 0 395 67346 1

A dog gets revenge on a cruel master.

★ ★ ★ Van Allsburg, Chris **Two Bad Ants** Houghton, 1988 ISBN 0 395 48668 8

We get an ant's eye view of a human's kitchen.

★ ★ ★ Van Allsburg, Chris **The Widow's Broom** Houghton, 1992 ISBN 0 395 64051 2

A witch leaves her magic broom behind, and the widow makes good use of its magical powers.

★ ★ ★ Wiesner, David **Tuesday** Houghton, 1991 ISBN 0 395 55113 7

Frogs ride airborne lily pads around a village one magical night.

★ ★ ★ Yolen, Jane **Encounter** Harcourt, 1992 ISBN 0 15 225962 7

The arrival of Columbus and his men is seen through the eyes of a Taino boy, living on the island on which Columbus has landed.

★ ★ ★ Young, Ed **Lon Po Po: A Red Riding Hood Story from China** Putnam, 1989 ISBN 0 399 21619 7

The illustrations in this book are fascinating as the wolf appears and disappears in the pictures.

CHAPTER 12

Appalachia

⬗ COMMENTS

It is possible to take one area of the country and investigate it through literature coming from and set in that area. Although the Appalachian Mountains extend from Maine to northern Georgia, the area typically referred to as Appalachia is that part of the mountainous area of our country that extends from southwestern Pennsylvania to Georgia. The area is rich in folklore and has been the setting and inspiration for many good books for young people. We can approach a study of history and geography of the United States through the literature from and about Appalachia.

Cynthia Rylant grew up in the coal mining area of West Virginia, and most of her books are set there. This theme could easily lead to an author study of Rylant and her work.

As with the study of any region, students should not be left with the idea that the area, in this case Appalachia, is a museum frozen in time for our viewing purposes. This is a very real danger in this particular area of study because much of the literature we are about to discuss is set in the Great Depression. Also, although much of Appalachia is still an economically depressed area, it is important that students not go away from the study convinced that the entire area and everyone in it is in dire straits.

⬗ PICTURE BOOK STARTER

Keeping the avoidance of stereotyping in mind, a good book with which to start the study is **Appalachia: Voices of the Sleeping Birds**, by Cynthia Rylant and illustrated by Barry Moser. The author starts with the dogs who run free, for the most part, in the rural mountain areas and goes from them to their owners and to the houses they live in. The people she talks about are mostly coal miners who live in company housing, although she brings in people who leave the area for awhile to become doctors or lawyers and such, but usually come back. Moser's illustrations resemble a photograph album, and Rylant's affection for the people and the area is apparent.

The book avoids stereotypes and the "museum" quality we talked about earlier by pointing out the differences among the people and by bringing descriptions into the present, as in:

"Some have shiny new cars parked in their driveways and some have only the parts of old cars parked in theirs. Most have running water inside the house, with sinks in their kitchens, washing machines in their basements, and pretty blue bathrooms. But a few still have no water pipes inside their houses and they carry their water from an old well or a creek over the hill..."

▶ ACTIVITIES

After reading *Appalachia: Voices of the Sleeping Birds*, some students may be ready to go directly to nonfiction sources for further information. Be sure they consult the **Reader's Guide to Periodical Literature**, for the area is often the subject of magazine articles. Others may want to head for novels set in the region. If you can hold them back a little bit and suggest that they peruse one of the picture books listed below, they may get a better base from which to work.

Appalachia: Voices of the Sleeping Birds should open up some discussion first from people who know the area. How accurate is the book? How does it jibe with previous information? How do the author/illustrators know so much about the area? The blurb on the book jacket gives some information in that direction. Also, Rylant has written two brief autobiographies. **Best Wishes** (Richard Owen, 1992 ISBN 1 878450 20 4) is short and easy to read, with photographs of the author in her Ohio home, as well as the one in which she grew up. A slightly more difficult autobiography is **But I'll Be Back Again** (Beech Tree, 1993 ISBN 0 688 126537). The latter book might be of more interest to middle school students because of its frequent references to the Beatles and because the roots of most of the rest of her writing are clearly defined.

Webbing is a technique often used in the classroom because it is a graphic means of outlining and of organizing brainstorming results. Creating a web together encourages divergent thinking and can draw in students who might have thought the topic had little interest for them. Later, students searching for a topic for writing, investigation, or discussion may find inspiration by examining the web. Such a web of Appalachia might start out looking like this:

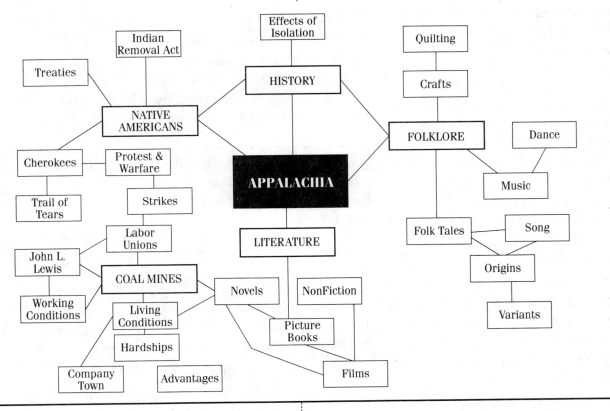

http://www.ced.appstate.edu/appalachia/history/ is an excellent Web site that offers a brief history of Appalachia and its role in American history. Compare the statements here with those that could be made about your own area.

As students discover and read some of the literature, they can add the titles to their web. Various new items added to the web can be connected to more than one item already there. When that happens, students get a sense of the connections stretching out in many directions and of the way things interconnect. When the web ceases to be of use, replace it with something more useful, such as a time line or chart. To facilitate finding and using the related literature, a chart such as the following may be useful:

Books on Appalachia

PICTURE BOOKS

Author/Title	Time	Summary of Book	Topics
Rylant **Appalachia: Voices of Sleeping Birds**	Present	The kinds of people and animals who live in Appalachia.	Dogs Names Homes
Rylant **When I Was Young in the Mountains**	1950s	A little girl talks about living in a coal-mining community long ago.	Country store Outhouses Pumps Coal Mining

NOVELS

Author/Title	Time	Summary of Book	Topics
Lowry **Rabble Starkey**	present	A mother and daughter become extremely involved with the house-hold of the mother's employer. Mrs. Bigelois mentally ill and nearly causes the deathp of her own son.	Mental illness Family Mother/ Daughter Friendship Single Parent
Paterson, **Come Sing Jimmy Jo**	Present	The youngest child of a family of country singers is left at home with his grandmother while the others are on tour.	Country music Families Talent Jealousy Grandmothers

FOLKTALES

Author/Title	Summary	Motifs
Chase **The Jack Tales**	Many of these stories are variants of more commonly known folk talesAll of them surround the character of Jack, the trickster.	Tricksters Little one outwitting big ones
Moser **Polly Vaughn**	A traditional ballad is the inspiration for this story of feuding mountain families.	Feuds Romance

NONFICTION

Author/Title	Summary of Book	Topics
Beale **Only the Names Remain**	The story of the forced removal of the Cherokee Indians from the Smoky Mountains to Oklahoma.	Indian removal
Bial **Mist Over the Mountains**	Photographic essay on the area.	Land
Rylant **But I'll Be Back Again**	A picture book autobiography about growing up in Appalachia.	Author's adolescence

When I Was Young in the Mountains was Rylant's first book. The illustrations, by Diane Goode, caused the book to be named an honor book for the Caldecott Award, but Rylant didn't like Goode's illustrations. She said they made everybody look too neat and tidy and not as she remembered them. Look at all the picture books written by Rylant. Which of her illustrators do you think best capture her images?

Look at maps of the area commonly called Appalachia. What percentage of it is mountainous? What effect would this have on the lives of its inhabitants? How many of the big cities in those states are located in the mountains? Why would this be?

Look at other mountainous areas of the world—the Rockies, the Swiss Alps, and the Himalayas. Do they share the same problems and benefits as Appalachia? Why or why not?

Quilting is one of the many handcrafts popular in Appalachia. Make a list of the patterns used in quilting. Use cloth or cut paper to duplicate a block of eight squares for each pattern. Can you see the relevance of the name?

Visit the Web site at **http://www.appalachia.com/**, which is a shopping site run by a Coalition of Independent Artisans, Craftspeople, and Merchants from the Southern Appalachians, to get some idea of the products being sold.

Coal mining was the basis of economy for some of Appalachia. Why did the demand decrease? What effect did that decrease have on the area?

Find out about John L. Lewis and Mother Jones and their work with coal miners. What, if any, were the long-term effects of their work?

Various linguistic researchers have said that the language spoken in parts of Appalachia is very close to the original language spoken by the early European settlers in North America. What factors would make that likely?

Many years ago, a folklorist named Lomax made recordings of folk songs sung by inhabitants of Appalachia. Many of those songs are sung by Jean Ritchie and are available in her book **Folk Songs of the Southern Appalachians** (University Press of Kentucky, 1997 ISBN 0 813 10927 2). Play and sing some of the songs and find variants of them.

Invite a fiddler, and a banjo and bass player to play Appalachian tunes, or clog dancers to show their skills.

Have a storytelling festival using Richard Chase's collected stories of Appalachia or some other source (see below).

These collected stories from the mountains are vividly retold and could serve as the starting point for an investigation of the folktales of Appalachia. Many have strong roots in the folktales of the British Isles and can lead to an investigation of their roots or those of the people who told them.

While the reading of novels is going on, gather small groups together frequently to discuss such things as stock characters, stereotypes or the lack of such, underlying themes, author's purpose, and skills in story-telling.

How many of the authors of these novels have intimate knowledge of the area? Research author books and the Web for such information.

The fact that the novels listed below are set in a wide range of time periods, from the Civil War to the present, allows us to look at change and permanence in the area. How do events such as World Wars I and II affect the people as reflected in these novels? Is there a difference in quality of life there from then to now?

⊱ BOOK LIST

▶ Picture Books

★ ★ ★ Bates, Artie Ann **Ragsale** Houghton, 1995 ISBN 0 395 70030 2, illustrated by Jeff Chapman-Crane

The portrait-style illustrations make this story of a family's delight in a succession of rag sales work.

★ ★ ★ ★ Hendershot, Judy **In Coal Country** Knopf, 1987 ISBN 0 394 98190 1

Chalk is aptly used to portray this account of life in a coal-mining town.

★ ★ ★ ★ Houston, Gloria **My Great-Aunt Arizona** Lamb HarperCollins, 1992 ISBN 0 06 022606 4, illustrated by Susan Condie

Another picture book to help build a feeling for Appalachia is Gloria Houston's biographical picture book. Houston tells the story of her great aunt, who, even as a little girl, had travel in her soul, but never got out of the mountain community where she lived. She became a teacher and encouraged her students to go to the places she visited "only in my mind."

★ ★ ★ Ransom, Candice **When the Whippoorwill Calls** Morrow, 1995 ISBN 0 688 12729 0, illustrated by Kimberly Bulcken Root

Polly and her parents love their life in the holler of the Blue Ridge Mountains. Conveniences are few, but the simple pleasures are many. Then, their land-lord sells out to the government. Their home will be part of the Shenandoah National Park, and Polly's family moves down to the flatlands. Their house there is a "glory, white-painted, with inside taps and electric lights," but the family know they've lost something precious.

★ ★ ★ Rylant, Cynthia **Appalachia: The Voices of Sleeping Birds** Harcourt, 1991 ISBN 0 15 201605 8 See above.

★ ★ ★ ★ Rylant, Cynthia **The Relatives Came** Simon & Schuster, 1986 ISBN 0 02 777220 9

This is less a story than a description of a wonderful family reunion. The relatives drive all the way from Virginia, drinking pop and eating crackers and observing the terrain before they literally drive into our yard (knocking down the fence as they do so). From that moment on they eat, sleep, hug, fix things, take pictures, sing, play instruments, and celebrate being together with not much in the way of material things, but a great deal of love.

★ ★ ★ ★ Rylant, Cynthia **The Old Woman Who Named Things** Harcourt, 1996 ISBN 0 15 257809 9

In an effort to keep from being lonely, the woman gives a name to everything she cannot outlive. When a puppy presents itself, the woman faces a dilemma. What if she names it, and then it dies?

★ ★ ★ ★ Rylant, Cynthia **When I Was Young in the Mountains** Dutton, 1992 ISBN 0 140 54875 0, illustrated by Diane Goode

This was Rylant's first book. It describes the time in the author's childhood when she lived with her grandparents in the mountains. The book is a hymn of praise to the simple life.

▶ Novels

★ ★ ★ ★ Burch, Robert **Ida Early Comes Over the Mountain** Puffin, 1990 ISBN 0 140 34534 5

This novel is strong on family, with a deliciously eccentric central character. Ida does indeed come over the mountains of northern Georgia to the door of the Sutton family, looking for work at a time when they are in need of household help. More important, the motherless children are in need of attention and love. This story, set in the Great Depression, deals with values, prejudice, and the concept of family.

★ ★ ★ Caudill, Rebecca **Did You Carry the Flag Today, Charley?** Yearling, 1988 ISBN 0 440 40092 9 illustrated by Nancy Grossman

This is a book that is short and quite easy to read. Charley Cornett can't wait to start "Little School" in the mining country where he lives with his parents and his nine brothers and sisters. They've told him all about school, and he's especially interested in the reward given to the most helpful child—the honor of carrying the flag. Charley is sure that he'll carry it often, but so many strange new things can be seen at school (a sink with water, for instance) that his own stubborn curiosity and independence combine to keep him in trouble.

★ ★ ★ Hamilton, Virginia **M.C. Higgins, the Great** Simon & Schuster, 1974 ISBN 0 02 043490 1

Sarah's Mountain has been home to the Higgins family ever since Great-great-grandmother Sarah ran away north to Ohio and to freedom carrying her baby, and her presence is very real to these later generations. Now, the beauty of their land is threatened by the slag heap, left by the strip mining going on in the area. The slag, which accumulated on the edge of the flattened mountaintop, is poised over their house. To his horror, M.C. Higgins learns that the slag is precariously balanced. With enough rain, it is ready to shift and bury the house and them. It is his nightmare.

★ ★ Houston, Gloria **Littlejim** Beach Tree, 1993 ISBN 0 688 1212 8

Littlejim is trying to find out what it is to be a man and he's having a tough time of it. Although the time is World War I, and there are references to it, it is not the focus of this brief novel. Littlejim's father and uncle have a lumber business which, is thriving due to the war effort, but otherwise the Appalachian setting is peaceful. The drama concerns the attempts, often futile, of scholarly, talented Littlejim to earn his father's respect and love. Unfortunately for Littlejim, his father is an insensitive and often brutal man.

★ ★ ★ ★ Lowry, Lois **Rabble Starkey** Houghton, 1987 ISBN 0 395 43607 9

We mustn't let students get the impression that everybody in Appalachia is a coal miner or moonshiner, however. *Rabble Starkey* is set in the fictional town of Highriver, West Virginia, and Mr. Bigelow, one of the main characters, is a real estate salesman. The personalities, rather than the area, dominate this novel. Rabble is a wonderful and beautifully defined character, as are most of the others in this sensitive book about love and mental illness and what makes a family.

★ ★ ★ ★ Naylor, Phyllis Reynolds **Shiloh** Atheneum, 1991 ISBN 0 689 31614 3

This is another novel set in Appalachia that is not difficult to read and may bring in the dog lovers. The Newbery Award-winning book tells about Marty, whose family, and particularly his father, has a strong sense of right and wrong. When Marty finds and befriends an abused dog, Shiloh, and his father demands that he return Shiloh to his owner, Marty must choose between deceit and truth. This simple book is better than most animal stories. The characters are well drawn, and even Shiloh's cruel owner has his reasons for behaving as he does.

★ ★ ★ Naylor, Phyllis **Shiloh Season** Atheneum, 1996 ISBN 0 689 80647 7, illustrated by Barry Moser

This is the second in the Shiloh series of books by Naylor. Marty, having been able to keep Shiloh legally now for more than a month, sets about trying to reform Judd Travers, Shiloh's previous and abusive owner. Judd wants Shiloh back, but has made a deal with Marty because Marty saw him shoot a deer out of season.

★ ★ Naylor, Phyllis **Saving Shiloh** Atheneum, 1997 ISBN 0 689 81460 7, illustrated by Barry Moser

This is the third book in the miniseries about Shiloh and involves the redemption of Judd Travers, the villain who first abused Shiloh. Judd has turned his life around, but his past deeds and reputation catch up with him when he is accused of murder and some robberies. He does, indeed, save Shiloh.

★ ★ ★ ★ Paterson, Katherine **Come Sing, Jimmy Jo** Dutton, 1985 ISBN 0 525 67167 6

Paterson has turned her sure writer's hand to Appalachia in this book. Jimmy Jo Johnson's family are country singers. As the story begins, Jimmy Jo has been left behind with his grandmother in the mountains, being considered too young to travel on the road with the group. His grandmother was once part of the group but is now considered too old. It is she who encourages Jimmy Jo to sing, and when he finally gets his chance, he outshines his father and mother and becomes the focal point of the group and the cause for their rise to "big time."

★ ★ ★ Reeder, Carolyn **Grandpa's Mountain** Camelot, 1993 ISBN 0 380 71914 2

Carrie stays with her grandparents every summer in the old family house in the Blue Ridge Mountains. Now, however, Grandpa is engaged in battle. The authorities want to take his land, along with that of his neighbors, to build the Shenandoah National Park. Many of his neighbors are glad to sell out and locate elsewhere, but Grandpa has vowed to fight on until the end. Carrie learns that some things are worth fighting for, even against the odds.

★ ★ ★ Reeder, Carolyn **Shades of Gray** Simon & Schuster, 1989 ISBN 0 02 775810 9

Set in the Piedmont region of Virginia, this novel tells how 12-year-old Will Page feels strongly about the Civil War, which has just ended. He has good reason, because he lost his whole family in what he thought was a just but hopeless cause. Now, he has been sent to live with relatives who he believes to be traitors. They choose not to take sides and have suffered almost as much as he has for their cause. Good dialogue about courage should follow the reading of this book.

★ ★ ★ Reeder, Carolyn **Moonshiner's Son** Simon & Schuster, 1993 ISBN 0 02 775805 2

It's Prohibition, and Tom's family is making good money making and selling moonshine liquor. His father makes the best whiskey around, and Tom is proud of that until he meets the preacher's daughter. She's a rabid temperance lady, and before he knows it, Tom is standing up to Pa and defending his decision not to go into the family business.

★ ★ ★ ★ Rylant, Cynthia **A Fine White Dust** Dell, 1987 ISBN 0 440 42499 2

It's the visit of the traveling Preacher Man to the small North Carolina town that changes everything. It gives new impetus to 13-year-old Peter Cassidy's struggle to reconcile his own deeply felt religious beliefs with the different beliefs and nonbeliefs of his family and friends. Peter is so taken by the Preacher and his message that he plans to run away with him as a kind of apprentice/helper when the man leaves town. Peter, having written a farewell note to his parents, leaves home and waits for the Preacher Man at a prearranged location. He waits, but the Preacher Man, it turns out, has already left town with Darlene Cook. In an act of great loyalty, Rufus, Peter's friend, has followed Peter and, hidden, has also waited. He gets the devastated Peter home. This is a crisis of belief for Peter. He learns about human frailty.

★ ★ ★ Rylant, Cynthia Rylant **Missing May** Orchard, 1992 ISBN 0 531 05996 0

This Newbery Award-winning novel is set in West Virginia. It's a wonderful book about love and death. After the death of the beloved aunt who has raised her, 12-year-old Summer and her Uncle Ob leave their West Virginia trailer in search of the strength and the reason to go on living. They are aided by Cletis, the neighborhood boy who has his own mission: he wants to visit Charleston and see the capitol building.

★ ★ ★ ★ White, Ruth **Belle Prater's Boy** Farrar, 1996 ISBN 0 374 30668 0

This wonderful novel is set in a small coal-mining town in Appalachia. We've used this book for one of our focus books, and more extensive information and activities on it can be found on page 211.

▶ **Poetry**

★ ★ ★ ★ Rylant, Cynthia **Waiting to Waltz** Bradbury, 1984 ISBN 0 02 778000 7

These are poetic vignettes of the Appalachian people and of a young girl's feelings growing up in a small Appalachian town.

▶ **Folklore**

★ ★ Chase, Richard **American Folk Tales & Songs, and Other Examples of English-American Tradition As Preserved in the Appalachia Mountains and Elsewhere in the United States** Dover, 1971 ISBN 0 486 22692 1

The title may be long but it's self-explanatory, and the book is a valuable source of information on the folklore of Appalachia.

★ ★ ★ Chase, Richard **Grandfather Tales** Houghton, 1973 ISBN 0 395 06692 1

This large collection of tales from Appalachia is written down by a master storyteller. Here are variants of many well-known tales made for the telling.

★ ★ ★ Chase, Richard **The Jack Tales** Houghton, 1943 ISBN 0 395 06694 8

This is Chase's first collection of tales starring Jack, the young but resourceful boy whose deeds include giant killing.

★ ★ Haley, Gail Mountain **Jack Tales** Dutton, 1992 ISBN 0 525 44974 4

This is another anthology of mountain tales also involving the trickster hero Jack. The book's wood engravings greatly enhance the tales.

★ ★ ★ Hooks, William **The Three Little Pigs and the Fox: An Appalachian Tale** Aladdin, 1997 ISBN 0 689 80962 X, illustrated by S. D. Schindler

Hooks gives us the Appalachian version of "The Three Pigs." The tale is witty and should lend more interest to the search for variants of common tales.

★ ★ Kidd, Ronald **On Top of Old Smokey: A Collection of Songs and Stories from Appalachia** Ideals, 1992 ISBN 0 824 98569 9, illustrated by Linda Anderson

There are 11 songs and three Jack tales in this collection. The illustrations are striking.

▶ **Audio Tapes**

★ ★ ★ **Listening for the Crack of Dawn** August House Audio, P.O. Box 3223, Little Rock, AR 72203 1991

We have cassette tapes in which storyteller Donald Davis tells four stories about Appalachia in the 1950s. The tapes are entertaining in and of themselves, but are also good examples of oral history gathering. His book by the same title contains these tales and many others (August House, 1990 ISBN 0 87483 130 X).

▶ **Nonfiction**

★ Anderson, Joan **Pioneer Children of Appalachia** Houghton. 1986 ISBN 0 899 19440 0, with photographs by George Ancona

These photographs were taken in a living history museum in West Virginia and do well at evoking the time and people.

★ ★ ★ Bial, Raymond **Mist Over the Mountains: Appalachia and Its People** Houghton, 1997 ISBN 0 395 73569 6

This is a photographic essay. This beautiful book also works to eliminate the stereotypes some people may hold of the people and the land.

★ ★ Rylant, Cynthia **But I'll Be Back Again** Beech Tree, 1993 ISBN 0 688 12653 7
See above.

★ ★ ★ Rylant, Cynthia **Best Wishes** Owens, 1992 ISBN 1 878450 20 4
See above.

CHAPTER 13

Mythology

► COMMENTS

The study of mythology appears in almost every school curriculum and the best place for a deeper study of it is in the middle school. As Bullfinch says in the introduction to his *Mythology*:

> The religions of ancient Greece and Rome are extinct. The so-called divinities of Olympus have not a single worshipper among living men. They belong now not to the department of theology, but to those of literature and taste. There they still hold their place, and will continue to hold it, for they are too closely connected with the finest productions of poetry and art, both ancient and modern, to pass into oblivion.

To study mythology is to study our language, for it is replete with mythology- related words. It's also a study of the cultures that produced that mythology; in this case predominantly those of Greece and Rome. Because so many of the bodies in our solar system are named for those cultures' gods, goddesses, and heroes, a study of mythology can link to astronomy and science. The buildings and statues created to honor or commemorate those creatures lead to a study of art and architecture.

Then, of course, there are the stories themselves, which offer explanations of natural phenomena or human behavior. It's easy to think of them as unrelated to present reality until you uncover such relationships as those of Ares, the Greek god of war, who is accompanied in battle by his sister Eris, the goddess of strife, and his sons Demos, the personification of dread, and Phobos, the personification of fear. Strife leading to war accompanied by dread and fear is a statement of reality in any culture.

► PICTURE BOOK STARTER

If there ever was a picture book intended for middle school students, it's Charles Mikolaycak's **Orpheus** (Harcourt Brace, 1992 ISBN 0-15-258804-3). The myth itself should appeal to the romanticism in many students, and the illustrations and allusions to other myths, plays, art, and stories that make up the book should keep everyone involved.

When you first show it to the students, be prepared for snickers and smirks, because the characters have a statue-like nudity, tastefully draped, of course. Although there are no genitalia shown, there are some naked breasts. If you think this is too distracting, read the book aloud ignoring the illustrations and let the students look at them later individually.

► ACTIVITIES

Once the giggling is over, take time to enjoy the book together. You need more than one reading—first to enjoy the story, then to enjoy the illustrations, and then to pick up the "facts" in the myth itself. By the end of the story, the author has given us may threads to follow, and his starting spots are as good as any.

It's difficult to keep the relationships, actions, and provinces of the gods and goddesses straight. A computer database is a useful tool in so doing. Fields should include:

> Name of god, goddess, or hero
> Father
> Mother
> Siblings
> Children
> Domain or special province
> Deeds
> Relations or interactions with humans

Ask that students enter such information as they find it.

Another possibility is to use a computer program that genealogists use, such as "Family Tree" or "Reunion," to enter such information. These programs allow a quick construction of a family tree that will show interrelationships easily and can be enlarged for display.

The myth of Orpheus and Eurydice, the story of two lovers and of the power of love and music, has inspired so many works that merely following up on them, reading and listening to the results of those efforts, will take some time. Each venture can lead to even more divergent research activities, artwork, and writing. Themes of sorrow and grief, the dangers of looking backward, music having the power to enchant, overcoming seemingly impossible odds, and unrequited and doomed love, are just some of the motifs in the myth. Art and music appreciation activities, and an exploration of other art forms that echo or portray this myth specifically or any myths, are surely possible for a middle school classroom that starts with Mikolaycak's *Orpheus*.

Sometimes such a complicated field of exploration works best if the class starts some planning charts to organize what needs to be done.

What We Know	What We Need to Find Out	Where We Might Find It
Orpheus was a hero, not a god.	Were there other heroes? Who were they? What did they do?	Library Internet
Many paintings have been done about Orpheus and Eurydice	Who painted them? Are they at all like these illustrations? Did Mikolaycak use any of them as inspiration for his art? Which ones do we like best?	Art museum Art books Local art college Internet
Orpheus was part of a mythological voyage	Who else was on that trip? What ship was it? Who were the Sirens?	Mythology books Internet

A web might work well next. Construct it as a class activity. It might take a format similar to this:

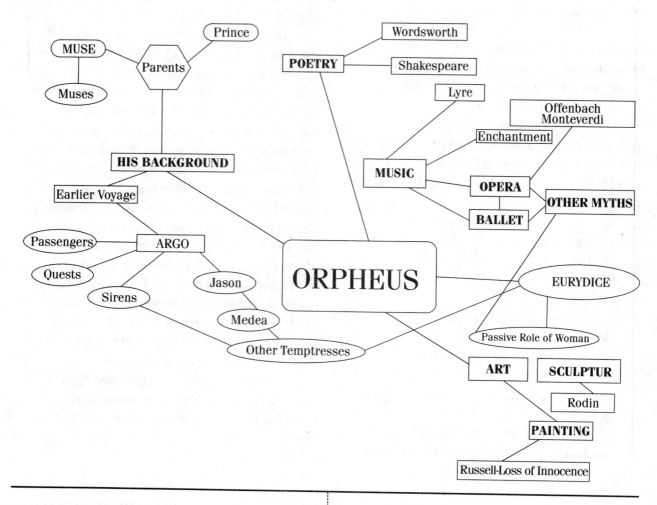

The web would have taken an entirely different direction if it concentrated on myth alone. Actually, any of the boxes or circles above could become the center for divergent or extension webbing.

There are so many allusions to other mythological figures in Mikolaycak's retelling that it is worth charting them in some kind of flow chart, perhaps something like the following:

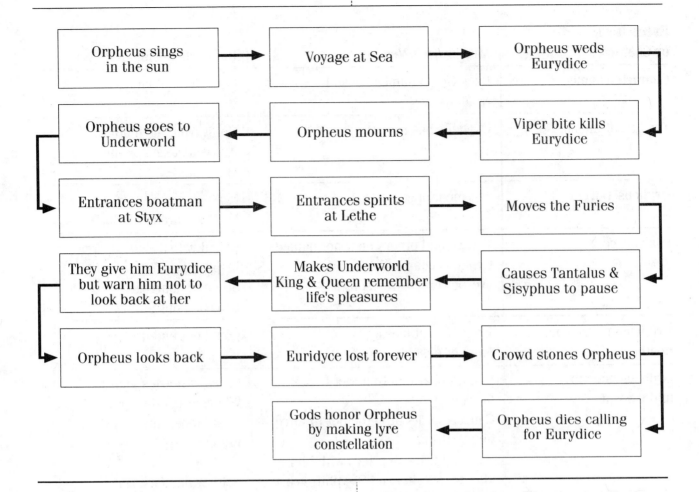

Students can find a subject for further research and reading at every point on the flow chart. For example: when Orpheus sings to the sun, we can find out why he would do such a thing. What did the ancient Greeks and Romans think about the sun god? Who was he? Are there other poems and chants that are addressed to the sun or moon? Do I like any of them? Can I write one? Can I set it to music?

At another point on the chart, Orpheus causes Sisyphus and Tantalus to pause in their labors. What were those labors? Why were they so doomed? What are other impossible tasks in mythology and folklore? What references are made to those two inhabitants of the Underworld in other literature?

Later, Orpheus looks back at Eurydice and loses her forever. Are there other myths where looking back was fatal? How does this relate to the story of Lot's wife in the Bible?

A chart contrasting two or more versions of this myth might come next:

Event, Item, or Character	Mikolaycak's Version	Bullfinch's Version
Character names	Uses Greek names for gods & goddesses	Uses Roman names
The gift of music	Orpheus has it	Got it from his mother It was fostered by the Thracians
Orpheus' parents	Not mentioned	Mother—muse Father—Thracian prince
Sea voyage	Voyage and others on it not named Orpheus charmed sea and overpowered Siren song	Sailed with Jason on Argo Inspired oarsmen Stopped quarrels Drowned out Sirens
Orpheus mourns her death	Wandered aimlessly Sang of despair	Could not endure it
Orpheus goes to underworld	Causes boatman to forget to ask for coin Causes spirits at Lethe not to force him to drink Causes Furies to grieve with him Makes Tantalus and Sisyphus cease	Cerebus relaxes guard Wheel of Ixion stops Sisyphus & Tantalus stop Furies weep Neither named
Names of King & Queen of Underworld	Queen Persephone King unnamed	
Songs	Shorter, less complicated	Longer
Eurydice returned to Orpheus	Warned not to look back at her	Warned not to look back at her
Orpheus looks back and loses her	Eurydice smiles forgivingly	Eurydice cries, "Farewell!"
Orpheus' death	Stoned by crowd Threw head in river Drowned calling out her name	Torn apart by Maenads Head thrown in river
Memorial	Gods make constellation of Lyre to honor the love	Head found and buried by Muses Nightingales sing at tomb
MAJOR DIFFERENCE	More of a story, fewer details	More names, history, and details

That last category is important because it sums up all the otherwise insignificant details.

Look back at the illustrations in Mikolaycak's book. The figures are nude or nearly so. Why would Mikolaycak portray them that way? Come to think of it, why are so many renditions of gods and goddesses in sculpture and painting nude? Why did they make so many statues of them, anyway? Has anyone used mythological figures as subjects for art or music created recently?

The myth of Orpheus has been used in a modern young adult novel, **Orfe,** by Cynthia Voigt (see booklist below).

It is, of course, an easy step from the myth of Orpheus to a study of Greek and Roman mythology or, for that matter, into the mythology of any civilization. Defining and recognizing myth might be the next step. Usually a myth is defined as a story explaining a natural phenomenon or basic truth. Using that definition, most of the pourquoi tales fall into this category: "Why the Bear Has a Stubby Tail," "Why the Sun and the Moon Are in the Sky," "How the Tides Came to Rise and Fall." These are all myths. Many of these tales are folktales and make easily accessed reading. They are also relatively easy to compose, and writing pourquoi tales can become a classroom activity.

Another myth that has been used in many art forms is that of Icarus. Use Jane Yolen's **Wings** for an excellent picture book version of that myth. Students may realize that they need to read more mythology to find out more about Daedalus. The same or similar activities that were outlined above from the book *Orpheus* could be done with *Wings*.

While some are exploring that direction, others may want to find remnants or allusions to the myth of Icarus in other works of literature. Lynd Ward's wordless novel, **The Silver Pony**, certainly falls into that category and also brings the mythological figure of Pegasus into play. Chris Van Allsburg's picture book, **The Wreck of the Zephyr**, concerns a boy whose reach, like that of Icarus, is too high.

Brueghel's painting, *The Fall of Icarus*, shows a farmer in the foreground plowing his field and a ship sailing by while Icarus falls unnoticed into the sea.

W. H. Auden's poem, "Musee des Beaux Arts," is available at **http://www.mathematik. uni-stuttgart.de/CIP/wojnowmo/labyrinth/ musee.html**. It is inspired by the painting and, in the second verse, Auden remarks on how everything turns away from the tragedy. The plowman may have even heard Icarus cry but for him it was not "an important failure." The ships "had somewhere to get to and sailed calmly on."

Lois Lowry relates that painting and poem in her acceptance speech for the Newbery Award which she received for "Number the Stars." That speech can be found in the August 1990 issue of *Hornbrook Magazine*.

The painting can be found in many art books, as well as on the Web at **http://sunsite. unc.edu/wm/paint/auth/bruegel/**.

The more formal myths step closer to religion, and many are or were part of the belief system of their culture of origin. Finding out how much the myths of Greece and Rome were truly believed and how many of them were considered just good stories involves some serious historical research.

There are several places on the Internet where computer users are amassing information on mythology. Try **http://www.desy.de/ gna/interpedia/greek_myth/gods.html# GreekGods** for a site which boasts information on Greek and Roman mythology. Just searching the Internet via Lycos Search Engine with the word "Orpheus" produced more than 500 citings, including a painting by Elsie Russell, *The Loss of Eurydice* (1994, oil on linen, 48"x52"), which can be viewed on screen. We also found a review of the movie *Black Orpheus*, a Cannes Festival winner in 1959 in which a guitar-playing bus driver falls in love with an innocent country girl named Eurydice.

The study of the **Iliad** and/or the **Odyssey** can be the culminating literary activity for this theme. If you do so, try using Paul Fleischman's thought-provoking **Dateline: Troy** as the introduction. (This is a focus book (see page 171).) Fleischman places current newspaper articles and headlines in juxtaposition to the tale, making the reader aware of the timelessness of it. For instance, when Hecuba is frightened by the Oracle's prophecy about the baby in her womb, the facing-page headline reads: "Reagan's Use Astrology," and the article tells how Nancy Reagan used an astrologist's readings to decide on her husband's activities.

After showing the students a few of those headlines, pause in the reading of Fleischman's book to ask them about current events along those lines or suggest that they search magazines and newspapers for relevant articles.

Listing cause and effect of the actions and reactions of the gods during the *Iliad* or the *Odyssey* is a way of keeping some of the action and characters straight.

Make wordlists of everyday words that are based on the names from mythology. Start with: cereal, atlas, and gas. Suggest that students find graphic ways of showing how those words originated; for instance—a picture of Ceres surrounded by cereal boxes.

The symbols of the gods and goddesses also make an interesting discussion topic. We use the symbol of Mars for men and Venus for women in many academic papers and documents. Are there more appropriate ones? What is that saying about the nature of men and women?

While exploring mythology can take a lifetime of research, a more surface exploration is feasible in a middle school classroom. There are many good books on Greek, Roman, and other mythology, as well as many books that deal with individual myths.

Besides the aforementioned Web sites, the following contain useful mythological information:

http://members.tripod.com/~comonline/ report.html gives a brief introduction to the gods and goddesses of Olympus;

http://www.webcom.com/shownet/ medea/bulfinch/welcome.html is an electronic version of *Bullfinch's Mythology*, easily searchable and very informative;

http://pubpages.unh.edu/~cbsiren/myth. html offers links to many mythology sites.

BOOK LIST

Picture Books

★ ★ Climo, Shirley **Atalanta's Race** Clarion, 1995 ISBN 0 395 67322 4

Spurned by her father, the king of Arcadia, because of her sex, Atalanta learns to be a great runner and refuses to marry anyone who cannot outrun her.

★ ★ ★ Fisher, Leonard Everett **Theseus and the Minotaur** Holiday, 1988 ISBN 0 823 40703 9

This beautifully illustrated book makes a nice contrast to Yolen's *Wings*, which covers some aspects of the same story.

★ ★ Hutton, Warwick **Odysseus & the Cyclops** McElderry, 1995 ISBN 0 689 80036 3

One tale from the story of Odysseus, when he and his men become hostages of Polyphemus, is related and illustrated.

★ Hutton, Warwick **Persephone** Simon, 1994 ISBN 0 689 50600 7

We concentrate here on the story of Persephone and her mother, Demeter. Hutton's illustrations are as stately and graceful as his prose in this myth, which explains the reason for seasons.

★ Hutton, Warwick **Perseus** McElderry, 1993 ISBN 0 689 50565 5

Perseus, the beheader of the gorgon Medusa, confronts the evil king who sent him there. Also covered in this picture book is the rescue of Andromeda.

★ ★ ★ Mikolaycak, Charles **Orpheus** Harcourt Brace, 1992 ISBN 0 15 258804 3
See above.

★ ★ ★ Orgel, Doris **Ariadne, Awake!** Viking, 1994 ISBN 0 670 85158 2

Most stories about the Minotaur and the labyrinth concentrate on Theseus, but this concentrates on Ariadne, who fell in love with him.

★ ★ ★ Van Allsburg, Chris **The Wreck of the Zephyr** Houghton, 1983 ISBN 0 395 33075 0

This story, told by an old man to a younger one, explains why the ruins of a sailboat are found high above the sea on a cliff. He tells of a boy in the village, who, years ago, was an excellent sailor and demanded to know how to fly above the waves.

★ ★ ★ Ward, Lynd **Silver Pony** Houghton, 1973 ISBN 0 395 14753 0

Here is a wordless novel of a boy and a flying horse. Like Icarus, they fly too high. Even the chapters are indicated wordlessly.

★ ★ ★ Yolen, Jane **Wings** Harcourt, 1997 ISBN 0 152 1567 1, illustrated by Dennis Nolan

This is a beautifully illustrated, lyric retelling of the myth of Daedalus and Icarus in which the gods and goddesses in the clouds react to the action of the humans below.

Novels

★ ★ ★ Katz, Welwyn W. **Out of the Dark** McElderry, 1993 ISBN 0 689 80947 6

Ben and Keith's mother has been murdered, and they've gone with their father to a small town in Newfoundland to get their lives back together again. Keith begins carving a Viking ship that helps him remember the myriad of myths the family told together. Those myths help everyone accept the loss of their mother.

★ ★ ★ Voigt, Cynthia **Orfe** Atheneum, 1992 ISBN 0 689 31771 9

The story of Orpheus and Eurydice is paralleled in this modern novel of two outcasts who meet in elementary school and reestablish contact in their teens. Enny becomes Orfe's manager, breaking her away from one band and making her very successful with another. Then, Orfe falls in love with Yuri, a drug addict, who eventually is led away from her by his druggy friends into a life of hell.

Longer Mythology

★ ★ ★ Fleischman, Paul **Dateline: Troy** Candlewick, 1996 ISBN 1 56402 469 5

Fleischman has done an amazingly clever retelling of the Trojan War. His introduction states that: "Though their tale comes from the distant Bronze Age, it's as current as this morning's headlines." He then makes visual parallels through newspaper collages throughout the book. This is a focus book (see page 171).

★ ★ Philip, Neil **The Adventures of Odysseus** Orchard, 1997 ISBN 0 531 30000 5, illustrated by Peter Malone

This is an interesting retelling of the 10-year journey of the Trojan War hero, during which his own pride and the actions and reactions of the gods beset the traveler at every turn.

★ ★ ★ ★ Sutcliff, Rosemary **Black Ships Before Troy: The Story of the Iliad** Delacorte, 1993 ISBN 0 385 31069 2, illustrated by Lee Alan

Sutcliff tells the story of the Greeks' 10-year siege of Troy with such skill that the great story bursts into life. Lee's misty watercolors add a nice dimension to Sutcliff's prose, which becomes only slightly tedious during some battle scenes.

▶ Anthologies of Mythology

★ Bellingham, David **Goddesses, Heroes and Shamans: The Young People's Guide to World Mythology** Kingfisher, 1994 ISBN 1 856 97999 7

This is a handy and comprehensive encyclopedia of mythology with brief entries and descriptions.

★ ★ ★ D'Aulaire, Ingri & Edgar **The d'Aulaire's Book of Greek Myths** Doubleday, 1962 ISBN 0 385 01583 6

This anthology of tales has been around longer than most, but nobody's ever explained the gods and goddesses and their relationships better.

★ ★ Graves, Robert **Greek Gods and Heroes** Laurel Leaf, 1995 ISBN 0 440 93221 1
These are well-told tales of the familiar heroes and Olympians.

★ ★ Low, Alice **Macmillan Book of Greek Gods & Heroes** Simon & Schuster, 1985 ISBN 0 02 761390 9

This is a survey of the tales and relationships between and among the Olympians.

★ McCaughrean, Geraldine **Greek Myths** McElderry, 1993 ISBN 0 689 50583 3, illustrated by Emma Chichester Clark

These 17 stories from the myths are told in an arch and amusing manner, making them appealing read-alouds.

★ Osborne, Mary Pope **Favorite Norse Myths** Scholastic, 1996 ISBN 0 590 48046 4, illustrated by Troy Howell

These tales from the Nordic cultures are well and dramatically told, and the introduction shows their relevance to this study.

★ Waldherr, Kris **The Book of Goddesses** Beyond Words, 1997 ISBN 1 885 22330 7, illustrated by Linda Schierse Leonard

Twenty-six different goddesses from many cultures are depicted, and their deeds explained.

CHAPTER 1

Animal Stories

› COMMENTS

One genre of books for young people, that of animal stories, has been thoroughly covered in literature. Because the genre is so vast, you can find good books on a variety of reading levels on the subject. The theme is mostly literary, although you can extend it into science easily enough. It bridges naturally from survival stories (see page 61). In fact, many books can fit easily into both categories.

Like other rich themes in literature, it easily divides and diverges, letting students follow the paths of greatest interest for them. There are books about human relationships with pets and about human encounters with wild animals. There are books in which humans play a distant role or are not present in the story. Some books make humans of animals, and they are really stories about ourselves in fur or feathers. Many picture books for the very young fall into this category. In other books, the animals behave like animals but have some human emotions or actions. Books such as **Charlotte's Web** and **The Jungle Book** fall into this category. Still other books are completely nonanthropomorphic and tell of animal behavior and survival without endowing them with human thoughts.

› PICTURE BOOK STARTER

You might like to introduce the theme with Donald Hall and Barry Moser's picture book, **I Am the Dog: I Am the Cat** (Dial, 1994 ISBN 0 8037 1504 8). This book does well comparing the basic differences in nature between the two beasts as the animals alternate, giving us their views of the world. It's an easy step from here to science. The anthropomorphism is easily identified here.

› ACTIVITIES

Students might like to write about animals with which they have had special relationships or animals that interest them at this point. Many favorite readings from their childhood are apt to fall into this genre, and making a list of them may help to get students talking about the genre. Putting their favorite books in a scatter graph may help to visualize the various genres and subcategories better. Such a graph might have as one axis "realism to fantasy," while another might be "human to animal." This would make each axis a continuum along which the book titles or the characters in the books could be placed. It might look something like this:

```
Fantasy |
         |    Mathias
         |
         |           Babe
         |
         |
         |
         |
         |
Reality  |                        Shiloh
         |_____
              Human              Animal
```

With additional picture books about animals for students to read and browse through, you can expose them to the vast amount of written and illustrative material that this genre includes. Put out copies of Michael J. Rosen's picture books, **Purr: Children's Book Illustrators Brag About Their Cats** and **Speak!: Children's Book Illustrators Brag About Their Favorite Dogs**. These two delightful browsers should get kids talking about their favorite authors and illustrators, as well as about the pets they favored. A class book made up of one-page writings and drawings from pet owners would be a logical next step.

Encourage students to talk about their picture book discoveries and to relate them to personal experiences they have had with animals. Any of these picture books can lead to science research as students extend the facts found in the books to whole studies of animal behavior.

A good read-aloud for the animal stories genre might be one of the strongest recent books about dogs: Phyllis Reynolds Naylor's Newbery Award-winner, **Shiloh** (Simon & Schuster, 1991 ISBN 0 689 31614 3). More than the usual boy-and-his-dog story, *Shiloh* is a book in which ethics are called into question and no easy answers are given.

Students choosing to stay within the dog, cat, or horse books can research various breeds, deciding why the authors might have chosen a certain breed or mix of breeds for their animal characters.

Do the same for wild animal characters in their books. Research nonfiction sources to find out about the main personality and physical characteristics of these animals, as well as their typical predator/prey relationships of the animal. Which is the author using? Which is the author omitting or ignoring?

In some of the books, human characters have a relationship with wild animals. How realistic is that relationship? For instance, in **Julie of the Wolves**, a young girl is more or less adopted by a wolf pack. Find out what various wolf experts think about the idea. Visit Web sites for further information about wolves. Find Web sites about the animal or animals featured in their books.

There are formulas within this genre that are easy to identify:

protagonist gets pet, protagonist almost loses pet, protagonist appreciates pet,

hero gets pet, pet teaches hero life lessons, pet dies.

The best of the books avoid such formulae or give them unexpected twists. Didacticism, sentimentality, and inconsistent anthropormorphism can ruin the literary quality of a book, and discerning readers may begin to notice the presence or absence of these qualities on their way to becoming more critical readers. Put the formula at the beginning of this paragraph on the board and ask that students see which of the novels that they are reading would fit or almost fit the formula.

Try another formula, such as:

Home ——> away ——> home.

After students fit some books they are reading or have read to either of those formulae, suggest they write such a bare-bones outline about the book they're currently reading.

While the students are reading their novels, gather them together for discussions about such topics. Lead in questions such as: Did you know this was going to happen next? Is the action believable? Are the animals too good to be true?

Make a silhouette of the central animal character in a book. On the silhouette, put words to describe it. Make arrows from each of these descriptive words to a justification for it from the book. Here's one about **Babe, the Gallant Pig**

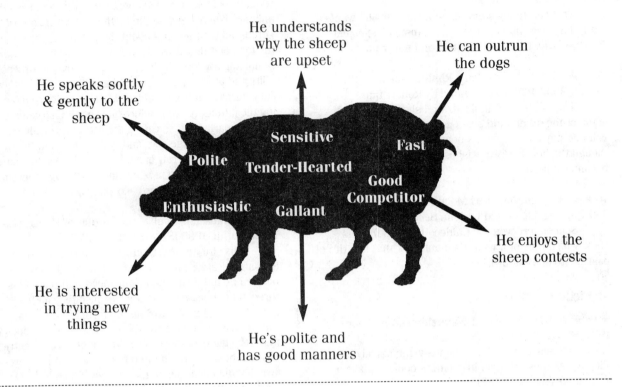

He understands why the sheep are upset

He can outrun the dogs

He speaks softly & gently to the sheep

He is interested in trying new things

He's polite and has good manners

He enjoys the sheep contests

Sensitive

Polite

Tender-Hearted

Fast

Good Competitor

Enthusiastic

Gallant

📖 BOOK LIST

▶ Picture Books

★ ★ ★ ★ Bunting, Eve **Red Fox Running** Clarion, 1993 ISBN 0 395 58919 3, illustrated by Wendell Minor

This beautifully illustrated book follows a red fox in search of food in the winter landscape.

★ Carrick, Donald Carrick **Harald and the Giant Stag** Clarion, 1988 ISBN 0 89919 514 8

Carrick's book is set in medieval times and tells of a young serf's attempt to save a stag from the Baron's hunt.

★ ★ ★ Cowcher, Helen **Tigress** Farrar, 1991 ISBN 0 374 47781 7

Cowcher has villagers in conflict with the people in the wildlife preserve over a tigress and her cubs.

★ ★ Rosen, Michael J. **Purr: Children's Book Illustrators Brag About Their Cats** Harcourt Brace, 1996 ISBN 0 15 200837 3

Rosen and 40 other illustrators pay tribute to their various felines, past and present. The large illustrations speak louder than the text and have the added advantage of showing us the illustrators' art styles.

★ ★ Rosen, Michael J. **Speak!: Children's Book Illustrators Brag About Their Favorite Dogs** Harcourt, 1993 ISBN 0 15 277848 9

Profits for this book and the one above go to an animal charity. As in *Purr*, it's the artwork that dominates this book, in which illustrators tell about their favorite dogs.

★ ★ ★ San Souci, Dan **North Country Night** Doubleday, 1990 ISBN 0 395 41319 X

This is another wintry picture book that brings us a great horned owl, as well as several other woodland creatures, in simple prose with elegant illustrations.

★ ★ ★ Segal, Lore **The Story of Mrs. Lovewright and Purrless Her Cat** Knopf, 1985 ISBN 0 394 86817 X, illustrated by Paul O. Zelinsky

This is a funny story about a woman who wants a cat to love her and be loved by her. Instead, she gets Purrless, who refuses to be held and never purrs.

★ ★ ★ Weller, Francis Ward **Riptide** Philomel, 1990 ISBN 0 399 21675 8, illustrated by Robert Blake

This is more of an illustrated short story than some of the others and gives us a golden retriever who will not stay away from his beach patrol duty, even though the beach patrol wishes he would—until he becomes a hero.

★ ★ ★ ★ Yolen, Jane **Owl Moon** Philomel, 1987 ISBN 0 399 21457 7, illustrated by John Schoenherr

Schoenherr won the Caldecott Award for this book, which tells of a winter's night walk that is a rite of passage to spot an owl.

▶ **Fiction**

★ ★ ★ ★ Adams, Richard **Watership Down** Simon, 1974 ISBN 0 02 700030 3

Animals that act like humans verge quickly into allegory, as they often do in Adams's books. This is a focus book (see page 139).

★ ★ Ball, Zachary **Bristle Face** Holiday House, 1962 ISBN 0 8234 0915 5

This novel is set in rural Mississippi and gives us Jase Landers, who is 14 and orphaned and runs away from an abusive uncle. Headed toward Memphis, Jase meets the dog he later calls Bristle Face. The dog's unusual appearance (half dog and half porcupine?) belies his foxhunting talent, which is instrumental in getting Jase's friend Lute elected to sheriff and accepted by the Widow Jarkey. This is a book that packages a strong adventure story in gentle love and humor.

★ ★ ★ Bauer, Marion Dane **A Question of Trust** Scholastic, 1994 ISBN 0 590 47923 7

Their mother has moved out; their father is withdrawn. Charlie and Brad are furious. The boys hope to force their mother to move back home by refusing to see her or to answer her phone calls. When a stray cat has kittens in their tool shed, the boys know that their father would forbid them to keep the cats, but are sure that, when their mother comes home, she'll let them keep the animals. When they find the mother cat eating one of the kittens, all their feelings about their own mother come to the fore, and they drive the mother cat away from the remaining live kittens, determined to show their responsibility and their superior parenting abilities. The mother cat returns, and Brad realizes that she has been mothering the kittens, as well. Before he can tell Charlie this, Charlie nearly kills the cat. At the vets, a reconciliation is affected between the boys and their father, and they learn that the cat was merely behaving naturally when a kitten dies. The boys end up in a tearful reunion with their mother and make a start toward accepting her decision.

★ ★ ★ Branscum, Robbie **The Murder of Hound Dog Bates** Puffin, 1995 ISBN 0 14 037593 7

This story is short, funny, and very accessible. Sassafras Bates, commonly known as Sass, finds his beloved hound dead and is convinced that one of his three aunts poisoned the dog, because they all hated him. The aunts work hard on the farm and they have raised Sass since he was a baby, but Sass now hopes to make the guilty party confess. The aunts are eccentric characters who love him in different ways and, therefore, handle his accusations uniquely. When Kelly O'Kelly starts courting one of the aunts after agreeing to help Sass solve the mystery, Sass feels doubly betrayed.

★ ★ ★ ★ Burgess, Melvin **The Cry of the Wolf** Tambourine/Morrow, 1990 ISBN 0-688-11744-9
This is a focus book (see page 153).

★ ★ Byars, Betsy **Tornado** HarperCollins, 1996 ISBN 0 06 026449 7

Byars gives us short, easy-to-read stories told by Pete, the hired man, to entertain and distract a family huddled in their storm cellar during a tornado warning. The title, however, is that of the dog who is the hero of these tales, which have a gentle humor.

★ ★ ★ ★ Campbell, Eric Campbell **The Place of Lions** Harcourt, 1990 ISBN 0 15 21031 9
See page 63.

★ ★ Dexter, Catherine **Gilded Cat** Morrow, 1992 ISBN 0 688 09425 2

Animal stories can be set in any era, and Catherine Dexter's time-travel story takes us back to ancient Egypt. Maggie buys a funny-looking statue at a yard sale that turns out to be a mummified cat from ancient Egypt. Drawn into the spiritual world of ancient Egypt, Maggie undertakes to reunite a boy Pharaoh with his pet cat, only to find herself under the spell of an evil magician from the past. Maggie learns spells that first excite and later terrify her. The magician's spells posess Maggie, then her friend Donnie, and eventually threaten the life of her family. This is a scary, can't-put-it-down kind of book. The author creates a believable spirit world. The pace is swift, and the suspense is sustained. When Maggie's young brother is bitten by a conjured scorpion, we share her terror as the scorpions take over the house.

★ ★ ★ Erickson, John **Hank the Cowdog Series** Gulf Publishing Company

This series of books must be mentioned here. These stories are not great literature, but they are very funny. Pompous and officious Hank is the animal equivalent of Barney Fife, and he and his cohort, Drover, attempt to solve mysteries both existent and imaginary on the ranch they supposedly guard. Because of their accessibility and humor, these books may appeal to kids who are unmotivated by more serious literary works. The writing is more clever than it may appear on the surface. Often, events occur more or less off-camera, which the reader must infer from the reading. Give yourself a laugh and try one.

★ ★ ★ ★ Fox, Paula **The One-Eyed Cat** Simon & Schuster, 1984 ISBN 0 02 735540 3

Compelled to try a new rifle just once, in spite of his parents' disapproval, Ned does so and shoots at something in the night. Shortly thereafter, Ned sees a one-eyed cat whose eye has been shot out. Convinced that it was he who injured the cat, Ned is overwhelmed with guilt. Mr. Scully, his elderly neighbor, befriends the cat, as Ned's guilt causes him to become obsessed with the cat. Ned's father is a minister, and both of his parents exhibit such trust in Ned that it compounds his guilt. His anxiety pervades his entire life. In spite of being physically ill and weak, Ned's mother is a strong woman who tries to help him understand and deal with what he has done.

★ ★ ★ ★ George, Jean **Julie of the Wolves** HarperCollins, 1972 ISBN 0 06 021943 2
See page 98.

★ ★ Hall, Lynn **Flying Changes** Harcourt, 1991 ISBN 0 15 228790 6

Horse stories fall into this category, too, and one of the best horse-story writers is Lynn Hall. The scene here is Liberal, Kansas, and 17-year-old Denny is there with her grandmother, a horse trainer, trying to get over a love affair with a rodeo rider. Her father and mother return after many years of separation between themselves and their daughter. Her father is now wheelchair-bound, and their relationship is stormy, to say the least. The hard work of training the horses helps Denny cope with them all.

★ ★ Henkes, Kevin **Protecting Marie** Greenwillow, 1995 ISBN 0 688 13958 2

Henkes is insightful in his portrayal of a 12-year-old girl and her parents. Fanny's mother is fortyish, beautiful, and the anchor of their family. Her father is 60, moody, a talented artist, and demanding. Both, however, adore their only child and reach out to her in remarkably open ways. Fanny's relationship with her mother is open and loving. Her father, however, has given her reason to distrust him. Once, he brought her a puppy and then found the puppy's antics so distracting to his work that he made her give the puppy away. Now, her father is blocked in his painting, depressed about turning 60, and often angry and withdrawn. He wants, even demands, understanding from his wife and daughter. His wife gives that understanding quite consistently. Fanny alternates between hating and loving him. When he brings her another dog, this one grown and well trained, she hesitates to love the dog and, after she does so, she lives in constant fear that her father will take him away. The book is not action-packed, but the relationships among the three main characters are thoroughly explored, and you end up envying Fanny for her parents, irascibility and all.

★ ★ ★ ★ Jacques, Brian **Redwall** Putnam, 1987 ISBN 0 399 21424 0

Slightly less challenging than **Watership Down**, although almost as long and also dealing with animals with human behavior, is Brian Jacques' *Redwall* series. This book is the first volume, and here mice and other woodland creatures defend an abbey against invasion by a pack of villains.

★ ★ ★ King-Smith, Dick **Babe, the Gallant Pig** Knopf, 1997 ISBN 0 679 87393 7

This book was the inspiration for the movie *Babe* and tells the delightful story of a prize-winning, sheep-herding, ultra-polite pig.

★ ★ ★ ★ Naylor, Phyllis Reynolds **Shiloh** Simon & Schuster, 1991 ISBN 0 689 31614 3
See page 98.

★ ★ ★ Peck, Sylvia **Kelsey's Raven** Morrow, 1992 ISBN 0 688 09583 6

   A tamed wild animal makes a nice bridge here, and a good book that features such a creature is this one. When Kelsey and her best friend, Sam, find a raven trapped in the chimney, the old, ailing bird becomes Kelsey's pet. Kelsey's fantasy-type dreams have become troubling. In them previously, she and Sam have sped away from various foes on horseback, racing to their castle, leaping across the moat to the slowly rising drawbridge which pulls up before their pursuers can follow. Now, the dreams are changing; something has gone wrong. Kelsey's dreams parallel and at times foreshadow her waking life, where the chimney sweep becomes the new man in her mother's life, and where Kelsey and Sam are torn apart by jealousy. This is a well-grounded story interspersed with a fantasy world of almost mystical dreams. Those dreams, the relationship between Kelsey and the Raven, and the Joan of Arc play in which her mother is currently playing the title role, all add class and depth to the classic contemporary tale of a single mom falling in love, and best friends in trouble. The symbols are never oversimplified, and life is exposed as complex and illusory, never pat.

★ ★ ★ Rawls, Wilson **Where the Red Fern Grows** Bantam, 1984 ISBN 0 553 25585 1

   This book will be familiar to many students from their encounters with it in elementary school. If they have not heard or read it previously, however, they may want to read it now. The sentimental tale of Billy and his two hunting dogs, Old Dan and Little Ann, takes place in the Ozarks, where the team takes first place in a hunting contest. When one of the dogs is killed, the other pines away from loneliness. It's a guaranteed tearjerker.

★ ★ ★ Spinelli, Jerry **Wringer** HarperCollins, 1997 ISBN 0 06 02491373
This is a focus book (see page 204).

★ ★ ★ Westall, Robert **The Kingdom by the Sea** Farrar, 1990 ISBN 0-374-44060-3
See page 66.

▶ **Nonfiction**

★ ★ ★ Jackson, Carolyn **The Flying Ark** W.H. Freeman, 1990 ISBN 0 7167 6594 2

   Don't let the title fool you. This is a fascinating book about how animals for zoos are transported, usually by air. Each kind of animal presents a different problem, and in telling us how they are moved about, the book tells us a lot about the animal itself.

★ ★ ★ ★ Paulsen, Gary **Woodsong** Bradbury, 1990 ISBN 0 02 770221 9

   This book of essays makes a good bridge between stories about domestic and wild animals, as well as making a step into nonfiction reading, because it deals with experiences Paulsen has had with his sled dogs and animals of Alaska and northern Minnesota. There is acceptance and respect for animal life, especially that of sled dogs, in all its harsh reality. A good portion of the book relates the author's experiences in running the Iditarod. These are good adventure and outdoor stories that should appeal to outdoor enthusiasts and to animal lovers.

CHAPTER 15

Sports

COMMENTS

A theme about sports is ideal for middle school. For one thing, in spite of the popularity of the subject, it is seldom approached within the school curriculum, so it hasn't been done to death. It's almost all-inclusive as far as subject areas are concerned. It can be studied as physical science: projections and laws of motion, for instance. Its connection with history is obvious, and it can also be studied sociologically: group dynamics, effects of competition, and self-concept. For music, there are not only songs about sports, but the uses and abuses of bands as part of competitive sports. Mathematics is easily included, not only for statistics and their analysis, but for calculations about possible human speeds and feats based on current knowledge. There are also, of course, the economics of sports, and that can be treated either mathematically or sociologically. Physical education includes health and safety, as well as the various sports themselves. So, once again, grab the teachers from those many disciplines and see how many will cooperate on a sports theme.

PICTURE BOOK STARTER

Playing Right Field by Willy Welch, with illustrations by Marc Simont (Scholastic, 1995 ISBN 0 590 48298 X). If you can find it, get the tape of the song on which the book is based, recorded by Peter, Paul, and Mary. The narrator is out there in right field, the poorest player on the team—and he knows it. He was picked last, and he knows this is the position that gets almost no action in a Little League game. He is distant from the action in more ways that one, but as he tells us, "It's important, you know." At first, he doesn't really believe it, and we know that, but suddenly he becomes aware that things are happening and he's in the right place at the right time—right field. Read it together. Sing it with the trio. Some kids may be willing to share their experiences of being chosen last or of being an unexpected hero.

ACTIVITIES

To establish what formula writing is, make a list of the formulas common in sports fiction such as:

Weak player becomes hero during big game.

Hero shows weakness during big game.

As books are read for the theme, add formulas to the list.

Some authors take formulas such as those above and twist them in such a way as to lift the story above the formula. Others follow a formula, but their level of writing is such that we are hardly aware of the familiar plot. Use these and other observations to conduct dialogues on the books read.

In many novels, some characters, often the main ones, grow or change in the story while others remain pretty much as they were to begin with. Use this dichotomy to make a chart such as the following:

Title	Characters who changed
Characters who remained static	Moment of change

In Chris Crutcher's novel, **Stotan!** (see below), the boys discuss "Stotan" behavior as a cross between stoic and Spartan behavior. Students will need to find out what each of those terms mean, but then can discuss or write about moments in their lives, in and out of sports, when such behavior was expected of them or when they showed such behavior.

Stay literary for a bit and construct another dichotomy in which the true climax of a work of fiction takes place during a game or in another venue.

Further discussion about the above topic might debate whether or not sensitive and Stotan behavior are mutually exclusive.

There are many debates, of course, that a theme on sports can and should engender.

Make sure that students use nonfiction sources to buttress their arguments for or against such practices as hunting and dog racing, which almost automatically encourage people to take a stand. Other debate material could be: the purpose of team sports in educational institutions, the amount of money involved in professional and amateur sports, the purposes and results of athletic scholarships, sexism and racism in sports, the use and abuse of sports' fame, and the role of sports heroes. Should some sports be outlawed or drastically changed?

It may be time to analyze each student's chosen sport as far as physical science is concerned. Put the laws of motion on the board and figure out together the way those laws are demonstrated in each sport. Design experiments to demonstrate them. What can be measured and how?

Find out about changes in equipment for each sport over the years and determine the price, if any, that has been paid for increased safety. Should further protection be added to any of the examined sports?

Pick ideal teams for a sport, selecting players based on statistics, and follow your hypothetical team through a season, calculating wins and losses.

Look at artistic depictions of sports, both photographic and otherwise.

Read some newspaper and magazine sports columns, and compare the writing styles and literary quality of the work.

▧ BOOK LIST

▶ Picture Books

★ ★ ★ ★ Blake, Robert J. **Akiak** Philomel, 1997 ISBN 0 399 33798 9

Within these 32 pages, you get striking and informative illustrations; an exciting story; and hooks to math, geography, science, and history. The endpaper maps show us the Iditarod trail and some of its topography. The text gives us a day-by-day account of a woman, Mick, and her dog team, but the star of the book is the lead dog, Akiak. At least, she starts out as the lead dog. She's run this race before and always got her team into top places, but she's never won. At 10, this will be her last chance to win. On day four, Akiak's paw is injured, and Mick replaces her and makes arrangements to fly her home. Akiak, however, has other ideas, and she escapes her handlers and determines to catch up with her team. At the first two stations, trail volunteers try to catch her, but soon everybody, including the reader, is rooting for Akiak.

★ ★ Bottner, Barbara **Nanna Hannah's Piano** Putnam, 1996 ISBN 0 399 22656 7, illustrated by Diana Cain

Our narrator loves baseball with a passion and loathes the piano lessons his mother insists upon. His grandmother Hannah's passion is dance, and when she hurts her ankle and can't do the tango, he teaches her how to catch a fly ball. She teaches him how to play "Take Me Out to the Ball Game" on the piano. Their four-handed rendition of that song brings other young baseball fans to the window as a most appreciative audience.

★ ★ ★ Golenbock, Paul Bacon **Teammates** Harcourt Brace, 1990 ISBN 0 152 00603 6

Branch Rickey recruited Jackie Robinson, the first African-American player in the major leagues, for the Cincinnati team. This picture book tells a bit about the results of that inclusion and of the racism that was rampant in baseball at the time. Then PeeWee Reese declared Jackie Robinson his teammate.

★ ★ Ketteman, Helen **I Remember Papa** Dial, 1998 ISBN 0-8037-1848-9 illustrated by Greg Shed

This is a sweet and sentimental story about a boy and his father. Money is scarce, and the boy has been saving his pennies to buy a baseball glove. His father has done the same to buy boots. On a trip to town to see a ball game, the boy sees just the glove he wants. At the game, however, he loses his money. His father buys the glove with his boot money. The boy polishes his father's old boots and resolves to pay back the money.

▶ **Novels**

★ ★ ★ Bloor, Edward **Tangerine** Harcourt, 1997 ISBN 0 152 01246 X

Paul is legally blind, but he doesn't let the kids at his new school find that out. He plays soccer well and makes friends with his quick wit and skills. His older brother, Erik, is their father's pet, however, for Erik is a football star, and football is the town's and his father's passion. Erik is also evil, and may well have been involved in the accident that injured Paul's eyes. There's an underground fire spilling smoke and stench, and clouds of mosquitoes everywhere in the bizarre town of Tangerine. Lightning strikes frequently and even kills a football player, but the games go on. Eventually, Erik's

behavior—the gang killing of a boy—becomes too much even for his father to deny.

★ ★ ★ ★ Brooks, Bruce **The Moves Make the Man** HarperTrophy, 1995 ISBN 0 06 447022 9

This is a deeply disturbing book. It is funny, stark, and deceptively simple. Jerome Foxworthy—13, ace student, the first black student in an all-white school, and a basketball fanatic—narrates this story of his friendship with Bix. Bix's game is baseball, but Jerome recognizes in his skill the same passion and technical accuracy that Jerome has for basketball. It is clear from the beginning, however, that Bix is deeply disturbed. Convinced that the best way to show up his stepfather, who was a college basketball star, is to beat him at his own sport, Bix is taught the game of basketball by Jerome. Bix, although a quick learner, refuses to learn the feints and tricks so much a part of Jerome's game. He insists compulsively, almost hysterically, that such moves are lies and that he must be totally truthful. This is a focus book (see page 150).

★ ★ ★ Brooks, Bruce **What Hearts** HarperCrest, 1992 ISBN 0 06 021132 6

Told in four stories, each set at a crucial time in a boy's life, this book gives us a longitudinal study of a gifted child. We start with the departure of Asa's father. Then, Asa's mother announces that she is marrying Dave, much to Asa's disgust. Dave is difficult, inflexible, and antagonistic. He and Asa have a difficult time from the beginning. Asa is a gifted and talented student and athlete. When Dave coaches the baseball team, the sport at which Asa excels, Asa is furious. Dave deliberately hits Asa with a hard-thrown ball, and the fight deepens. When his mother's mental illness becomes apparent, however, Dave and Asa must combine efforts to cope.

★ Chapin, Kim **The Road to Wembley** Farrar, 1994 ISBN 0 374 34849 9

This is an accessible soccer story in which fifth-grader Marty Regan, a poor and rejected transplant from America to this school in England, becomes a gofer for a professional soccer team. The coach is a former soccer hero, but the team is up against it this year. Through gritted determination, the team makes it to the finals at Wembley. There is a lot of soccer (English football) discussion here, as well as drama.

★ Christopher, Matt **Baseball Turnaround** Little Brown, 1997 ISBN 0 316 14275 1

This is just one of many works of sports fiction by Matt Christopher. In this one, a boy with a secret moves to a new town hoping to make a new start on the baseball team there, but soon meets someone who knows all about his past. A probation officer proves helpful, and with much of the stress gone, Sandy proves to be capable of change and growth.

★ ★ ★ ★ Cohen, Barbara **Thank You, Jackie Robinson**
Beech Tree, 1997 ISBN 0 688 15293 7

Sam Green is nuts about baseball. His mother runs an inn in New Jersey, and Sam's best friend is Davy, the African-American cook at the inn, who is as crazy about baseball as Sam. They especially admire Jackie Robinson, the first black man in major league baseball. Together, Davy and Sam set out to see a game at each ballpark within a day's drive of their home. They can't go any farther than that because, in these days of segregation, Davy is not allowed in any restaurant or hotel. When Davy has a heart attack, Sam musters up his courage and gets past many obstacles to get Jackie Robinson's autograph on a baseball for Davy, somehow convinced that the ball with make him better.

★ ★ Crutcher, Chris **Athletic Shorts** Laurel Leaf, 1996 ISBN 0 440 21390

Although each of these six stories has something to do with sports, growing up is a more prominent theme. All but one of these stories contains a character from one of Chris Crutcher's novels. "A Brief Moment in the Life of Angus Bethune" outlines a tender, funny time in the life of a boy whose mother and father are each living with their gay partners. "The Telephone Man" brings us Jack, an emotionally damaged young man from **Crazy Horse Electric Game** (see below), as he is rescued from a Chinese gang by an African-American, calling his father's racism into question. The final story deals with the fear of AIDS. Most of the stories take place in small towns in Montana or Idaho.

★ ★ ★ Crutcher, Chris **The Crazy Horse Electric Game**
Dell, 1991 ISBN 0 440 20094 6

Willie Weaver does well at most sports. Perhaps that's because he comes from a family of sports heroes. His girlfriend, Jenny, is also into sports. He pitches for his school's baseball team, and in a crucial game against the Crazy Horse team, he gains greater acclaim. The team presents him with an inscribed cane shaped like a baseball bat. Soon afterward, Willie fractures his skull while water skiing. Resuscitated by Jenny, he lives, but he is partially paralyzed and his speech is halting. He must now use the ceremonial cane in order to walk. After a series of other catastrophes, Willie drops out of school before turning his life around.

★ ★ ★ Crutcher, Chris **Ironman** Laurel Leaf, 1996 ISBN 0 440 21971 X

Bo Brewster blows up at his football coach, who attempts the same bullying tactics that Bo has experi-
enced from his father. Forced to attend a therapy group dealing with anger, Bo finds that writing letters to Larry King that he will never mail is as valuable as the group sessions, which are led by a Texan of Japanese descent. Bo begins training intensively for a triathlon—swimming, biking, and running. His father is rooting for his chief competitor, even giving him a bike, in the hope that losing will teach Bo a lesson.

★ ★ Crutcher, Chris **Running Loose** Laurel Leaf, 1986 ISBN 0 440 97570 0

Unlike Bo, in **Ironman**, Louie Banks has his father's support when he defies his football coach during his senior season. The racist coach demands that Louie make an illegal hit against an opponent. Louie is thrown off the championship team, even though he had earned a starting spot, and is nearly thrown out of school. Things get worse when his girlfriend, Becky, is killed in an automobile accident.

★ ★ ★ Crutcher, Chris **Staying Fat for Sarah Byrnes**
Greenwillow, 1993 ISBN 0 688 11552 7

Sarah has been disfigured since the age of three, and overweight Eric is her only friend. Now in a psychiatric hospital, Sarah is catatonic, but Eric visits her daily while trying to keep up his work on the swim team. When she finally speaks, it is to tell Eric of her escape plans. Knowing that her father, Virgil, is dangerously psychotic, Eric gets help from Lemry, a sympathetic teacher. Together, they try to find Sarah's mother while fending off attempts from the father to find her. Eventually, Virgil stabs Eric, but all ends well—perhaps too well for this otherwise taut novel.

★ ★ ★ Crutcher, Chris **Stotan!** Greenwillow, 1986 ISBN 0 688 05715 2

A "Stotan" is a cross between a stoic and a Spartan as defined by the boys' swimming coach. The swim team pushes beyond exhaustion to a euphoric state as they live together for a week in Lion's apartment. There, they share moments from their past when Stotan behavior was required. Walker, the protagonist in this gritty novel, attempts to sort out his feelings about these stories of the past, and also find a way to help his teammates in the coming weeks. Nortie is beaten by his father, and Jeff becomes terminally ill. The boys complete three legs of a four-man relay in tribute to Jeff.

★ Dygard, Thomas J. **Infield Hit** Puffin, 1997 ISBN 0 140 37935 5

A transfer student for junior year, Hal intends to use his baseball skills as entry to the social scene. His father was a professional baseball star, but Hal hopes to conceal that fact. The team player he replaces at second base is furious, and Hal must deal with that as well as the relationship with his father.

★ Glenn, Mel **Jump Ball: A Basketball Season in Poems** Lodestar, 1997 ISBN 0 525 67554 X

We could easily have listed this book under poetry, for it is indeed a book of poems. However, the poems combine to make a story as a bus carrying a basketball team crashes on an icy road. We get multiple points of view as players' fans, teachers, and parents, as well as witnesses, give testimony to the events.

★ Heymsfeld, Carla **Coaching Ms. Parker** Simon & Schuster, 1992 ISBN 0 02 743715 9

The faculty/student annual baseball game is a big deal at Westbend Elementary, and when the fourth graders find out that their teacher dreads it because of her lack of skill in the game, they volunteer to coach her. She has a lesson to teach, as well. This is an easily accessible book with some humor and good sports talk.

★ Hoffius, Stephen **Winners and Losers** Simon, 1993 ISBN 0 671 79194 X

There's a rivalry between Daryl and Curt, both on and off the track team, but when Daryl suffers a heart attack during a race, Curt becomes the focus of Daryl's father's ambition, as well as Daryl's. Daryl's father is cruel and relentless in his pursuit of winning, driving his son beyond endurance.

★ Hughes, Dean **End of the Race** Atheneum, 1993 ISBN 0 689 31779 4

Jared and Davin compete on the track team. Davin, being black, feels great pressure from his father to be better than his white teammates. Jared is almost equally pressured by his father to achieve, but sees no race problem in their almost entirely white community in Utah. Davin has a lesson to teach him about racism, both conscious and not. The true challenge lies in whether or not they can be real friends.

★ ★ ★ Kehret, Peg **Searching for Candlestick Park** Cobblehill, 1997 ISBN 0 525 65256 6

Spencer's mother and father are divorced, and he misses the time he had with his father. Most of it, however, was spent just watching the Giants' baseball games on TV. Now, he and his mother have had to move in with his Aunt May. When told he must give up his cat, Foxey, Spencer decides to run away. He has had a postcard from his father saying that he visits Candlestick Park in San Francisco every day. Spencer determines to find his father there and go to live with him. Running away with a cat isn't easy, and Spencer has to steal money, food, and a bicycle to do so. He is often in great danger, but

he has the good fortune to trust the right stranger, Hank, who gets Spencer to call his mother, and gives him money for a bus ticket to San Francisco. Leaving Foxey with Hank is hard, but Spencer knows it's best for the cat. He does find his father in Candlestick Park, where his father is working as an usher, but his father cannot or will not let him stay.

★ Ketchum, Liza **Twelve Days in August** Holiday House, 1993 ISBN 0 823 41012 9

Alex and Rita are twins, and their family comes to town just as soccer practice begins. Alex's obvious ability galvanizes the team, and native son Todd greatly admires Alex. Another player, Randy, is threatened by both Alex's talent and what he perceives to be Alex's sexual orientation, and determines to make Alex quit the team. Randy's actions almost cause a tragedy, as peer pressure becomes a focal point of the novel.

★ Klass, David **Danger Zone** Scholastic, 1996 ISBN 0 590 48590 3

Jimmy Doyle is a basketball hero in a small town in Minnesota, and he's picked to be on the Dream Team for a tournament in Italy. However, he's the "wrong" color and from the wrong place to suit the other players on the team. They, in turn, face racism from the fans in Europe. That's trauma enough, but then Nazi terrorists become a much more real danger to the team.

★ Korman, Gordon **The Toilet Paper Tigers** Apple, 1995 ISBN 0 590 46231 8

Corey's Little League team is sponsored by the Feather Soft Bathroom Tissue Company, and that's humiliating enough. Then Kristy, the coach's grand-daughter, becomes team manager. It's enough to make a fellow quit, but then Kristy starts to make changes–for the good! This is comic ground, and Korman treads it well.

★ Lee, Marie G. **Necessary Roughness** HarperCollins, 1996 ISBN 0 06 025124 7

Like Soto's **Taking Sides** (see below), this novel concerns a culture clash between inner city and subur-ban kids, as well as an ethnic conflict. Chan and his twin sister, Young Kim, have moved from Los Angeles to a small town in Minnesota, where they receive a cool reception, not only because of their race, but because of their uncle's disgrace running the grocery store that the Kims take over. Chan is assaulted by his football team-mates. Fortunately, they gain quick acceptance from their landlady, Mrs. Knutson, as the family struggles to make the grocery store a success, only to be hit head-on with tragedy.

★ Manes, Stephen **An Almost Perfect Game** Scholastic, 1995 ISBN 0 590 44432 8

Every summer, Jake and Randy go with their grandparents to their hometown minor league baseball games. Jake and Grandma are compulsive about keeping up their scorecards, while Randy and Gramps are more relaxed about the game. This summer, however, things change. It soon becomes apparent, to Jake at least, that his scorekeeping controls rather than records the game.

★ ★ Nelson, Vaunda Micheauc **Mayfield Crossing** Camelot, 1994 ISBN 0 380 72179 1

It's the time of forced busing, 1960, and the African-American kids from Mayfield Crossing are having a rough time of it. They liked their old school, where they enjoyed playing baseball together. The new, big Parkview School has been all white, and students there react with anger and fear at the integration of Mayfield students. Meg Turner is the only black student in her fourth grade, but she has a compassionate teacher. Her brother, Billie, is less fortunate. Even he can't keep Meg out of trouble. A challenge to a baseball game between Mayfield kids and Parkview kids seems to help.

★ Patneaude, David **The Last Man's Reward** Albert Whitman, 1996 ISBN 0 807 54370 5

The bet is on. The neighborhood is made up of company-owned apartments, and their parents are all looking to move. The boy who ends up as the last of the bunch to live in the apartment complex wins a valuable Willie Mays rookie baseball card that the kids hid in an abandoned mine. Five boys are competing, and each has his own reasons for wanting to be that last man.

★ Powell, Randy **The Whistling Toilets** Farrar, 1996 ISBN 0 374 38381 2

The sport is tennis, and Ginny is a rising star about to participate in a big tournament. Stan, her former partner, is hired on to coach her out of a slump. Stan's having problems coming to grips with his own past and future. During the summer, it's hard to tell who's coaching whom as Ginny helps Stan come to grips with the truth about himself, and love comes into play, in this sometimes very funny novel.

★ Savage, Deborah **To Race a Dream** Houghton, 1994 ISBN 0 395 69252 0

Harness racing is the focus of this book set at the turn of the century in Minnesota. Dan Patch, the legendary race horse, is quartered hear Theodora's farm, and she dreams of becoming a harness driver, much to her parents' dismay. Her older sister, Claudia, has chosen music as her career, and they much prefer her choice to Theodora's. Then, Claudia contracts polio, and the family's attention is diverted from Theodora, who disguises herself as a boy to gain work as a stable hand and get started on her dream.

★ ★ ★ ★ Slote, Alfred **Finding Buck McHenry** HarperCrest, 1991 ISBN 0 06 021652 2

Jason loves baseball, although his playing skills are only mediocre. Cut from his Little League team, he is crushed and unburdens himself on the school janitor, Mack Henry. It turns out that Mr. Henry knows a lot about baseball, especially about the Negro League. Jason knows nothing about such a league; his extensive collection of baseball cards gives no indication of it. A trip to the card store, however, turns up a card for Buck McHenry, who may or may not be Mr. Henry.

★ ★ ★ ★ Smith, Robert Kimmel **Bobby Baseball** Yearling, 1991 ISBN 0-440 40417 7

This book is much better than the title implies. Bobby dreams, writes, and plays baseball. His father made it to professional baseball, although he never got to the major leagues, but Bobby has his own path figured out. He will become a great Little League pitcher and then go right to the semi-pros, into the major leagues, and on to the Baseball Hall of Fame. He secures a place on the team his father coaches in spite of his father's feeling that he'd be better off on another team. Bobby is sure he'll be an outstanding pitcher and refuses all advice to try for second base. He becomes the pitcher, and that's the beginning of the end of all his dreams.

★ ★ Snyder, Zilpha Keatley **Cat Running** Delacorte, 1994 ISBN 0 385 31056 0

It's the time of the Great Depression. Cat Kinsey is a fast runner, but because her father refuses to allow her to wear slacks, she does not run in a school sports day. Zane Perkins, however, does run, and he wins. Cat's family looks down on families like the Perkins, calling them "Okies," even though they come from Texas. Cat resents Zane's victory until she meets his little sister, Sammy, and deals with her own intolerance.

★ Soto, Gary **Taking Sides** Harcourt Brace, 1991 ISBN 0 15 284076 1

Transplanted from the barrio in California to a tree-lined suburb, Lincoln Mendoza feels torn when his new basketball team is slated to play against his old team. Lincoln is sure his coach is racist and looks down on him because of his Mexican heritage. Add to that the fact that his mother is dating a Caucasian, and his old friends think he's betraying them. Which side shall he take in each of those dilemmas, or need he take a side at all?

★ Wallace, Rich **Shots on Goal** Knopf, 1997 ISBN 0 679 98670 7

Set in the same Pennsylvania town as the author's **Wrestling Sturbridge** (see below), and told in the present tense, we have here the story of Barry and Joey, friends since grade school and avid soccer players. There's a power struggle as each boy tries to find his role on the team, and, as if that's not enough to break up a friendship, they're vying for the same girl.

★ ★ Wallace, Rich **Wrestling Sturbridge** Knopf, 1996 ISBN 0 679 87803 3

Small-town Pennsylvania is the narrow confines of this novel, and Ben is determined to escape the fate of most of its youth—employment in the town's cinder block factory. Previously, he was a second stringer on the wrestling team, content to be his friend Al's wrestling partner. Al is the team's best hope for the championship, a position Ben determines to take over. This is a quest story in which the main character does not achieve his goal.

★ Weaver, Will **Farm Team** HarperCrest, 1995 ISBN 0 06 023589 6

Billy's dream is to play on a summer baseball team in a nearby city, but his father's jail sentence precludes that. Billy must tend the farm in his father's absence. His mother organizes a team of her own, however, using migrant workers, neighbors, and even the family dog. The bonding that takes place among the team members is strong. Their success is such that the literal "farm team" challenges the city team to a game.

★ Yee, Paul **Breakaway** Groundwood Books, 1997 ISBN 0 888 99289 0

Here the heritage is Chinese-Canadian, for a change. Eighteen-year-old Kwok is resentful of his father and of working on the family's pig farm in 1930s Vancouver. He faces racism at school, but rejects contacts in Chinatown. Soccer is his game, and he hopes to use it as his entry to college, which is his mother's dream, as well. His father sees no reason for Kwok to leave the farm. The friction between generations is the focus of the book. The ending is not what you'd expect, although Yee prepares us for it.

▶ **Nonfiction**

★ Aylesworth, Thomas G. **The Kids' World Almanac of Baseball** Pharos Books, 1996 ISBN 0 886 87787 3

Here are records and facts galore, and plenty of chances to revel in statistics, trends, and trivia.

★ Christopher, Matt **Baseball Jokes and Riddles**, Little Brown, 1996 ISBN 0 316 14081 3, illustrated by Daniel Vasconcellos

There's more in this book than the title implies, as anecdotes about baseball are interspersed throughout the book.

★ ★ Mochizuki, Ken **Baseball Saved Us** Lee & Low, 1993 ISBN 1 880 00001 6

This story is set during World War II, when Japanese-Americans living on the West Coast were put into prison camps. The injustices of the prison camp are the background for this well-written baseball book in which the prisoners used the game as a vehicle for establishing both diversion and pride.

★ ★ ★ Paulsen, Gary **Woodsong** Puffin, 1991 ISBN 0 140 34905 7

All of these essays are not about sports as such, but some center around hunting and fishing. Others deal with dog racing. They're all beautifully written and show the author's strong connection with the out-of-doors.

★ Ward, Geoffrey C.
Shadow Ball Knopf, 1996 ISBN 0 679 86749 X
25 Great Moments Knopf, 1996 ISBN 0 679 86751 1
Who Invented the Game Knopf, 1996 ISBN 0 679 86750 3

These books are taken from the PBS television series on baseball and offer an alternative to the usual sports books for young people. They are full of captioned photographs, but the approach is historical, and the text is not too complicated.

▶ **Poetry**

★ ★ ★ Janeczko, Paul **That Sweet Diamond** Atheneum, 1998 ISBN 0 689 80735 X, illustrated by Carole Katchen

This is a delightful collection of baseball poems that are seldom found elsewhere. Many are small, but all are right on target.

★ Morrison, Lillian **At the Crack of the Bat: Baseball Poems** Hyperion, 1992 ISBN 1 562 82176 8

There are 44 poems about baseball in this very good anthology.

★ Morrison, Lillian **Slam Dunk: Basketball Poems** illustrated by Bill James Hyperion, 1995 ISBN 0 786 80054 2
There are 42 poems in this anthology by a variety of poets, including Eloise Greenfield and Mary Swenson. Some are tributes to superstars.

CHAPTER 16

Humor

COMMENTS

The difficulty in writing and talking about humor is that, in the process of analyzing it, we can destroy it. Most of us like to laugh, however, and we can sometimes entice students who are less than avid readers into books by introducing them to some genuinely funny writers. We can even identify some of the devices that make us laugh, and thus become aware of some of the authors' techniques without ruining their books. Senses of humor vary widely, however, and we should remember that what makes one person laugh can disgust or at least turn away others.

Since humor writing often appeals to a wide range of ages, this genre can help bridge the gap between young adult and adult literature. Such writers of adult humor as Dave Barry and Patrick McManus address topics with a humor that can be shared by younger readers and listeners.

PICTURE BOOK STARTER

The Stinky Cheese Man and Other Fairly Stupid Tales by Jon Scieszka, illustrated by Lane Smith (Viking, 1992 ISBN 0 670 84487 X). This humorous book of revisionist and playful presentations of well-known fairy tales is fun for a diverse group of students. Its 10 complete stories are clever, amusing, and true to

their name: "fairly stupid." These presentations have unique versions, such as modern, "hip" changes; combinations of more than one tale; new and different endings; and truly unusual twists, and the print itself is part of the humor.

ACTIVITIES

It may be best to approach the subject through what is already familiar to most middle school students: comics. "Calvin and Hobbs" is a popular comic strip that can invite laughter on a variety of levels. "Doonesbury" is more political. "Far Side" cartoons are apt to be more subtle and absurd. Encourage readers to make similar or more refined statements about them.

Also encourage readers to post their favorite comic strips and cartoons. Start a lift-the-flap riddle board, with absurd riddles on the cover and the answers under the flap. The riddles, jokes, and cartoons can be placed on a bulletin board in such categories as: school-related, parents, friends, etc. Other categories can be developed as readers become more involved in the task.

For many readers, the idea that an essay or any other piece of writing can be laugh-out-loud funny is a new one. Play one of the tapes of Patrick McManus's essays, such as **The Night the Bear Ate Goombaw** (Durkin Hayes, 1990 ISBN 0 886 46261 4). Follow the listening experience by showing the students some of the books of his collective essays.

The humor writers can be likened to the cartoon makers: Mark Russell is often political and can be compared to "Doonesbury." Dave Barry often writes about the frustrations of parenting and running a home. Begin making such relationships between and among the humor writers encountered in the study.

Humor writing can also be compared to television programs. Some funny novels are very much like situation comedies, in which a humorous character reacts to various events within his or her life. **The Best School Year Ever**, by Barbara Robinson, is such a book. In it, the Herdman family is developed almost as a single unit, and they react to the various situations in which they find themselves much to our delight and laughter. On a bulletin board, set "Situation Comedy" as one category into which students can place their humor readings.

Other humor writing is more like *Saturday Night Live* in that a series of skits and monologues are presented for our amusement. Patrick McManus and Dave Barry sometimes work in that venue. Use "Skits and Commentary" as another category. You categorize humor, of course, not because it fits so well into neat boxes, but because the reasons you put a given piece of humor writing into a particular category can set off an interesting discussion.

Slapstick humor is evident in many of the *I Love Lucy* episodes and in some writings, such as **Harris and Me**, by Gary Paulsen, and some of Patrick McManus' work. Students can find and identify that kind of humor.

Dialogue can be witty. *Seinfeld* relies on that kind of humor. Lois Lowry's Anastasia books have many humorous conversations, especially between Anastasia and her parents.

At this point, it might be wise to start a humor circle wherein readers share their

funny discoveries by reading aloud. The leader may want to start by reading aloud from Patrick McManus' **The Grasshopper Trap** or any other compilations of his humor column in *Field and Stream* magazine. McManus combines slapstick humor with a tongue-in-cheek style. His writing is for adults, and his vocabulary may challenge some readers. However, his subject matter, hunting and fishing, should appeal to readers who like outdoor life. Try reading the chapter, "The Human Fuel Pump" from the above-mentioned book, or "The Swamp." There's a section in that latter chapter where an action has to be assumed because it is not described. One paragraph ends with the sentence, "I knew there was no way we wouldn't be through the swamp by sundown." The next paragraph begins with "Immediately after sundown, one of the first things I noticed about the swamp was that it had become excessively creepy." The reader is left to imagine what must have occurred throughout that day to leave them still in the swamp after dark.

Books of jokes and cartoons are good things to have in the classroom. They may not be great literature, but they may be the only actual reading some students will do of their own accord. It's a place to start.

There are many picture books, including those by Dr. Seuss, in which much of the humor and subtlety is missed by younger readers while being snatched up and enjoyed by more mature ones. Get kids to bring in books they laughed at when they were little, and see if they still find them funny. For instance, William Steig's **CDB!** is letter talk accompanied by sketches that may help to decipher some of them. This is not as easy as you might think.

There are many tongue-in-cheek revisions and extensions of fairy tales currently available (see below). Assemble some of these for a sharing circle one morning. Let students take turns sharing their favorites.

In Avi's **"Who Was That Masked Man, Anyway?"**, real life is less than satisfying for Frankie Wattleson. His brother is home from the war, wounded and depressed. A mysterious lodger has rented Frankie's room. His only refuges are the radio dramas of Captain Midnight, the Lone Ranger, and Superman. Frankie tries to live the lives of these heroes, ferreting out the evil scientist (the lodger) with the aid of his good friend, Mario. The book is very funny, and all the text is dialogue. Use it for reader's theater. Use multiple copies of the book and suggest that partners decide on one chapter to present to the class with or without partners.

Uses of humor in our society can be approached through the classroom. What role does humor play in students' scholastic lives? Class clowns may be persuaded to talk about the ways in which they have made people laugh, and whether or not their humor hurts anybody, emotionally or physically. Teachers who use humor in their teaching can be interviewed to see what effects they think it has on education.

Go from the classroom to society in general. Conduct interviews with family members and ask what makes them laugh. Which comedians do they enjoy? Do they read humor columns in magazines and newspapers? comic strips? What old movies were their humor favorites?

≥ BOOK LIST

▶ Picture Books

★ ★ ★ Alexander, Lloyd **Fortune Tellers** Dutton, 1992 ISBN 0 525 44849 7

A young carpenter seeks a fortuneteller to learn about his future. Will he be rich, famous, and happy? Will he find his true love? He is conditionally assured of a very bright future, but the advice is self-fulfilling: he will be rich if, the fortune teller says, he earns large sums of money, happy if he avoids misery, and live a long life unless he dies early.

★ ★ Birdseye, Tom **A Regular Flood of Mishap** Holiday, 1994 ISBN 0 8234 1070 6

Our narrator explains that she was just trying to help by rescuing her grandfather's fishing pole, but each attempt at fixing things leads to another disaster. There are many outrageous puns.

★ ★ ★ Breathed, Berkeley **Goodnight Opus** Little, 1993 ISBN 0 316 10853 7

This is **Goodnight Moon** gone mad. Students who remember that story as an early childhood favorite should enjoy this zany book.

★ ★ ★ Breathed, Berkeley **Red Ranger Came Calling** Little, 1995 ISBN 0 316 10881 2

This is **Polar Express** as seen through a fun house mirror. A little boy who's shunted anywhere but home spends his Christmas with a distant aunt. He considers himself to be the Red Ranger of Mars, and in this role, he confronts an old man remembered by many islanders to be Santa Clause. The man is failing fast, but does seem to be surrounded by elfish-looking men. Daring him to prove himself, the boy asks for a Red Ranger Tweed Bicycle. The old man misunderstands but delivers. It's a one-joke book, but it works.

★ ★ ★ ★ Cazet, Denys **Never Spit on Your Shoes** Orchard, 1990 ISBN 0 531 05847 6

Arnie has just returned from his first day of first grade. He's got lots to tell his mother about the day. As he does so, we are treated to a look at the whole story. This one should be funny for anyone with a memory of his or her first day of school.

Charlip, Remy **Arm in Arm** Parents, 1969 ISBN 0 691 2610

Tiny images fill pages full of jokes, riddles, and puns.

★ ★ ★ Cole, Brock **The Giant's Toe** Farrar, 1986 ISBN 0 374 42557 4037 0

This is a humorous prequel to *Jack and the Beanstalk*.

★ ★ ★ Everett, Percival **One That Got Away** Clarion, 1992 ISBN 0 395 56437 9

This is a book of puns in a pseudo-Wild West tale.

★ ★ ★ Johnston, Tony **The Cowboy & the Black-Eyed Pea** Putnam, 1992 ISBN 0 399 22330 4

This is a Texas version of *The Princess and the Pea*.

★ ★ Koscielniak, Bruce **Geoffrey Groundhog Predicts the Weather** Houghton, 1995 ISBN 0 395 88398 9

There aren't many books about the origins of Groundhog Day, and this explanation is as good as any. It's also a fine satire on the media. Geoffrey Groundhog wakes up on the second of February, doesn't see his shadow, and walks to the local newspaper and announces that spring will come soon, and it does. By the next year, the media have done their job. Geoffrey's picture is plastered all over town. When he wakes, bright television lights keep him from seeing much of anything.

★ ★ ★ Pilkey, Dav **'Twas the Night Before Thanksgiving** Orchard, 1990 ISBN 0 531 05905 7

This is a parody, as the title implies, but the names for the turkeys that are rescued are hilarious, and the whole premise is funny.

★ ★ ★ Scieszka, Jon **The Frog Prince, Continued** Viking, 1991 ISBN 0 670 83421 1

Life isn't "happily ever after" for the Frog Prince and his wife.

★ ★ ★ Scieszka, Jon **The Stinky Cheese Man and Other Fairly Stupid Tales** Viking, 1992 ISBN 0 670 84487 X, illustrated by Lane Smith
See above.

★ ★ ★ Smith, Lane **The Happy Hocky Family** Puffin, 1996 ISBN 0 14 055771 7

This looks like the dullest book ever and it's meant to look that way. It's a spoof on pre-primers and other early readers.

★ ★ ★ Stanley, Diane **Saving Sweetness** Putnam, 1996 ISBN 0 399 22645 1

This is a tongue-in-cheek Western melodrama involving a sweet, innocent little orphan girl and a bungling sheriff who just doesn't get the message.

★ ★ Steig, William **CDB!** Simon and Schuster, 1987 ISBN 0 671 66689 4
See above.

★ ★ ★ Yolen, Jane **Sleeping Ugly** Putnam, 1981 ISBN 0 698 11560 0

This turnabout of the Sleeping Beauty fairy tale contains some delightful puns, especially in the moral.

★ ★ ★ ★ Yorinks, Arthur **It Happened in Pinsk** Farrar, 1987 ISBN 0 374 33651 2

Irv Irving is unhappy and it's hard to see why. Irv wants more. He envies everyone. And then, one day, it happens. Irv loses his head. His wife's reaction? "Oh, Irv!...Every day you lose something. Your keys. Your glasses. Now this." Ever resourceful, she quickly makes him a head out of a pillowcase and some old socks, but Irv's troubles have just begun. While searching for his missing head, he is variously identified as a criminal, a long-lost uncle, and a deadbeat, before he finds his head being used as a dummy in the window of a hat shop.

▶ **Novels**

★ ★ Avi **Romeo & Juliet: Together (and Alive!) At Last** Avon, 1987 ISBN 0 380 70525 7

Slapstick humor is combined with a sidewise look at human behavior in this school story. When our narrator realizes that it is his duty to bring two lovers—who have never even communicated—together, he casts them as the leads in Romeo and Juliet. Everything that can go wrong, does.

★ ★ ★ Avi **"Who Was That Masked Man, Anyway?"** Orchard/Jackson, 1992 0 531 05457 8)
See above.

★ ★ ★ Birdseye, Tom **I'm Going to be Famous** Holiday, 1986 ISBN 0 8234 0630 X

Birdseye tells us of Arlo Moore, who has decided to be in *the Guiness Book of World Records* for eating the most bananas in less than two minutes. The current record is17. Arlo's attempt soon becomes a school-wide effort to break many Guiness records, and much hilarity results in this fast-paced, very accessible book.

★ ★ ★ Burgess, Barbara Hood **Oren Bell** Dell, 1991 ISBN 0 440 40747 8

This is a very good book with great characters and very funny situations. It's about an African-American seventh grader who must contend with the goings-on in his Detroit neighborhood, many of which are dangerous, if not life threatening. However, his strong family and their humor make it all possible.

★ ★ ★ ★ Cooper, Susan **The Boggart** Aladdin, 1993 ISBN 0 689 80173 4

It seems like great news when the Volnik family learns they have inherited a Scottish castle. However, it turns out to be a ruin inhabited by the Boggart. When a desk is sent from the castle to the Volniks' Canadian home, the Boggart comes in it. His clash with modern technology is very amusing.

★ ★ ★ ★ Curtis, Christopher Paul **The Watsons Go to Birmingham: 1963** Delacorte, 1995 ISBN 0 385 32175 9

This book has some very funny sections and a wonderful depiction of the Watson family. There is, however, the horror of the bombings in Birmingham, toward which the book builds. It starts with humor and ends with tragedy. The Watsons—Mother, Father, older son Byron, next son Kenny, and daughter Joetta—live in Flint, Michigan. Most of the first part of the book is devoted to the hijinks, many of them hilarious, of Byron, who walks on the edge of delinquency. Often it's the tears and protests of the little sister that keep Byron from being badly punished. Although his parents are loving and have great senses of humor, they are finally pushed into doing something drastic about Byron. They will take Byron to his grandmother's, in Birmingham, and he will stay with her for awhile. The trip to Birmingham brings the children to their first experience with segregation. After a warm welcome at their Grandmother Sands' house, it is Kenny, not Byron, who gets in trouble. He nearly drowns, and it is Byron who saves him. The real climax comes when the church Sunday school that Joetta is attending is bombed. Fortunately, she escapes injury, but it is some time before the family realizes this. The horror of it all is too much for Kenny, however. The family, including Byron, come back to Michigan, and, again, it is Byron who saves the day by helping Kenny accept the unfairness of the tragedy.

★ ★ ★ Hamilton, Virginia **Willie Bea & the Time the Martians Landed** Greenwillow, 1983 ISBN 0 688 02390 8

It's Halloween 1938, and Willie Bea's extended family has gathered at their grandmother's house in rural Ohio. Aunt Leah hears the Orson Welles radio broadcast about Martians landing on earth. The antics, misunderstandings, and results of the half-heard program create havoc and humor.

★ ★ ★ Johnston, Julie **Hero of Lesser Causes** Joy St. ISBN 19920 316 46988 2

This book is both funny and sad. Keely's brother, Patrick, who was such an enthusiastic comrade, is lost in his despair since he became paralyzed from polio. Now, Keely has done everything she can think of to draw

him out, but nothing works. What of her own life? She's almost 13. Shouldn't she be growing up, dressing more maturely, keeping a level head? She loves her fantasy of growing up to be a hero on a silver steed. Not a heroine, she says; they only stay at home while the hero goes off to save someone. She is impetuous, always plunging headlong into things with unshakable enthusiasm. As our narrator, Keely pulls us along with her energy and wit. A tale of courage and friendship and everyday heroes, this book is light and funny, firmly grounded in real life even while it shares with us Keely's and Patrick's struggles to reestablish a relationship, and Patrick's enormous struggle to live again.

★ ★ ★ Lillington, Kenneth **An Ash-Blonde Witch** Faber, 1987 ISBN 0 571 14625 2

This is a fairly sophisticated novel set in the 22nd century. The village of Urstwhile tries to retain its backward look while the resident guardian of morals, Prudence, and a mysterious blonde stranger both set their sights on Simon, the farmer.

★ ★ ★ Paulsen, Gary **Harris and Me: A Summer Remembered** Bantam, 1993 ISBN 0 440 40994 2

This is one of the funniest books ever written. A city boy spends a summer on a Minnesota farm with Harris, who manages to contrive one adventure after another, all of which are doomed, and all of which provide hilarious slapstick humor.

★ ★ Robinson, Barbara **The Best Christmas Pageant Ever** HarperCollins, 1988 ISBN 0 06 440275 4 Although most of your kids will have encountered this book earlier, they may enjoy looking at it again for the slapstick and humorous commentary on the Herdman family's attempt to take over the Christmas pageant.

★ ★ ★ Townsend, Sue **The Adrian Mole Diaries** Grove, 1986 ISBN 0 380 86876 8

Two books are combined in one in this book about an adolescent boy, Adrian, who worries about everything: pimples, diet, Princess Di, and his parents' divorce. The book is funny and, at times, quite touching. Adrian is an only child, and his parents are about to break up. He writes copious entries in his diary and sends off letters to the BBC, interpreting the replies in his own way. Adrian also worries about being a virgin. He's in love with the new girl in his class, although he worries about her higher social standing. His mother is having an affair, as is his father, so he has even more to worry about. When his parents get back together, Adrian learns he's about to become a brother. Much to his surprise, he adores Rosie, his new baby sister, and checks her vital signs constantly.

▶ Series Books

The following series books are situational, family-oriented, funny books that are particularly well written:

The Anastasia books by Lois Lowry (published by Houghton Mifflin).
The Alice books by Phyllis Reynolds Naylor (published by Atheneum).
The Bingo Brown books by Betsy Byars (published by Viking).
The Besseldorf books by Phyllis Reynolds Naylor (published by Atheneum).

Another series of books that is fun to read is that about Hank the Cowdog, by John R. Erickson (Gulf Publishing, 1992 ISBN 0 87719 213 8). The stories are narrated by Hank, who refers to himself as chief of security at the ranch, assisted by his not-so-able second in command, Drover. The books are written in a sort of hard-boiled detective narrative, but Hank is so inept and so transparent in his attempts to cover his mistakes that the laughter is almost guaranteed.

▶ Essays

McManus, Patrick
★ ★ ★ ★ **A Fine and Pleasant Misery** Holt, 1987 ISBN 0 805 00032 1
★ ★ ★ **The Grasshopper Trap** Holt, 1985 ISBN 0 03 000738 0
★ ★ ★ **The Good Samaritan Strikes Again** Owlet, 1993 ISBN 0 805 029222
These are just a few of the many collections of essays by Patrick McManus. Many are also available as audiotapes from Durkin Hayes Publishers.

▶ Nonfiction

★ ★ ★ Mowat, Farley **Owls in the Family** Little, 1961 ISBN 0 316 58641 2
Based on the author's own memories, this book tells of two owls who lived with the family and set the household on end.

CHAPTER 17

Quests

➤ COMMENTS

This theme could include almost every work of fiction and many works of nonfiction listed elsewhere in this book. It crosses genre, and is intended to allow students to follow their own interests in reading, while finding means of commonality among their choices. Leland Jacobs defined "story" as "one or more characters on a quest." Exploring that concept with readers may show them another way of looking at and analyzing books. It can also provide an outline for writing students' own stories.

Finding the characters and defining their quests is usually the easy part. In most stories the quest is stated somewhere early in the text. In some, however, the quest is implied.

➤ PICTURE BOOK STARTER

Barbara Cooney's beautiful picture book, **Miss Rumphius** (see below), is one that many of your students will have encountered in grade school, but its beauty and meaning may have eluded them then. Now, they can enjoy the illustrations and the story of a woman determined to fulfill her quest—actually, multiple quests—before her life is complete.

➤ ACTIVITIES

The story of Miss Rumphius may lead students to discuss or even just think about their own personal goals and ambitions. Making the world more beautiful is also a subject worthy of discussion from the book, and students can make up a list of ways in which they could accomplish this quest soon.

The character or characters on the quest are not always successful. Sometimes, they just plain fail, usually learning something on the way. Other times, they fail to achieve the original objective, but get something else instead. Sometimes, they achieve their aim, but are unaware of it. Other times, they think they achieve their goal, but do not really do so. Sometimes, more than one quest is going on at the same time by various characters in the book. Occasionally, the goal can be achieved only by one, and others are thus thwarted in their quest. In other books and stories, disparate characters join in a common search. Students can start categorizing familiar stories along these lines.

In **Tom Sawyer**, Aunt Polly's quest is to raise Tom to be a respected member of society. Tom's quest is to outwit Aunt Polly, run free, and explore the world. Huck's quest is to retain his freedom. These might be represented graphically in this way:

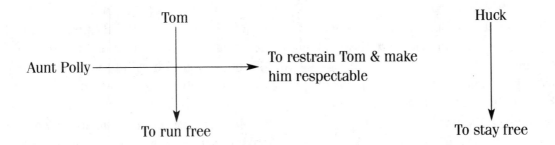

The diagram shows that, if Tom gets his way, Aunt Polly can't get hers, but Huck's quest is independent of both of them. Because *Tom Sawyer* is episodic, many chapters can be seen as individual quests. For instance, in "The Glorious Whitewasher," there are several quests that can be defined and plotted in different ways:

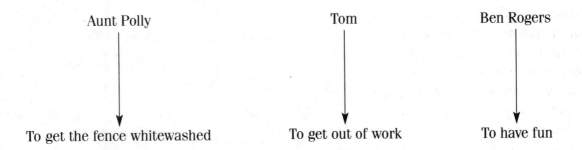

If we define Aunt Polly's quest in this way, everybody is a winner. If, on the other hand, we define Aunt Polly's quest as "to punish Tom," the result and the diagram are different:

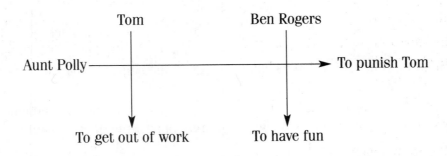

In this setup, Aunt Polly's and Tom's quests are at crossed purposes. If she is successful, Tom is not, and vice versa. Because Ben's and Tom's quests are parallel, they can both be winners.

Carrying the quest analysis further, if a character in a story sets out on a quest and the story simply tells how he or she did it, the story is apt to be boring. Most writers add barriers, abettors, and interveners to make the plot less simplistic and more interesting. They can be identified in a diagram, as well. In the diagram above, Aunt Polly is an intervener in Tom's quest. Ben Rogers is an abettor. Usually, but not always, abettors and interveners have their own quests, which can be shown or ignored in a given diagram.

Looking at a novel or short story in this way can be an aid to thinking about the motivations of any and all characters within. Students may wish to show their stories' content graphically in terms of quest in a form similar to this:

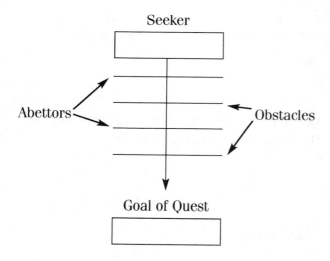

Charting a story along these lines could provide a new means of analysis. The same outline could serve as a way of setting up a story yet to be written. If students first conceive of a character and delineate that character with some descriptive phrases, they can then imagine what that character could conceivably want. By placing the character at the top of the page and the goal at the bottom, and deciding whether or not their character is going to be successful, they can then picture the story about to be written in terms of a quest. Deciding what obstacles the character will encounter and what characters and events will help that character, the writer can work with them on the page. The result could be a working outline for the story. Of course, there can and probably should be other characters with congruent or divergent quests, so similar outlines could be developed for them. Some young authors might find writing easier after using such a setup.

This graphic analysis is not the only means of contrasting and comparing books about quests and journeys. The motivation behind the quest is worth discovering and discussing. Is it selfish? high-minded? a search for things material or otherwise? Are those undertaking the quests doing so willingly or under duress? Are the abetting or intervening characters well-developed or cardboard characters, there for a single purpose? Is the plot realistic? idealistic? fantastic? And, what happens as a result of the main character's journey? Are people better off? Is the person on the quest better off?

Most fairy tales are quests of one sort or another. Snow White seeks refuge from her stepmother and a way to achieve adulthood on her own. Rapunzel seeks a rescuer from her cruel imprisonment. Jack seeks the treasures at the top of the beanstalk. Cinderella wants to go to the ball. Her abettor is the fairy godmother; her obstacles are the lack of costume and conveyance, and the actions of her stepsisters and stepmother. Encourage students to make a similar quest analysis of different fairy and folktales.

As with other themes in this book, the setting up and use of a chart may make the reading clearer and suggest opportunities for dialogue. The chart for quests may start like this:

NOVELS

Book	Questors	Quest	Abettors	Obstacles	Outcome
Hilgartner **"Colors in the Dreamweaver's Loom'**	Zan	Prevent the taking of the territory of the	The twins The dreamweaver	Vemathi Khedathi	Territory is secured Returns to her father
Jacques, Brian **Redwall**	Matthias Cluny	Defend the Abbey Capture the Abbey			
Paulsen **Dogsong**	Russell	Find his own song	Oogruk		
Voight **Homecoming**	Dicey and her siblings	Find a home	Each other A few strangers	Lack of food People wanting to separate them Some family members	Home with Gram
Adams **Watership Down**e	Fiver	Find a safe hom	Hazel	Rogue Rabbits	Safe Warren
Lowry **The Giver**	Jonas	Become the Giver Save the twin Find out if there is an "elsewhere"	The Giver	The rules of his society	Unknown

Students might, as a result of investigating the theme of quests in literature, choose to think about their own quests: Do they have a goal? Do they have long- and short-term goals? What are they doing to achieve them? Ask students to write down two of their personal goals. Encourage them to be concrete and realistic.

Give students a form in which the days of a week are marked off in half hour segments. Students should fill in the blocks of time that are used for required activities such as sleeping and school attendance, putting an X through those time slots. For a week, students write in what they are actually doing during the remainder of the time. Later, students can assess how much of their flexible time was spent working toward either on of their goals.

BOOK LIST

▶ Picture Books

★ ★ ★ Cole, Brock **The Winter Wren** Farrar, 1984 ISBN 0 374 38454 1

The winter seems endless, and Simon and his sister Meg set out to wake up spring. Winter, in the person of an old man, throws ice at the children and turns Meg into a winter wren. She then tells Simon how to counteract Winter's evil. He sows wheat where Winter has sown sleet, plants an apple tree where Winter has cut off the apple buds, and finally chases Winter home. The allegory is sweet and well done.

★ ★ ★ ★ Cooney, Barbara **Miss Rumphius** (Puffin, 1985 ISBN 0 14 050539 3)
See above.

★ Polacco, Patricia **The Bee Tree** Philomel, 1993 ISBN 0 399 21965 X
There are two quests here: to find the bee tree, and to attain knowledge through learning to read.

★ ★ ★ ★ Seymour, Tres **Hunting the White Cow** Orchard, 1993 ISBN 0 531 07085 9, illustrated by Wendy Anderson

The white cow has run off and proves to be an elusive quarry as more and more people attempt to catch her. A young girl repeatedly asks to join the quest and is refused. The dialogue is very funny.

★ ★ ★ ★ Steptoe, John **The Story of Jumping Mouse** Lothrope, 1984 ISBN 0 688 01902 1

This Native American folk tale tells of the quest of a little mouse who dreams of finding the far-off land. Along the way, he is often tempted to give up his dream. He gives away his sight and his smell to other noble beasts, but his dream is strong, and he achieves his quest, thanks to the help of a frog. The story can be taken as an allegory of age and death or as the simpler story it seems to be at first glance.

★ ★ Thompson, Colin **How to Live Forever** Knopf, 1996 ISBN 0 679 87898 X

Inside a library, a boy steps out of a cookbook and attempts to find the title book, which he finds listed on a catalogue card. His quest is full of literary characters.

★ ★ ★ ★ Van Allsburg, Chris **Jumanji** Houghton, 1981 ISBN 0 395 30448 2

The quest here is a simple one—finish the game and call out "Jumanji."

★ ★ ★ ★ Yolen, Jane **Owl Moon** Philomel, 1997 ISBN 0 399 21457 7, illustrated by John Schoenherr

A child and his father are on a winter night's quest to see the owl.

▶ Novels

★ ★ ★ ★ Adams, Richard **Watership Down** Simon & Schuster, 1974 ISBN 0 02 700030 3

A group of rabbits set out on a quest to establish a new home after their previous one is threatened by developers. This is a focus book (see page 139).

★ ★ ★ Alexander, Lloyd **The Arkadians** Dutton, 1995 ISBN 0 525 45415 2

Alexander gives us elements of both Greek mythology and the *Canterbury Tales* in this quest story about the castle bean counter, who sets out to find the goddess, Lady of Wild Things.

★ ★ ★ Alexander, Lloyd **The Iron Ring** Dutton, 1997 ISBN 0 525 45597 3

This is a quest for honor that becomes a rite of passage. The young king, Tamar, engages in a dice game with King Jaya and loses everything. Furthermore, the iron ring which appears on his finger shows him to now be Jaya's slave. Duty-bound, Tamar sets out for Jaya's remote kingdom accompanied by his old teacher, Rajaswami. Alexander weaves in some of the myths and legends of India as the journey continues, with Tamar picking up more and more companions on his quest, including Mirri, a cow-tender, Hashkat, the king of the monkeys, and Garuda, a grumpy eagle.

★ ★ ★ Babbitt, Natalie **Search for Delicious** Farrar, 1969 ISBN 0 374 36534 2

Prime Minsister DeCree is commanded by the king to construct a dictionary of important words. When disagreement breaks out at court regarding the definition of "delicious," Vaungaylen, DeCree's son, is sent on a quest to find the perfect definition. What he finds is discord everywhere, and he changes his quest mid-route.

★ ★ ★ Barron, T.A. **The Merlin Effect** Philomel, 1994 ISBN 0 399 22689 3

Kate is on a quest to find the Horn of Merlin, an object guaranteed to bring eternal life to those who approach it. Convinced that it is on a sunken Spanish ship off the coast of Mexico, Kate, her father, and two other researchers study the strange phenomena reported in the area.

★ ★ ★ Cooper, Susan **Over Sea, Over Stone** Harcourt, 1966 ISBN 0 02 042785 9

The three Drew children find a treasure map and use it in an attempt to find the Holy Grail.

★ ★ ★ Creech, Sharon **Walk Two Moons** HarperCollins, 1994 ISBN 0 06 023334 6

Sal's mother left her and has not returned. Now, Sal and her paternal grandparents set off on a quest to find her.

★ ★ ★ ★ Hilgartner, Beth **Colors in the Dreamweaver's Loom** Houghton, 1989 ISBN 0 395 50214 4

Zan's father was a famous author. When he dies suddenly, Zan walks off into the wilderness of Vermont, where she becomes part of a fantasy world and aids the people who live in it in their quest to save the forest. Zan stays in this world for five months, learning the language and becoming involved in the forest dwellers' struggle with a group of city dwellers that wants to take part of the forest by force. Because the people of the forest do not believe in taking up arms, they need to find another way to stop the aggressors. Zan brings together a company of other "outsiders" to save their forest. The company must include one of each of the different peoples in the region and must venture to the heart of the desert to ask for the assistance of the fickle gods who sometimes intervene on behalf of the people. An engrossing fantasy, this book brings together elements of coming of age, of tolerance and understanding among people of different values and cultures, of questions of fate and free will, and of acceptance of each individual's "gifts." None of these is done with a heavy hand, and the plot is fast moving.

★ ★ ★ ★ Jacques, Brian **Redwall** Avon, 1987 ISBN 0 380 70827 2

The gentle mice of Mossflower Abbey are under attack by the dreadful Cluny the Scourge. Matthias, a young and valiant mouse, reads the signs on an ancient tapestry and undertakes the quest to free Mossflower. This is the first in a lengthy series of novels set in the Middle Ages.

★ ★ ★ Juster, Norton **The Phantom Tollbooth** Knopf, 1961 ISBN 0 394 81500 9

In this classic, which is full of word play, Milo sets off on a quest to rescue a lost princess.

★ ★ ★ Lowry, Lois **The Giver**

This is a focus book (see page 180).

★ ★ ★ Paulsen, Gary **Dogsong** Bradbury, 1985 ISBN 0 02 770180 8

Russell Susskit is a 14-year-old Eskimo boy sent by one of the elders on a quest to find his own "song" and achieve a harmony with the old traditions.

★ ★ ★ ★ Philip, Neil **Odysseus** Orchard, 1996 ISBN 0 531 30000 5, illustrated by Peter Malone

The story begins with the sacking of Troy and ends with Odysseus' return to Ithica in this quest from antiquity. See page xxx for other myths involving quests.

★ ★ Pullman, Philip **The Ruby in the Smoke** Random, 1985 ISBN 0 394 89589 4

This is a swashbuckler in which Sally Lockheart, the beloved daughter of a merchant lost at sea, undertakes the quest to solve the mystery of his death.

★ ★ ★ Sutcliff, Rosemary **The Light Beyond the Forest: The Quest for the Holy Grail** Puffin, 1994 ISBN 0 14 037150 8

Sutcliff's rendition of the Arthurian legend is beautiful and complex.

★ ★ ★ Turner, Megan **The Thief** Greenwillow, 1996 ISBN 0 688 14627 9

Gen, the thief, is freed from the royal dungeons to join an expedition attempting to recover a precious gemstone hidden in mazes under the river. Insulted by the others on the quest because of his low birth, Gen's victory is all the sweeter.

★ ★ ★ ★ Voigt, Cynthia **Homecoming** Atheneum, 1981 ISBN 0 689 30833 7

The Tillerman children are abandoned by their mentally ill mother in a parking lot at a mall. Dicey leads her siblings on a quest for home, heading toward the only one she knows—her Aunt Cilla's in Bridgeport, Connecticut. When that home proves untennable, they continue their journey to an unknown grandmother's home in Maryland.

★ ★ ★ Westall, Robert **Blitzcat** Scholastic, 1989 ISBN 0 590 42770 9

Lord Gort is a black cat owned by a soldier in the British army during World War II. When she is separated from her master, Gort sets out on a quest to find him.

CHAPTER 18

Poetry

COMMENTS

By the time kids get to upper grades, some of them have been turned off to poetry. Already, some teachers have made each poem an obscure puzzle where there is one answer to "What does it mean?" and many students have decided that, whatever it means, it makes no difference to them. However, this is a wonderful age for poetry. Students can now find relevence to their own lives in the work of Frost, Angelou, Dickinson, Hughes, and many, many others. Teachers can help in the search for meaningful interpretations by filling in some definitions and allusions, by giving information about the lives and experiences of these poets, and by finding poems that work for them and for their students.

PICTURE BOOK STARTER

Susan Jeffers's illustrations for **Stopping by the Woods** (Dutton, 1978 ISBN 0 525 40115 6) were controversial because the "Santa Claus" image she finds in the lines is not consistent with the mood many people gain from them. That very divergence, however, makes the picture book all the better for our use. Many of the students will have been introduced to the poem in the elementary school, but just in case they have not, let students read the poem in its entirety before looking at Jeffers's rendition

and then encourage them to voice their feelings about her interpretation and theirs.

Along these same lines, look through Dan Fox's **Go In and Out the Window**, in which well-known songs of childhood have been illustrated with paintings from the Metropolitan Museum of Art. Besides showing the role of illustration in the interpretation of meaning, the idea that songs are poems is one that may be new to some students.

ACTIVITIES

To establish an affinity for some poetry, you may want to start with voices that speak to the teenage experience. In some books, the poet has provided us with his or her autobiography in poetry. Try Lee Bennett Hopkins's **Been to Yesterdays: Poems of a Life**. The book is a series of connected short poems covering one year—the 13th—in Lee Bennett Hopkins's life. During that time, he faces his parents' divorce, his grandmother's death, and his move from Pennsylvania to New Jersey. The economy of words and lines, and the things the reader must infer from words not spoken make this a worthwhile step into poetry. Another story in poem, this time in free verse, is Karen Hesse's **Out of the Dust**. This book won the Newbery Award for 1997 and is one of our focus books. See page 173 for further development of that book. It's a story set in the 1930s in the Dust Bowl. A third story in verse is **Who Killed Mr. Chippendale?**, by Mel Glenn. Mr. Chippendale, a high school English teacher, is murdered, and through a series of poems we witness the event and its aftermath from many perspectives, including that of the murderer. Also by Mel Glenn is **Jump Ball: A Basketball Season in Poems**, which tells of a bus accident and its aftereffects. In Glenn's **The Taking of Room 114: A Hostage Drama in Poems**, a teacher goes mad and takes the students in Room 114 hostage.

Suggest that students select one of the above for independent reading, meeting together frequently to discuss their observations of and reactions to the stories, as well as the effect that poetry has on them.

While that's going on, turn to two books of short poems by a single poet, Cynthia Rylant. **Waiting to Waltz** is a wonderful book of sketches, both in charcoal and in poetry, of the author's teenage years in Beaver, West Virginia. This is free verse, and all of the poems are accessible. There is little hidden meaning here that must be uncovered, but the author's ability to sketch in a character or a scene makes this book special. A sort of companion book is **Soda Jerk**, in which the same years are seen through the eyes of a teenage boy in a small town. The illustrations in *Soda Jerk*, by Peter Catalanotto, make a fine contrast to the sketches by Stephen Gammell in *Waiting to Waltz*. Catalanotto's work is impressionistic and uses muted colors to point out the isolation in the book. Much of this author's work is autobiographical.

Paul Janeczko, whose work is usually that of anthologizing the work of other poets, has written a book of related poems, **Stardust Otel**. These are free verse poems written from the perspective of a 15-year-old boy looking at his parents (ex-flower children), friends and neigh-

bors. They make an interesting contrast to Rylant's work.

Make a list of the subjects Rylant uses for her poems in these two picture books and suggest that students begin keeping a folder of ideas for writing poetry or prose into which some of these ideas might fit. Usually, it's better not to demand that students begin writing poetry. As this theme is being explored, many students will begin to express their ideas in poetry and, if the atmosphere is right, they'll want to share them with you and with the class. The way you accept and encourage these efforts will often determine how many others try their hand at it. It's also a good idea to prime the pump yourself by sharing your efforts in poetry writing.

It's time to bring out anthologies with many different poems by different poets that speak to the teenage generation. Paul Janeczko has created some of the best anthologies of poetry for these audiences. He chooses poems that are not often seen elsewhere, and his choices are very much in tune with young adult readers' tastes. Put out a few anthologies by Janeczko, among others, and ask kids to find one poem they'd like to share. Suggest several different ways to share it—by reading it aloud (after having plenty of time to practice), by presenting it visually (with or without calligraphy or illustration), by asking others to read it aloud in verse choir and its variations, or by setting it to music, or in a film, slide, or multimedia presentation.

A sort of "found" poetry can be created by asking students to choose one particular line of poetry that has meaning or beauty for them. Play a piece of music and ask students to read their line aloud, whenever they think it is appropriate, as the music plays. Another use of single lines is to ask students to find a work of art that suits their line and display the two together.

Seymour Simon's picture book, **Star Walk**, juxtaposes poems with photographs of stars and planets. After viewing it together, suggest that students compile a similar work in which photography and poems are combined.

Valerie Worth's poems are short and non-threatening. She often provides close-up, almost slow-motion looks at common objects and things. After sharing a few from her book listed below, suggest that some students might like to try some of her techniques.

Looking at a single work of poetry together takes great skill on the teacher's part to allow students to voice their reactions and interpretations to a work without creating the feeling that there is one correct way to view it. A good way to get past the latter temptation is to choose a lesser-known poem which no one (including the teacher) knows precisely how to interpret.

Robert Frost and Emily Dickinson created so many poems, which are, on first look, simple to understand but they contain allusions or symbols which may reach beyond those familiar to some students. Encourage students to play with such symbols, relating experiences with the object. Do some free-wheeling with the symbol, thinking of possible experiences that could influence one's interpretation of it. See if any of them apply to the poem. Does it make any meaning clearer for the students?

Sometimes mythological or literary figures or items are alluded to in a poem and teachers or other students may be able to supply the background information to help others gain meaning from the poem.

For poems in great contrast to the ones above, read aloud one of the more boisterous sections from **Beat Voices**. These poems often express rebillion and rage from the sixties.

Students might like to start looking at their own songs for lyrics. Posting the lyrics from a current hit can accomplish three things: that music is a form for poetry, that poetry has

relevence to their lives outside of school, and that some of the lyrics they treasure are quite good, while others fail without the accompaniment. Suggest that someone post lyrics from a different song each day.

Sometimes a single poem has been produced as a book with illustrations. While this may help us gain meaning from a poem, students need to understand that the illustrations are only one person's—the illustrator's—images and meaning. One such interesting book is Robert Frost's **Birches** with impressionistic illustrations by Ed Young. The watercolor paintings in this 32-page book have the effect of encouraging us to stop and look at each spread. They slow our reading of the poem to a pace where each phrase stands out. Because the poem is repeated in its more accustomed format on the last two pages, we can read it again at our own pace, with our own visions of that boy flinging outward from the treetops to come back and begin again.

One activity that helps enliven the study of poetry is to set poems to familiar music. If the music selected differs greatly from the supposed mood of the poem, hilarious results can be achieved. Almost everything Emily Dickinson wrote can be set to the tune of "Yellow Rose of Texas." The aforementioned "Stopping by Woods on a Snowy Evening" also goes to that tune, as well as to "Hernando's Hideaway," "The Doxology," "When the Saints Go Marching In," "Yankee Doodle," and many, many others. Try a silly poem, such as Richard Armour's "Pachycephalosaurs," available in **Sing a Song of Popcorn**. An iambic pentameter poem, it can be sung to any of the tunes listed above and many more. Put the poem on the overhead and, before students have a chance to read through it all, start them singing the first verse to "The Battle Hymn of the Republic." Switch to "Yankee Doodle" for the next verse, and so on. Use "America the Beautiful" (with harmony, if possible) for a rousing rendition of the last two verses. Encourage students to find other tunes that fit the poem and try them out. Such activity has the same effect of scanning a poem—a much less interesting activity. It also lets you talk more about mood because of the inappropriateness of many of the song selections. Try it sometime when students' attitudes about poetry get too heavy.

Don't, however, allow too many poems to be trivialized in any of the above activities. Look at a piece of good but arresting poetry together, such as Robert Frost's "Out, Out..." It's on the Web at **http://www.columbia.edu/ acis/bartleby/frost/81.html**. Put it on an overhead and read it aloud in unison, moving the pacing along so that students get the flow of language. Reading it in this way eliminates the chore, for some readers, of deciphering the words and allows them to concentrate on the poem itself. The grim story in which a boy loses his hand and then his life is easily understood. Students will probably not be familiar with the source or meaning of the title and you may want to tell them about the Macbeth soliloquy from which it came.

The last sentence of the poem, "And they, since they were not the one dead, turned to their affairs," is very like the sentiment expressed in "Musée des Beaux Arts" by W.H. Auden (on page 93), and the painting he is referring to. All express the idea that life goes on around tragedies.

Paul Fleischman has written two books of poems (see below) in which two different poems are meant to be read aloud simultaneously. It takes some doing, but the effect can be interesting. Use them for some verse choir renditions.

By keeping the choices of poems varied and in students' control as much as possible, and the activities and searches for meaning open-ended, students will leave your room thinking that many poems speak to them.

⬧ BOOK LIST

▶ Books about Writing Poetry

★ Appelt, Kathi **Just People & Paper/Pen/Poem: A Young Writer's Way to Begin** Absey, 1997 ISBN 1 888 84207 5

The first half of the book contains the poems; the second half features the poet's suggestions for writing similar pieces.

★ ★ ★ Janeczko, Paul **Poetry from A to Z: A Guide for Young Writers** Atheneum, 1994 ISBN 0 02 747672 3

Janeczko speaks to the middle school student and, in warm and sometimes funny dialogue, suggests things for them to work with in writing poetry. Haiku, list poems, and many other poetry beginnings are presented.

★ Ryan, Margaret **How to Write a Poem: Speak Out, Write On!** Watts, 1996 ISBN 0 531 11252 7

This is a step-by-step brainstorming guide to the writing and publishing of poems.

▶ Picture Books

★ Adoff, Arnold **Slow Dance: Heart Break Blues** Lothrop, 1995 ISBN 0 688 10569 6, illustrated by William Cotton

Adoff speaks directly to teenagers, especially African-American teenagers, expressing their rage, humor, and concerns.

★ Bruchac, Joseph **Earth Under Sky Bear's Feet: Native American Poems of the Land** Philomel, 1995 ISBN 0 399 22713 X, illustrated by Thomas Locker

Short stories and poems from many cultures are illustrated with bold colors.

★ ★ ★ ★ Fox, Dan **Go In and Out the Window** Metropolitan Museum of Art, 1987 ISBN 0 8050 0628 1 See above.

★ ★ Frank, Josette **Snow Toward Evening** Puffin, 1998 ISBN 0140 55582 X

Locker's landscape paintings give us a year in nature.

★ ★ ★ Frost, Robert **Birches** Holt, 1988 ISBN 0 8050 0570 6, illustrated by Ed Young See above.

★ Frost, Robert **Stopping by the Woods** Dutton, 1978 ISBN 0 525 40115 6, illustrated by Susan Jeffers See above.

★ Janeczko, Paul **Stardust Otel** Orchard, 1993 ISBN 0 531 05498 5, illustrated by Dorothy Leech See above.

★ ★ ★ Janeczko, Paul **That Sweet Diamond: Baseball Poems** Atheneum, 1998 ISBN 0 689 80735 X, illustrated by Carole Katchen

This is an appealing series of baseball poems. Janeczko has chosen well, and few of these gems can be found elsewhere.

★ Rylant, Cynthia **Soda Jerk** Watts, 1990 ISBN 0 531 08464 7, with illustrations by Peter Catalanotto See above.

★ ★ ★ ★ Rylant, Cynthia **Waiting to Waltz** r, 1 02 778000 7, with illustrations by Stephen Gammell See above.

★ ★ ★ ★ Simon, Seymour **Star Walk** Morrow, 1995 ISBN 0 688 11887 9

This is a beautiful book in which full-color space photographs are matched with the words of great poets.

★ ★ ★ Wood, Nancy **Dancing Moons: Poems** Doubleday, 1995 ISBN 0 385 32169 4

Some of the poems and meditations in this book, which celebrate the Earth, are wonderful, and the portraits of Native American women are breathtaking.

▶ Longer Works

★ ★ ★ Glenn, Mel **Who Killed Mr. Chippendale? A Mystery in Poems** Lodestar, 1996 ISBN 0 525 67530 2 See above.

★ Glenn, Mel **Jump Ball: A Basketball Season in Poems** Lodestar, 1997 ISBN 0 525 67554 X

Various players, teachers, and family members react to a traffic accident involving their basketball team.

★ Glenn, Mel **The Taking of Room 114: A Hostage Drama in Poems** Lodestar, 1997 ISBN 0 525 67548 5 See above.

★ ★ ★ ★ Hesse, Karen **Out of the Dust** Scholastic, 1997 ISBN 0 590 36080 9

This is a focus book (see page 173).

★ ★ ★ ★ Hopkins, Lee Bennett **Been to Yesterdays: Poems of a Life** Boyds Mills Press, 1995 ISBN 1 56397 467 3 See above.

► Anthologies and Extended Works

★ Berry, James **Everywhere Faces Everywhere: Poems** Simon & Schuster, 1997 ISBN 0 689 80996 4

The poet grew up in the Caribbean and now lives in England. His poems both celebrate that life and exhort the reader to care about its injustices.

★ ★ ★ deRegniers, Beatrice Schenk, ed. **Sing a Song of Popcorn** Scholastic, 1988 ISBN 0 590 40645 0

Although many of these poems are intended for a younger audience, the diversity of illustrations is interesting, and some of the poems will be of interest to middle schoolers.

★ ★ ★ Dunning, Stephen, ed. **Reflections on a Gift of Watermelon Pickle** Lothrop, 1966 ISBN 0 688 41231 9

Black-and-white photographs illustrate this delightful anthology.

★ ★ ★ Fleischman, Paul **I Am Phoenix: Poems for Two Voices** HarperTrophy, 1989 ISBN 0 06 446092 4

As in the book below, these poems make duets for two voices. This collection is about the birds.

★ ★ ★ Fleischman, Paul **Joyful Noise: Poems for Two Voices** HarperCollins, 1988 ISBN 0 06 021852 5

Fleischman's poems, meant to be read aloud in pairs simultaneously, are all about insects.

★ ★ Fletcher, Ralph **Ordinary Things: Poems from a Walk in Early Spring** Atheneum, 1997 ISBN 0 689 81035 0

An adolescent boy takes a walk, and the poems become a sort of journal of his sights and thoughts. The images are well within the grasp of most middle school students.

★ Giovanni, Nikki **Ego-Tripping and Other Poems for Young People** Chicago Review/Laurence Hill, 1994 ISBN 1 55652 188 X, illustrated by George Ford

Giovanni gives an African-American look at life in poems that often illuminate and celebrate ordinary lives.

★ ★ ★ Giovanni, Nikki, ed. **Shimmy Shimmy Shimmy Like My Sister Kate: Looking at the Harlem Renaissance Through Poems** Holt, 1996 ISBN 0 805 03494 3

Giovanni has brought together some of the finest work by African-American poets. Many are difficult, but most are excellent.

★ Hearne, Betsy **Polaroid: And Other Poems of View** McElderry, 1991 ISBN 0 689 50530 2

Hearne's images are often oblique although always attainable, and many are uncomfortable. They are, however, quite good, and many will speak to middle school kids.

★ ★ Janeczko, Paul, ed. **Going Over To Your Place: Poems for Each Other** Simon, 1987 ISBN 0 02 747670 7

This is a collection about relationships.

★ ★ Janeczko, Paul, ed. **The Music of What Happens: Poems That Tell Stories** Orchard, 1988 ISBN 0 531 08357 8

This is not the usual collection of Longfellow and the like. These poems evoke a variety of moods and are more like short stories in verse form. The subjects cover a wide range, from school experiences to the Holocaust.

★ ★ ★ Janeczko, Paul, ed. **Looking for Your Name: A Collection of Contemporary Poems** Orchard, 1993 ISBN 0 531 05475 6

This anthology contains poems about Vietnam and other conflicts. Many of the images here are harsh and disturbing.

★ ★ ★ Janeczko, Paul, ed. **The Place My Words Are Looking For: What Poets Say About and Through Their Work** Bradbury, 1990 ISBN 0 02 747671 5

We not only get some very good poems, but we get comments by the poet about a particular piece. It is a wonderful collection of poems by 39 poets, most of whom are represented by at least two selections. Each poet has written an extensive comment about his/her work—sometimes about the feelings of being a poet, or sometimes about a specific poem. Cynthia Rylant says it's lonely and lovely being a poet, and X.J. Kennedy makes a lovely and apt analogy, comparing a poet to a fisherman with a surprise at the end of a line.

★ Kherdian, David, ed. **Beat Voices: An Anthology of Beat Poetry** Holt, 1995 ISBN 0 805 03315 7

These are poems from the sixties in which various poets who considered themselves rebels and outsiders express their feelings.

★ ★ Nye, Naomi Shihab **The Space Between Our Footsteps: Poems & Paintings from the Middle East and North Africa** Simon & Schuster, 1998 ISBN 0 689 81233 7

Displacement is a common theme in this beautiful book of poems, in which the paintings illuminate but never dominate the text. The frequently displaced people of the Middle East share their hopes and concerns.

★ ★ Philip, Neil **Earth Always Endures: Native American Poems** Viking, 1996 ISBN 0 670 86873 6

The photographs are so compelling that they almost overpower the poems, which are arranged to cover a full day, from dawn to dawn.

★ Wood, Nancy **Spirit Walker: Poems** Doubleday, 1993 ISBN 0 385 30927 9

These poems and faces speak of the Taos Pueblo culture, and they do so with great beauty and dignity.

★ ★ ★ ★ Worth, Valerie **All the Small Poems** Farrar, 1987 ISBN 0 374 40344 9

These are short, vivid poems about commonplace objects and things.

▶ Novels

★ ★ ★ Shalant, Phyllis **The Great Eye** Dutton, 1996 ISBN 0 525 45695 3

While other novels have poets as characters, this one stands above the crowd. Here we have a good story in which a budding poet comes to terms with her father's desertion through her own "parenting" of a guide dog, and writes very good poetry, as well. The poems could stand alone.

Section 3 :
Literary Study
Authors Techniques and Devices

USING PICTURE BOOKS TO IDENTIFY TECHNIQUES AND DEVICES

It's no longer considered revolutionary to use picture books with upper grade and middle school kids. One look at a book such as **Pink and Say**, and you know that few kids below third grade would be ready for the trauma within. There are, of course, many other wonderful books that are designed to appeal to older readers. The fact that a book has illustrations which are at least as important as the text does not assure its place among the younger set. (See page 72 for more information on the uses of picture books in the middle school.)

We can also use picture books, however, in order to isolate and study author techniques and devices. Some books that are obviously intended for younger audiences serve this purpose very well. Using a picture book to demonstrate these techniques allows you to isolate and define them quickly. Once the concept is clear, we can then step into more complicated works in order to find other examples.

FORESHADOWING

Start with that masterpiece of the 1960s, **Where the Wild Things Are**. It's a deceptively simple tale of home/away/home that many kindergartners have enjoyed for years. **Where the Wild Things Are** makes a good vehicle for a lesson on foreshadowing. Many middle school students will recognize the book from their own childhood. Let them reminisce for a few minutes, recalling details and reactions. Then read the book aloud, sharing the illustrations as you do so. (The text is so limited that you can easily read it upside down while they examine the illustrations.)

Explain that foreshadowing means giving the reader hints about what is to come, and then search together through the illustrations for such hints as: the picture of the wild thing drawn by Max and displayed on the wall long before he sails away, and the wild thing toy hanging from the clothesline. They may not recognize the blanket tent or the stool in it as foreshadowing until you get to the tent of the same color and pattern and the identical stool in the land of the wild things. Some students may spot the growing size of the illustrations, which they probably missed as little kids (even many adults miss that). That gives you a chance to show that Sendak also gave visual clues to the climax. The pictures grow larger until the "royal rumpus" starts.

Look through other picture books to find similar examples of foreshadowing. With those strong and obvious examples, you can easily move back into the longer works, looking for verbal foreshadowing in such books as Kathryn Lasky's **Beyond the Divide**, Will Hobbs' **Far North**, and Mary Downing Hahn's **Dead Man in Indian Creek**. The whole prologue to Lois Lowry's masterful **Autumn Street** foreshadows the action to come. The first paragraph of Gary Paulsen's **The Monument** (Delacorte, 1991 ISBN 0 385 30518 4, see page 136) is an obvious and clear example of foreshadowing. For a very accessible and clearly discernable example of the technique, check out **Hank the Cowdog: The Case of the Haystack Kitties** (Maverick Books, 1998 ISBN 0 87719 338 X). One of a very funny series of books, the second paragraph gives three concrete examples of foreshadowing.

CLIMAX

You can use picture books to identify climax. Dr. Seuss's **And to Think That I Saw It on Mulberry Street** was his first book, and is the prototype for many of his later books. Its climax is easily identified, as is its anti-climax. Again, the brevity of the picture book makes it so useful here.

Identifying the climax in novels is difficult because often many moments can be so identified within a single work. It isn't important that you agree on which of these several moments is the true climax, only that you can defend your choice. The climax of the aforementioned short novel **The Monument** could be when the townspeople see the sketches Mick has made of them, but also can be the moment in which the monument is revealed.

There are many less complicated techniques for which picture books are particularly useful: point of view, perspective, scene, mood, and characterization. Picture books are lots more fun than workbooks, yet they can help you teach grammar, usage, and literary criticism. For each of the techniques below, we have listed appropriate picture books before listing longer literary examples.

SYMBOLISM

Detecting symbols in a work of literature can be a source of total frustration as students try to guess the "right" answer to "What does this mean?" When used properly, however, this process is an important tool for brainstorming, while discovering the many layers of meaning in a given work. In the River chapter (see page 54), we talk about the river as a symbol for writers and readers, but there are many other symbols in literature that are worth exploring.

First, the picture books: Eve Bunting uses dandelions as a symbol of life and home in the picture book **Dandelions**, illustrated by Greg Shed (Harcourt, 1995 ISBN 0 15 200050 X). In Peter Sis's **Three Golden Keys** (Doubleday, 1994 ISBN 0 385 47292 7), the title keys are symbols with which Sis unlocks his childhood for his daughter to view. Sherry Garland's picture book, **The Lotus Seed** (Harcourt, 1993 ISBN 0 15 249465 0), is a symbol of a family's heritage.

One longer work with an obvious use of symbol is Marion Dane Bauer's **A Question of**

Trust (Scholastic, 1994 ISBN 0 590 47923 7). Here, a cat becomes the symbol for the boys' absent mother, and through their stormy relationship with the cat, many of the boys' feelings about their mother's desertion come to the fore and are worked through.

Carl Friedman's **Nightfather** (Persea, 1991 ISBN 0 89255 210 7) is a strong novel about the Holocaust, in which the father finds symbols everywhere which bring back the events of his imprisonment.

The title character in **Blue Heron,** by Avi (Avon, 1992 ISBN 0 380 72043 4), is a symbol of the heroine's life choice and of a kind of magic.

A Separate Peace, by John Knowles (Bantam, 1985 ISBN 0 553 28041 4), has several symbols, the most obvious of which are the two rivers, one dirty and one clean, that flow through the town.

The camera is both a symbol and a device in **Spite Fences**, by Trudy Krisher (Delacorte, 1994 ISBN 0 385 32088 4).

A geode with its drab facade and hidden crystals is a symbol for the main character in **The Stone-Faced Boy**, by Paula Fox (Aladdin, 1982 ISBN 0 689 71127 1).

The strange, windmill-like devices are certainly symbols in Paul Fleischman's **Whirligig** (Holt, 1998 ISBN 0 8050 5582 7).

Dust is a symbol and almost a character in Karen Hesse's **Out of the Dust** (see page 173).

The title is a symbol in **Painting the Black**, by Carl Deuker (Houghton, 1997 ISBN 0 395 82848 1). It refers to hitting the line between foul and fair in baseball. One of the main characters goes over that line in his personal life.

ALLEGORIES

The line between symbolism and allegories is blurred, and usually is a matter of length; an allegory being the expression by means of symbolic fictional figures and actions of truths or generalizations about human existence.

Several of the picture books discussed on pages 72-79 are allegorical in nature, as is Ferida Wolff and Kathy Osborn's **The Emperor's Garden** (Tambourine, 1994 ISBN 0 688 11651 5), in which the people of a village in old China seek the attention of the emperor. To this end, they cooperate on the construction of a beautiful garden. It isn't until they try to name the garden that conflict begins, as each laborer wants the garden named for himself or herself.

Little Blue and Little Yellow, by Leo Lionni (Mulberry, 1959 ISBN 0 688 13285 5), is either a very simple story about two blobs of color or an allegory about racism and prejudice. Chris Van Allsburg's **The Wretched Stone** (Houghton, 1991 ISBN 0 395 53307 4) is a none-too-subtle allegory about the evils of television.

Looking at longer allegories, the fictional African country with all the warfare within it is surely an allegory in Peter Dickinson's **AK** (Delacorte, 1990 ISBN 0 440 21897 7). Richard Adams' **Watership Down** (Simon & Schuster, 1974 ISBN 0 02 700030 3) presents a rabbit society as an allegory of the human condition.

▶ FLASHBACKS

Julie Downing's picture book, **Mozart Tonight** (Simon & Schuster, 1991 ISBN 0 02 732881 3), is all flashback.

Carrie, now a grown woman, flashes back to her childhood wartime experience in **Carrie's War** by Nina Bawden (HarperCollins, 1973 ISBN 0 397 31450 7). Another Carrie is undergoing psychiatric treatment in Zibby Oneal's **The Language of Goldfish** (Viking, 1980 ISBN 0 140 34540 X), and we get a series of flashbacks showing us the causes of her illness. There's extensive use of flashback

in Robert Cormier's **I Am the Cheese** (Dell, 1981 ISBN 0 440 94060 5).

▶ CLIFF HANGERS

A picture book that uses cliff hangers effectively and constantly is Remy Charlip's **Fortunately** (Simon & Schuster, 1964 ISBN 0 02 718100 6).

Avi uses cliff hangers in several of his books, but his most transparent and playful use of them occurs in his two-volume saga, **Beyond the Western Sea** (Orchard, 1996 ISBN 0 531 09513 4 and ISBN 0 531 09520 7). Each chapter in these books ends with a cliff hanger.

Sid Fleischman is also skillful with cliff hangers. His brief adventure story, **The 13th Floor** (Yearling, 1997 ISBN 0 440 41243 9), has a nice use of cliff hangers, as does **The Whipping Boy** (Morrow, 1987 ISBN 0 688 06216 4).

▶ ALTERNATING POINTS OF VIEW

Marcia Sewall uses alternating points of view in a picture book work of nonficiton, **Thunder from the Clear Sky** (Atheneum, 1995 ISBN 0 689 31775 1), telling the story of the conflict between the Pilgrims and the Native Americans.

Another picture book that uses several points of view of the same events is Ann Turner's **Mississippi Mud** (see page 18).

John Marsden's **Letters from Inside** uses alternating letters from two girls to tell the story. This is a focus book (see page 189).

▶ GOOD BEGINNINGS—FIRST PARAGRAPHS FROM WORKS OF LITERATURE

Note: The beginning paragraphs of novels can be used in a variety of ways. Obviously, they make a good literary quiz game: can you identify the book? Sometimes, when they are intriguing or exciting enough, the first lines make good teasers, enticing readers to want more of the story. Reading aloud some of the best of them may get some readers going. In our attempt to help children learn to read as writers, these beginning lines can be a point of focus for discussion. What do we know about a book from these few lines? What has the author helped us to know? What mood has she or he established? What do you want to know after this taste? Because some young readers skip over what they call description, they often miss these first lines unless special attention has been drawn to them. Reading and discussing other authors' opening lines can give students courage to step out differently in their own writing.

"Old Granny Greengrass had her finger chopped off in the butcher's when she was buying half a leg of lamb. She had pointed to the place where she wanted her joint to be cut but then she decided she needed a bigger piece and pointed again. Unfortunately, Mr. Grummett, the butcher, was already bringing his sharp chopper down."

The Peppermint Pig
by Nina Bawden

"It was not that Omri didn't appreciate Patrick's birthday present to him. Far from it. He was really very grateful—sort of. It was, without a doubt, very kind of Patrick to give Omri anything at all, let alone a secondhand plastic Indian that he himself had finished with."

The Indian in the Cupboard
by Lynne Reid Banks

"They murdered him.

"As he turned to take the ball, a dam burst against the side of his head and a hand grenade shattered his stomach. Engulfed by nausea, he pitched toward the grass. His mouth encountered gravel, and he spat frantically, afraid that some of his teeth had been knocked out. Rising to his feet, he saw the field through drifting gauze but held on until everything settled into place, like a lens focusing, making the world sharp again, with edges."

The Chocolate War
by Robert Cormier

"It was dusk—winter dusk. Snow lay white and shining over the pleated hills, and icicles hung from the forest trees. Snow lay piled on the dark road across Willoughby Wold, but from dawn men had been clearing it with brooms and shovels. There were hundreds of them at work, wrapped in sacking because of the bitter cold, and keeping together in groups for fear of the wolves, grown savage and reckless from hunger."

The Wolves of Willoughby Chase
by Joan Aiken

"When Mary Lennox was sent to Misselthwaite Manor to live with her uncle everybody said she was the most disagreeable-looking child ever seen. It was true, too. She had a little thin face and a little thin body, thin light hair and a sour expression. Her hair was yellow and her face was yellow because she had been born in India and had always been ill in one way or another."

The Secret Garden
by Frances Hodgson Burnett

"It was a dark and stormy night. In her attic bedroom Margaret Murray, wrapped in an old patchwork quilt, sat on the foot of her bed and watched the trees tossing in the frenzied lashing of the wind. Behind the trees clouds scudded frantically across the sky. Every few moments the moon ripped through them, creating wraith-like shadows that raced along the ground."

A Wrinkle in Time
by Madeleine L'Engle

"The first week in August hangs at the very top of summer, the top of the live-long year, like the highest seat of a Ferris wheel when it pauses in its turning. The weeks that come before are only a climb from the balmy spring, and those that follow a drop to the chill of autumn, but the first week of August is motionless, and hot. It is curiously silent, too, with blank white dawns and glaring noons, and sunsets smeared with too much color. Often at night there is lightning, but it quivers all alone. There is no thunder, no relieving rain. These are strange and breathless dog days, when people are led to do things they are sure to be sorry for after."

Tuck Everlasting
by Natalie Babbitt

"Listen. When I was a kid, I was crazy. Nuttier than a fruitcake. Madder than a hatter. Out of my head. You see, I had this obsession. This hang-up. It was all that mattered to me. I was in love with the Brooklyn Dodgers."

Thank You, Jackie Robinson
by Barbara Cohen

"If books could be more, could show more, could own more, this book would have smells... It would have the smells of old farms; the sweet smell of new-mown hay as it falls off the oiled sickle blade when the horses pull the mower through the field, and the sour smell of manure steaming in a winter barn. It would have the sticky-slick smell of birth when the calves come and they suck for the first time on the rich, new milk; the dusty smell of winter hay dried and storied in the loft waiting to be dropped down to the cattle; the pungent fermented smell of the chopped corn silage when it is brought into the manger on the silage fork. This book would have the smell of new potatoes sliced and frying in light pepper on a woodstove burning dry pine, the damp smell of leather mittens steaming on the back of the stovetop, and the acrid smell of the slop bucket by the door when the lid is lifted and the potato peelings are dumped in—but it can't."

The Winter Room
by Gary Paulsen

"The bear had been their undoing, though at the time they had all laughed. No, Mama had never laughed, but Lyddie and Charles and the babies had laughed until their bellies ached. Lyddie still thought of them as the babies. She probably always would. Agnes had been four and Rachel six that November of 1843—the year of the bear."

Lyddie
by Katherine Paterson

"Sometimes it's funny how we can't know things. I get cranky about that, but I'm always getting that way about something or other, so it doesn't matter.

"But it's still funny.

"Like if Python hadn't killed the chicken he wouldn't have been sent to prison, and I wouldn't have helped him escape. He wouldn't have become friend and led me to meet Mick so I could come to know all there is to know about art and life and sex and love and how Bolton, Kansas, is a microcosm of the world, even China, and I didn't know any of that was coming."

The Monument
by Gary Paulsen

"One day Grandfather wouldn't get out of bed. He just lay there and stared at the ceiling and looked sad."

Stone Fox
by John Gardiner

"I was nine years old, younger than Monty is now, the first time I hit my father and made him bleed. He was proud."

Shadow Boxer
by Chris Lynch

"The prairie was like a giant plate, stretching all the way to the sky at the edges. And we were like two tiny peas left over from dinner, Lester and me. We couldn't even see the soddy from out there—just nothing, nothing in a big circle all around us. We still had Cap then, and he stood very still, shaking his harness now and again while we did our work, throwing cow chips into the back of the wagon, me singing all the while. 'Buffalo chips, buffalo chips, won't you marry me? Oh, come on out, buffalo chips, and dance all night by the sea.' "

Prairie Songs
by Pam Conrad

"It was a cold wet afternoon in October when Rose Larkin came to live in the house at Hawthorn Bay. Rain dripped from the branches of the big horse-chestnut tree in the front yard and hung in large drops from the tangle of bushes around the house. Rose stood in the driveway, where Aunt Stella had left her, feeling that she had never been in a place more dismal in all her life."

The Root Cellar
by Janet Lunn

Section 4:
Focus Books

CHAPTER 1

Watership Down

★ ★ ★ ★

by Richard Adams
Avon, 1989
ISBN 0 380 00293 0

➤ COMMENTS

This compelling story works both as an allegory and as a fantasy, making it very useful for our purposes. The rabbit characters quickly assume believable personalities, so that we care about their success and fate while appreciating what Adams is saying about the human condition. There is a fairly recent sequel to the book, entitled **Tales from Watership Down** (Knopf, 1966 ISBN 0 679 45795 X). The classic story has been made into an animated movie that stays close to the book, with voices by John Hurt, Zero Mostel, and others. The book also inspired a song by Gerry Beckley.

➤ THE PLOT

A group of rabbits move to another location and, in the process, the essences of their characters are revealed and we begin to see the human corollaries. Fiver, who can see into the future, alerts the others that trouble, in the form of humans, is going to destroy their home, and so a group of the rabbits, led by Hazel decide to find a new home. Along the way, they come in contact with several other rabbit societies, each of which has its own form of government. Some members of those other societies join the group, seeking their own safe haven. The rabbits face great dangers; some are wounded and others lose their lives, but the survivors reach Watership Down, although, even there, they must defend it from attackers.

➤ TAKING IT DEEPER

Why do you think Adams chose to use rabbits as characters? Make a list of the words and characteristics you associate with rabbits.

Try rewriting the first few pages of the books to make the characters human. What does that do to the story?

Although these rabbits behave very much like humans, they exhibit some distinctly rabbit-like actions and reactions. List some of these rabbit behaviors and feelings, such as disliking woodland travel, dreading the river crossing, etc.

Name	Characteristics	Role
Fiver	Clairvoyant	Leader
Hazel	Shrewd, Hopeful	Cheerleader
Dandelion		Storyteller

Most of the characters in the story are rabbits, but a few other animal characters have roles. Kehaar, for instance, is a bird. What role does Kehaar play that a rabbit could not? List the other non-rabbit characters and their place in the story.

Each rabbit has its own character and role in the society. Make a chart such as the one above showing this.

Dandelion tells stories, each of which serves a different purpose. List those purposes. For instance, he tells the story of the King's Lettuce when they are visiting the strange rabbits of Cowslip's warren. It helps the others realize that these new rabbits don't share the heritage or knowledge of El-ahrairah.

Compare Dandelion's story, in which Frith created the world, to other creation stories.

There are many challenges to Hazel's leadership. Who are those challengers and how are the challenges resolved?

Is the OWSLA a necessary part of this society? What actions in the book would have changed if there were no OWSLA?

Look at the Lapine Glossary at the end of the book and see if all rabbit terms are defined. Which ones would you redefine or add?

Make maps of each warren described in the book, and show the different kinds of government in each.

Make a map of the rabbits' journey.

Outline or describe briefly the Lapine religion as revealed by Dandelion's stories.

Read some of the other books in which an animal society has been formed. Which of those societies do you think humans should copy?

Compare the society of *Watership Down* to the society in **The Giver** (see page 180).

What statements do you think Adams is making about human society?

▧ RELATED BOOKS

▶ Picture Books

★ ★ Banks, Lynn Reid **The Magic Hare** Camelot, 1994 ISBN 0 380 71562 7, illustrated by Barry Moser

There are 10 short stories in this picture book, all of which concern a trickster rabbit who is smart, helpful, and devious.

▶ Novels

★ ★ ★ Arkin, Alan **The Lemming Condition** HarperCollins, 1989 ISBN 0 06 250048 1

This story is about a society of lemmings, and Bubber, a young lemming, is excited about participating in the event each year when the lemmings plunge off the cliff into the sea. It's his friend the crow who asks questions like, "Can you swim?"

★ ★ ★ ★ Jacques, Brian **Redwall** Ace Books, 1998 ISBN 0 441 00548 9

This is the first in a series of books in which an animal society fights evil within and around an ancient monastery.

★ ★ Lawson, Robert **Rabbit Hill** Puffin, 1982 ISBN 0 140 31010 X

The animal society in this book is very much afraid of the new humans who have moved into the big house, but they soon find their fears unnecessary. This book has been around since the 1940s and has some dated aspects, but remains a vital book.

O'Brien, Robert **Mrs. Frisby and the Rats of NIMH** Aladdin, 1986 ISBN 0 689 71068 2

A laboratory has created a group of rats so intelligent that they have escaped to form their own society.

Nothing But the Truth: A Documentary Novel

★ ★ ★ ★

Avi

Orchard, 1991

ISBN 0 531 05959 6

 **COMMENTS**

Avi uses no direct conversation in this intriguing book, but the series of articles, letters, and transcripts of conversations that he does use propel the novel so well that the reader is hardly aware of this device. The idea that truth is different when viewed from various perspectives is nicely developed here.

THE PLOT

There has been bad feeling between ninth grader Philip Malloy and his English teacher, Miss Narwin, since the low grade she gave him disqualified him from the track team. When she reprimands him for humming while the national anthem is played, contrary to the rules, which call for silent attention, the battle is joined. This simple classroom incident of taunting behavior quickly assumes a life of its own as rules are applied without reason. Soon an inflamatory and distorted newspaper arti-

cle makes this a national story, and in the resulting conflagration, neither Philip nor Miss Narwin gets what they want. There are no winners in this war of words, and the truth is lost in the shuffle.

TAKING IT DEEPER

Which side are you on? Can you defend your position?

Which document do you find most revealing?

Every character in the book has his or her own agenda. Make a chart showing what each of them really wants. How many are successful in getting it?

There are no real villains here, only well-meaning people who don't communicate very well and who unwittingly shape the truth to fit their own needs. Look for spots in the novel where this occurs and think of ways someone could have changed the outcome.

One reporter does try to get the straight story. Why is his story never printed?

What makes this book believable?

For whom is this story a hollow triumph?

There is a good deal of irony is this story. Can you find it?

How does the title apply and what does it imply about the story? Although it concerns a search for the truth, there are many half-truths and untruths in the documents. For instance, the principal describes Phil's humming as loud and raucous. Can you find others?

▶ RELATED BOOKS

▶ Picture Books

★ ★ ★ Avi **The Bird, the Frog and the Light** Orchard, 1994 ISBN 0 531 06808 0

In this picture book fable, the light is that of truth and it points out the reality of a kingdom of riches the frog thought he owned.

▶ Novels

★ ★ ★ Babbitt, Natalie **The Search for Delicious** Farrar, 1985 ISBN 0 374 46536 3

A previously peaceful kingdom erupts in discord over the construction of a new dictionary, particularly over the definition of "delicious." Gaylen is sent to poll the kingdom in an effort to find the correct definition. What he finds is the seed of civil war.

★ ★ ★ L'Engle, Madeleine **Acceptable Time** Dell, 1989 ISBN 0 440 20814 9

This is part of the series of novels that began with **A Wrinkle in Time**. Here, Polly, the granddaughter of the original Meg and Calvin, comes to live with them in Connecticut and finds herself traveling back in time 3,000 years. where she deals with the eternal aspects of love and truth.

★ ★ ★ Lutzeier, Elizabeth **The Wall** Holiday House, 1991 ISBN 0 8234 0987 2

Hannah and her father are trying to survive in Germany after her mother's death. In a society in which telling the truth can get you killed, they must pretend that they are unaffected by her death. This is a focus book (see page 184).

★ ★ ★ Walter, Virginia **Making Up Megaboy** DK Press, 1997 ISBN 0 7894 2488 6

As in *Nothing But the Truth*, this brief novel uses no real narration to tell the story. We get newspaper and television accounts, as well as interviews expressing outrage at the crime. Many of the teenagers interviewed show themselves to be shallow individuals. There was indeed a crime, which no one denies. Robie shot Mr. Koh, the elderly Korean proprietor of a liquor store.

▶ Nonfiction

★ ★ Johnson, Lawrence E. **Focusing on Truth** Routledge, 1993 ISBN 0 415 07252 2

This book is a careful examination of approaches to historic truths as well as an exploration of the various theories of truth.

CHAPTER 3

Heartlight

★ ★ ★ ★

by T.A. Barron
Philomel, 1990
ISBN 0 399 22180 8

 **COMMENTS**

Although the book's theme of the role of death is a somber one, the writing is not. That's partly because of the attendant theme of love conquering all. The book has elements of physics, metaphysics, adventure, science fiction, and fantasy, broadening its appeal to many audiences. Even the author recognizes similarities in plot to Madeleine L'Engle's *Wrinkle in Time*, which many students will have read previously.

PLOT

Kate's grandfather has been working in his laboratory to uncover an unknown element in the heart of stars, called Pure Concentrated Light. He has succeeded in making a small amount of this magical substance, which has the power to liberate your "heartlight" so that you can travel to anyplace in space. Soon, his laboratory is plagued by a destructive presence, then the sun begins to lose power. Grandfather becomes "heartlight" and travels to a distant star, which he believes may hold the answer.

Kate, using a magical butterfly, joins him, and they begin a voyage into a world where Darkness and the Pattern are battling it out. They learn about the desire to live forever in contrast to the rightness of the pattern in which the death of one thing means the birth of something else.

TAKING IT DEEPER

What do you think the author's feeling about death is? Does that coincide with your own beliefs?

Investigate the philosophy about death in religions other than your own.

What if everyone lived even 20 years longer than expected today? 30 years? 100 years? What would it do to the quality of life? What accommodation would societies have to make?

Read or reread the sections of **Tuck Everlasting, Charlotte's Web**, and **Everywhere** (see below) which talk about life and death.

How do you understand the Sages' statement: "There are two kinds of death for a star, and they are as different as hope is different from despair."

"If you trust in the Pattern, you trust in yourself, and if you trust in yourself, your voice holds all the power of truth," is another quote from the book. Does it have any meaning for you?

Compare this book's philosophy about death with that in **The Giver**.

What did you think of grandfather's fate in the book? Would you have written it that way? How did the author help you accept it?

Make a Venn diagram comparing this book with *A Wrinkle in Time*.

◤ RELATED BOOKS

▶ Picture Book

Goble, Paul **Beyond the Ridge** Bradbury, 1989 ISBN 0 02 736581 6

This book presents a Native American view of death. We watch the spirit of an old woman leave her body and follow the voices from the next world as they lead her up a ridge. Descending from it, she finds her parents in a circle of teepees. We then shift back to the deathbed, where the family prepares her body and grieves for her.

▶ Novels

★ ★ ★ ★ Babbitt, Natalie **Tuck Everlasting** Farrar, 1975 ISBN 0 374 37848 7

The Tuck family has discovered a spring whose water gives eternal life. Winnie Foster, a 10-year-old who has led an overprotected life, stumbles on the family's secret and becomes their friend. A man in a yellow suit also learns their secret and threatens to sell the water to the highest bidder and to force Winnie to drink it, and thus remain a child forever. Mrs. Tuck kills him and is jailed and sentenced to be executed. Though the family knows she cannot be killed, they also know that, when the attempt is made to kill Mae, their secret will be revealed.

★ ★ ★ ★ Brooks, Bruce **Everywhere** HarperCollins, 1990 ISBN 0 06 020729 9

This is a short and very accessible book with layers of meaning beneath a simple text. Peanut's beloved grandfather may well be dying. When Lucy Pettibone, a black woman who claims to be a nurse, is called to the house, she brings her nephew, Dooley, to keep Peanut company while she and his grandmother tend to Grandfather. Peanut's grief and anxiety are overwhelming, and the gullible, vulnerable Peanut quickly grasps at Dooley's outrageous plan to switch the grandfather's soul with that of a turtle. The reader may be as fooled as Peanut is, for the book's resolution takes some careful

reading. The action takes place during one trauma-filled day. As the day draws to its climax, we're as repulsed and torn as Peanut and just as relieved at the resolution.

★ ★ ★ Hunter, Mollie **A Sound of Chariots** HarperCollins, 1972 ISBN 0 06 440235 5

Bridie is mourning the death of her father, Patrick McShane, in this novel set in Scotland. Then she comes across a line in a poem that puts into words her sense of transiency.

★ ★ ★ ★ L'Engle, Madeleine **A Wrinkle in Time** Dell, 1976 ISBN 0 440 99805 0

Meg, her brother, and a friend travel through time and space to rescue her father, who is held captive by an all-consuming power on the sinister planet Camazotz. They accomplish their travel through the use of a "tesseract"—in effect, a wrinkle in time. This they have learned from their other worldly neighbors: Mrs. Whatsit, Mrs. Who, and Mrs. Which.

★ ★ ★ ★ Lowry, Lois **The Giver** Houghton, 1993 ISBN 0 395 64566 2
This is a focus book (see page 180).

★ ★ ★ Paulsen, Gary **Tracker** Bradbury, 1984 ISBN 0 02 770220 0

John, who is 13, must track and kill a deer for his family's winter meat. In so doing, he finds himself drawn to the doe he is pursuing, which draws him ever deeper into the woods. John hates his role as hunter, and he cannot accept the fact that his grandfather is dying of cancer. For John, pursuing the doe until he can touch her and *not* give her death helps him to accept his grandfather's fate.

★ ★ ★ ★ Stolp, Hans **The Golden Bird** Dell, 1990 ISBN 0 440 40611 0

Daniel shares his daily experiences with us as he slowly understands that he is dying. He is 11 and has cancer. In the hospital for the last five months, he tells us of his daily experiences. His father died four years before and comes to Daniel in a dream. "Not yet, Daniel! Soon...soon...and then I'll make us both some tea." Three birds land on Daniel's windowsill: one blue, one green, and one golden. The golden bird goes to build a nest, and when the eggs inside have all hatched, Daniel is told, the golden bird will come back for Daniel. One of the other birds visits Daniel every day, flying magically through the window and bringing Daniel friendship and messages from the golden bird. Daniel is excited about going to the nest and about being with his father, but he is also frightened and in pain. He feels horrible about leaving his mother alone. By the time the golden bird comes for Daniel, his father is at his side, and leaving the world of the living no longer seems so difficult.

★ ★ ★ ★ White, E. B. **Charlotte's Web** HarperCollins, 1952 ISBN 0 06 026385 7

This classic has a strong theme of the inevitability and acceptance of death.

Truth to Tell

★ ★ ★ ★

by Nancy Bond
McElderry
1994 ISBN 0 689 50601 5

▶ COMMENTS

Don't let the apparent length of this novel
deter readers from tackling it. The print is
large and well spaced, making it no longer
than most books for young adult readers. One
of the strengths of this book is the literary allusions that abound. They are within the reach of
most readers, and they make a great introduction to allusions in more difficult works.
Art—and the way artists see and portray what
they see—is a focal point of the book. There is
also a good deal of information about New
Zealand and its landmarks. The author frequently uses flashbacks to tell the story.

▶ THE PLOT

Alice has been dragged to New Zealand from
Cambridge, England, by her mother, Christine,
who wants a fresh start. Christine has been
offered a job in Dunedin, New Zealand, as a
secretary and assistant to Miss Fairchild, who
is to write a book about the mansion,
Florestan, where they are all to live. They've
left behind a note for Len, Alice's stepfather,
telling him where they are and inviting him to
join them when he returns from a job he has
taken overseas. However, both Alice and her
mother are in some doubt as to whether he'll
ever show up. He does, however, and his irre-
sponsibility is often a trial to them both.

The mansion turns out to be in great dis-
repair; Miss Fairchild is petulant and
unreasonable; and Christine's job turns out to
be mostly that of housekeeper and nurse. Alice
is enrolled in school, which turns out not to be
so bad. Miss Fairchild is an artist whose work
is largely unknown and unappreciated. One of
Alice's friends from school, Margery, has been
inspired by Miss Fairchild's work to become an
artist herself.

Alice learns that she may well have been
lied to all her life by her mother, who has told
her that her biological father is Toby
Underwood and that Len is her stepfather.
Toby, she was told, was killed in World War II,
and her mother married Len shortly after-
wards. Alice and Len have had a wonderful
relationship—more friends than parent and

child. Now, it seems Christine lied about Toby, and that Len is Alice's real father.

▶ TAKING IT DEEPER

This book has many literary allusions. Do you know or can you find the source of any of these:

The poem "Young Albert and the Lion," which Miss Sallet quotes on page 172 of the hardbound book.

On page 128, it says that Margery made Alice feel "careless like James James Morrison Morrison Weatherby George Dupree in the poem."

Len quotes from a poem when he says, "Last night I saw upon the stair, a little man who wasn't there. He wasn't there again today—oh, cor, I wish he'd go away."

When they visit the albatrosses, they refer to the "Ancient Mariner."

Christine is reading "Sonnets from the Portuguese."

Alice reads, or tries to read *Rebecca*.

A parrot is named "Long John Silver."

Miss Fairchild tells Len, "It's a wise father that knows his own child."

The woman on the train is reading about the Borrowers to her child.

Tucker refers to *The Hobbit* and has an autographed book by J.R.R. Tolkien.

Some of the slang expressions the New Zealanders use are different than ours but you can usually get the meaning from the text.

"She's a real odd sock."
"I'll be along in a tick."
"Crikey Dick!"
"Having a kip."

What does Len mean when, after Christine says he always runs away from responsibility, "Aw, Chrissie, be fair. What about after the War? I didn't run then." And what does Christine mean when she replies,

"Maybe you should have. Perhaps it would have been better for us both."

Reread the letter from Charles Keating Murray that Miss Fairchild tore up. Can you find the condescension? What effect do you think it had on Miss Fairchild? on Mr. Murray?

There's a lot of information about albatrosses in one part of the book. Can you find pictures of them?

Some of the landmarks of New Zealand are in the book. Find more information about such things as:

Rotorua
The Gold Rush
Dunedin
Christ Church
The Otago Peninsula

On page 208, Alice relates to a painting by Miss Fairchild. Read the passage aloud and try to see what Alice sees. Later, on page 211, Alice says, "Well, I thought they'd just be paintings of flowers, like the ones in the dining room, I suppose. You know—decorative. But they aren't. I mean, not that they're ugly, but they're not comfortable. You couldn't just hang them on the wall and expect them to stay in the background." How does this relate to Mr. Murray's letter? What do you think about this kind of painting?

There are many flashbacks in the book. The first is on page 12. Find some and talk about flashbacks as a writing technique. See page xxx for this and other writing devices.

Why did Alice run away?

The relationship between Tucker and Jesse is very nice. How is it like and different from other relationships in this book and in real life?

Was Christine right to lie to both Len and Alice? What would Len's reaction have been if he'd known from the start that Alice was his daughter?

RELATED BOOKS

▶ Novels

★ ★ Gee, Maurice **The Fire Raiser** Houghton, 1992 ISBN 0 395 62428 2

This story, set in New Zealand at the beginning of the First World War, is about an emotionally disturbed child who becomes an arsonist.

★ Mahy, Margaret **The Good Fortunes Gang** Delacorte, 1993 ISBN 0 385 31015 3

A family moves from Australia to their father's native New Zealand to discover a raft of new family members.

★ ★ ★ Marriott, Janice **Letters to Lesley** Knopf, 1991 ISBN 0 679 81595 8

This very funny book is set in New Zealand and consists mostly of letters from Henry to Lesley, his pen pal. Henry is appalled by the recent behavior of his mother. She's become a women's libber, even signing petitions in the mall, and Henry has to cope with her new persona.

★ ★ ★ Mayne, William **Low Tide** Delacorte, 1993 ISBN 0 385 30904 X

As usual, Mayne combines realistic and mythic characters with great success. In this book, three children, one of whom is Maori, are swept away from New Zealand in a tidal wave to a deserted island inhabited by a Koroua, a mythical mountain creature.

★ Savage, Deborah **A Stranger Calls Me Home** Houghton, 1992 ISBN 0 395 59424 3

This is a fantasy, set in New Zealand, in which three friends search for their place in two conflicting cultures.

▶ Nonfiction

★ Keyworth, Valerie **New Zealand: Land of the Long White Cloud** Simon & Schuster, 1990 ISBN 0 87518 414 6

This is a good source for information about New Zealand. Although it's hardly exhaustive information, it does provide an overview and a good starting point for further research.

The Moves Make the Man

by Bruce Brooks
Harper & Row, 1984
ISBN 0 06 020679 9

COMMENTS

This is a strong book that should bring forth
some heated discussion among those who have
read it. Bruce Brooks has been criticized by
some members of the African-American community for writing so intimately of the black
experience when he himself is not black. This
provides further material for discussion.
Should books be written only by authors within
the same race and culture as their characters?
What about books with characters of several
cultures and races? Is it possible to do enough
research and have enough experience to portray a culture other than your own?

THE PLOT

This is a deeply disturbing book. It is funny,
stark, and deceptively simple. Jerome
Foxworthy—13, an ace student, the first black
in an all-white school, and a basketball fanatic—narrates this story of his friendship with a
white boy, Bix. Jerome tells us right from the
beginning that Bix has run off, so we are
almost prepared for the ending. Jerome first
shows us Bix as he first saw him, playing
shortstop in a Little League game. Although
Jerome's sport is basketball and he is at the
baseball game under duress, he is overwhelmed by the skill and grace of Bix's game.

Later, Jerome is given the dubious honor
of being the first and only black student at the
previously segregated white junior high.
There, he and Bix make stronger contact. Just
as the friendship is taking off, Bix has a
breakdown in class, which frightens Jerome.
Eventually, we learn that Bix's mother is
undergoing shock treatments in a hospital,
and Bix is living with his hated stepfather.
Convinced that the best way to show up his
stepfather, who was a college basketball star,
is to beat him at his own sport, becausethe
stepfather negates Bix's baseball success, Bix
is taught the sport by Jerome.

Bix, although a quick learner, refuses to
learn the feints and tricks that are so much a
part of Jerome's game. Bix insists compulsively, almost hysterically, that such moves are lies,
and that he must be totally truthful. Bix wins
not only the game, but the right to see his

mother in the hospital, although be has to compromise his principles in order to do so. Jerome goes with him to the hospital, and there witnesses a horrifying experience, in which the mother doesn't recognize her son. Bix plays out a scene using incredible "moves" and breaking his heart.

▷ TAKING IT DEEPER

This book has many very strong scenes. Read aloud one that especially affected you.

What's your opinion of Bix's father? Is he as awful as Bix thinks he is? What role does he have in his wife's condition?

One of the things that sets Bix off is the making of a mock apple pie. Can you think of some other things in our culture that might be called fakes? Do they bother you?

Brooks has Jerome refer to his race with some words that most of us find appalling. Do you think he was justified in their use? Does the fact that Brooks himself is white matter?

Bix ran. Should he have run? Could Jerome have done anything further to help Bix?

Would you have ended the book differently?

What does Brooks want us to think? What purpose might he have had in writing this book? Read some or all of his other books. Is there a common theme or thread in his writing?

There's a scene in **Rabble Starkey**, by Lois Lowry (see below), that is similar to the one where Bix visits his mother. After you've read both books, compare those scenes. Did one affect you more than the other? Can you figure out why?

Find out about *Brown v. the Board of Education* and the effects it had, both then and now. Find out about the first black students to enter previously white schools. Were any of their experiences similar to Jerome's?

What contact have you had with mentally ill people? Did those contacts help you learn anything about the illness? Have you read anything or seen anything on TV that informed you on the subject? What do you still need to know?

Find out about treatment for people who are suffering as Bix's mother is. Is shock treatment still used? Has its use changed over the years? What role does medication play in the treatment of similar conditions?

▷ RELATED BOOKS

(See also the theme on Sports, page 103.)

▶ Novels

★ ★ ★ ★ Lowry, Lois **Rabble Starkey** Dell, 1988 ISBN 0 440 40056 2

Two girls from very different backgrounds become friends. Veronica's mother is mentally ill, and Rabble's mother is the family's loving housekeeper. At one point Veronica's mother tries to drown Veronica's young brother.

★ ★ Moeri, Louise **The Girl Who Lived on the Ferris Wheel** Dutton, 1979 ISBN 0 525 30659 5

Til's life with her mother is awful. Her mother is mentally ill, and her physical abuse of Til is escalating, but when teachers question Til about her bruises, she runs from them. They think it's her father who is abusing her. Divorced, his only contact with Til is on Saturday's, when they spend most of their time at the amusement park, where he enjoys the Ferris Wheel, even though it frightens Til.

★ ★ Myers, Walter Dean **Hoops** Delacorte, 1981 ISBN 0 385 28142 0

It seems that Lonnie Jackson's only hope of getting out of the crime and violence of his Harlem neighborhood, is by succeeding in basketball. A has-been coach, Cal, appears to be the only one who can help.

★ ★ Neufeld, John **Lisa Bright and Dark** Phillips, 1969 ISBN 0 87599 153 X

Lisa is sinking into mental illness, and her family refuses to acknowledge the fact, even though friends and teachers voice their concerns. When Lisa tries to hurt three friends and then herself, they are forced to admit to her condition. One of Lisa's friends tells them of her own fight with mental illness and helps them find an institution that can help.

★ ★ ★ ★ Nolan, Han **Dancing on the Edge** Harcourt, 1997 ISBN 0 152 01648 1

This book won the National Book Award for young adult literature in 1997. It details a young girl's descent into madness in her search for truth about herself, her father, and her mother. Miracle was taken by caesarian surgery from the dead body of her mother, but the details of her mother's death have been withheld from her. Miracle's father, a writer who was a child prodigy, has disappeared in such a way as to give the appearance, to his daughter at any rate, of having melted away. His mother, Gigi, strengthens this belief and integrates it into her routines of fortune telling and other occult activities. Miracle yearns to become a prodigy like her father, but has, as yet, not discovered her talent. She is drawn to dance, but her grandmother and aunt react with alarm at any attempts she makes in that direction. It's her grandfather who surreptitiously funds her dance lessons. Miracle is, in the meantime, trying to bring her father back, even as she's trying to melt away herself and, in the process, incurring serious burns on her legs. Believing that it was a suicide attempt, Miracle's Aunt Casey brings in a psychiatrist and, much against Gigi's wishes, has Miracle committed to a sanitarium. It is there, with the help of the psychiatrist and her aunt, that Miracle breaks through the lies and self-serving denial with which the adults have surrounded her.

★ ★ ★ Oneal, Zibby **The Language of Goldfish** Viking, 1980 ISBN 0 140 34540 X

This book also deals with mental illness as we learn about a girl, Carrie, who refuses to grow up. She retreats into daydreams, disassociative behavior, and finally a suicide attempt.

▶ **Nonfiction**

★ Aaseng, Nathan **The Locker Room Mirror** Walker, 1993 ISBN 0 8027 0217 5

In this nonfictional book, Aaseng points out that substance abuse, racism, and violence in sports reflect those elements in society.

★ Greenberg, Harvey **Emotional Illness in Your Family** Macmillan, 1989 ISBN 0 02 736921 8

This book may be a good first step for those looking for information about mental illness and about community resources for helping the family as well as those afflicted.

★ Grunsell, Angela **Racism** Watts, 1991 ISBN 0 531 17279 1

On a slightly younger level than Linda Mizell's book by the same name (see below), this book takes a problem-solving approach to the issue of racism, using color photographs and graphics.

★ Lusane, Clarence **The Struggle for Equal Education** Watts, 1993 ISBN 0 531 11121 0

This history of African-American education starts with the post-Civil War era. It explores the concept of "separate but equal" and the Supreme Court decision that struck it down, as well as busing and other attempts to break down segregation in education.

★ Mizell, Linda **Racism** Walker, 1992 ISBN 0 8027 8113 6

This is a textbook on the history of racism in America, starting with Columbus and ending with the present day. It pulls no punches and should provide facts and figures as well as background information.

★ ★ ★ Myers, Walter Dean **Now Is Your Time** HarperCollins, 1992 ISBN 0 06 024370 8

Myers traces the history of African-Americans in this country by intermingling the heroes within his own family with the giants of the Civil Rights movement.

CHAPTER 6

The Cry of the Wolf

★ ★ ★ ★

by Melvin Burgess
Tambourine
1990 ISBN 0 688 11744 9

 COMMENTS

This book has an interesting premise that
could provide a model for students' writing.
The obsessed hunter vs. the altruistic hero is a
plot that has been used before, but seldom better than in this rather short novel.

THE PLOT

What if there were still wolves in England
and only a few people knew it? What if one of
those people was an obsessive, half-mad, but
extremely able hunter who was determined to
have the "honor" of killing the last wolf in
England? That's the basis of this spare,
unflinching short novel. We are with the last
wolf pups as they are born, barely minutes
before the slaughter begins. The female survives, wounded by The Hunter, with her last
pup, but only long enough to teach him a few
skills before she, too, is killed by the man.

The pup, named Greycub by the boy who
finds him, is reared by Ben and his family and,
being a social animal, waits in vain for the
sound or scent of a remaining wolf. Alas, this is

not to be, for he is the last wolf in England.
Regretfully leaving his human friends, he roams
for years searching for sign of his species.

In a bizarre but very fitting climax to the
story, Greycub becomes the hunter, and The
Hunter knows, too late, the feelings of becoming prey.

TAKING IT DEEPER

What would it be like to be the last surviving female or male of your species?

Are there any free wolves in England
today? How much danger of extinction are
they in today in America?

Investigate the debate between wildlife
preservationists and ranchers concerning
the reintroduction of wolves into Yellowstone
and other areas. After informing yourself of
the facts, conduct a debate in your class on
the subject.

Everybody in this book has a name except
The Hunter. Why would the author do that?

Read the book **A Family Goes Hunting**
(see below) for a nonfictional defense of hunt-

ing. Read Gary Paulsen's **Tracker** and **Woodsong** for other books in which hunters are portrayed sympathetically. Do the arguments for the activity make sense to you? Is it a sport? Is there a difference between killing a deer or killing a steer for meat? Do you or would you hunt? Write or talk about your feelings. Can you change someone's mind on the subject?

Wolves are often the villains in fairy tales. Does this influence our feelings about wolves in general? What would you do about it—ban fairy tales with wolves portrayed this way? rewrite the tales to reform the wolves? publish stories with wolves as good guys? ignore it?

Look at the story of *Little Red Riding Hood* and try substituting other animals for the part of the wolf. What changes? Does it still work? Why or why not?

Make a mural of images of wolves as perceived by children, environmentalists, artists, and the general populace.

Find the points at which the author gives the wolves human qualities. Could the story have been written without that anthropomorphic element?

Is The Hunter a serial killer? When and where does his obsession become madness?

When and how does passion become obsession?

View the movie *Moby Dick*, in which Captain Ahab is similarly obsessed. Is the outcome similar?

Investigate the term "Pyrrhic victory." Does it apply here?

◼ RELATED BOOKS

▶ Picture Books

Peet, Bill **Gnats of Knotty Pine** Houghton, 1975 ISBN 0 395 21405 X

This is an anti-hunting picture book in which the gnats of the forest join ranks to drive the hunters from the woods to save their fellow forest creatures.

▶ Novels

★ ★ Aiken, Joan **The Wolves of Willoughby Chase** Doubleday, 1989 ISBN 0 385 03594 2

Wolves in this Victorian melodrama are used to represent evil.

★ ★ ★ Cross, Gillian **Wolf** Holiday, 1991 ISBN 0 8234 0870 1

Cassy's mother and father are divorced, and she knows that he's a terrorist on the run. Her mother's boyfriend and she have a road show that brings the study of wolves to schools in a dramatic and exciting way. The activities they do would be fun to try in class. Eventually, Cassy equates the vulnerable and dangerous wolf to her own father. This is an unusual and fascinating book.

★ ★ ★ Cunningham, Julia **Drop Dead** Pantheon, 1965 ISBN 0 394 81089 9

We've included this title for two reasons: one of the characters, in this case, a good but enigmatic one, is called The Hunter. Also, the foster parent that Gilly, an orphan, is placed with is evil and driven, as is the villain in *Cry of the Wolf.*

★ ★ Curwood, James O. **Baree, the Story of a Wolf-Dog** Newmarket, 1992 ISBN 1 55704 075 3

This is a good adventure story, with a very accessible vocabulary, about an animal caught between the two sides of its nature. Though the good and bad characters in the book are just that—no shades of in-between—this is a well-written novel.

★ ★ ★ George, Jean **Julie of the Wolves** Bantam, 1987 ISBN 1 55736 053 7

This Newbery Award winner gives us a young girl lost on the tundra whose only hope of survival is being befriended by wolves. Within the very interesting plot is a lot of information about wolf pack behavior.

★ Hughes, Monica **Hunter in the Dark** Avon, 1984 ISBN 0 380 67702 4

A teenage boy, suffering from leukemia, comes to terms with death as he tracks and has the opportunity to kill a deer.

★ ★ ★ Paulsen, Gary **Tracker** Macmillan, 1984 ISBN 0 02 770220 0

John's grandfather, with whom John has often hunted, is dying. Although his grandfather seems to except that fact, John cannot. Deciding that he can bargain for his grandfather's life in some mystic way, John decides to track a deer, not to kill it, but to touch it.

▶ **Nonfiction**

★ ★ ★ Lawrence, R. D. **Wolves** Sierra Club/Little Brown, 1990 ISBN 0 316 51676 7

This is a beautiful book about wolves. The photographs are breathtaking, and the information is presented interestingly. There's a ton of information in this rather small volume.

★ ★ ★ Mowat, Farley **Never Cry Wolf** Little, 1963 ISBN 0 316 58639 0

Commissioned by the Canadian government to study wolves on the tundra, Mowat's nonfictional account of his experiences is funny and fascinating.

★ Patent, Dorothy **A Family Goes Hunting** Houghton, 1991 ISBN 0 395 52004 5

This is a nonfiction book that, through photographs and text, promotes the joys of hunting as a family sport. This is not a subject which is frequently addressed in kids' books, but it does present a viewpoint taken by most hunters: that they are culling a population in the absence of predators. It promotes responsible environmental behavior and claims that most hunters behave similarly.

★ ★ ★ Paulsen, Gary **Father Water, Mother Woods** Delacorte, 1994 ISBN 0 385 32053 1

These are short, often funny, essays on the joys of fishing and hunting. The experiences are mostly those of Paulsen when he was a boy and young man. They are so well written as to make a nonhunter rethink his or her position on the issue.

After the First Death

★ ★ ★ ★

by Robert Cormier
Dell, 1979
ISBN 0 440 20835 1

▷ COMMENTS

This is a strong, violent, compelling book. There are some schools, no doubt, where teachers will not be encouraged to focus on such strong young adult reading material. The plot is bleak and may even seem hopeless. The book contains swearing and some sexual references, although no sexual acts occur. The writing is very good, however, and the book forces us to confront very real aspects of ourselves and of others. As such, it makes worthwhile, if controversial, reading and discussing.

▷ THE PLOT

Terrorists from an unnamed land capture a camp bus loaded with children and their driver. Holding them hostage on a deserted railroad bridge in the woods, the terrorists hope to negotiate for the release of political prisoners, money, and the closing down of a secret government agency. They plan to kill the bus driver and one or two of the children to show they mean business. The bus that day was being driven by a young woman named Kate. At the hostage scene, we focus on her and on Miro, one of the terrorists. Kate has to perform heroically, although she finds nothing in her background that has prepared her for such a role. Miro, on the other hand, has spent most of his life in preparation for his role. Forced to deal with each other, they find each other incomprehensible.

We also focus on Ben, a young boy, whose father, a general in the secret government agency, has been remote. Ben has spent a lifetime attempting to live up to what he thinks are his father's expectations. We know from the beginning that Ben will play a major role in the hostage situation. We also know that he will be shot, although he will survive the bullet that goes through his chest. We also know that he feels he has, again, let his father down.

We focus on his father as well, as he comes face to face with Ben after the boy regains consciousness. We learn how he used and betrayed Ben for what he felt was the greater good.

◪ TAKING IT DEEPER

What do you think happened at the end? Did Ben kill himself? Why? When? What does happen to Ben's father? Does he kill himself?

There are many horror stories within this book. Which one got to you?

At the beginning of the book, Ben tells the shortest horror story in the world. What do you think of it?

Ben, his father, Kate, and Miro are the main characters of the book. What, if anything, do they have in common? What, in their backgrounds, prepared them for the roles they were to play at the bridge?

There are heroes and villains in the book. Which characters fit which roles? What makes a person or a deed heroic?

Many books concern the battle between right and wrong. Are there rights and wrongs here?

Why did the author create the character of Raymond? Does he represent innocence? humanity?

In the book, each main character makes discoveries about himself or herself. What do you think they are? Are any of those discoveries what you might discover in yourself?

What is an individual's responsibility to his or her family and/or government? What is worth dying for?

It is said that power corrupts and that absolute power corrupts absolutely. There is power in this book—that of the terrorists as a group, and of Artkin. There is also the power of Ben's father and of both governments. Is there abuse of power?

Cormier also deals with the issue of power in **The Chocolate War** and **Beyond the Chocolate War** (see below). What do you think he means to tell us about power? Do you agree?

Which death is the one you think is referred to in the title? What would you have named the book?

In this, as in many other Cormier books, the evil essentially goes unpunished. What do you think about that? Should he have ended the book differently?

Cormier has stated that evil occurs because we allow it to occur. Do you think that's true? What evidence can you present?

This book has been criticized, as have many of Cormier's books, for its violent content. How do you feel about that? Should young people be reading such books? How does this book differ from the violence on TV and in the movies, or does it?

◪ RELATED BOOKS

▶ Novels

★ ★ ★ Cormier, Robert **Beyond the Chocolate War**
Pantheon, 1985 ISBN 0 440 90580 X

A railroad bridge is a suicide scene in this book as well as in *After the First Death*. This is the sequel to *The Chocolate War*, and it takes place in the spring after the fund-raiser and its aftermath. The nefarious Brother Leon continues to misuse his power, this time by manipulating the grade of David Caroni, a high achiever. He does this is order to blackmail David into obtaining information about the activities of Jerry Renault.

★ ★ ★ Cormier, Robert **The Bumblebee Flies Anyway**
Pantheon, 1983

This bleak and disturbing novel has a wonderful element of hope. Cormier sets 16-year-old Barney Snow in a clinic where terminally ill patients are volunteers for experimental drug treatment. Barney believes he is there as a volunteer to help the other young people in the clinic, and he becomes very much involved with one patient and his sister. Eventually, Barney finds out that he, too, is terminally ill.

★ ★ ★ ★ Cormier, Robert **The Chocolate War** G. K. Hall, 1988 ISBN 0 8161 4528 8

A parochial boys' school in Massachusetts is the setting for this power struggle. The acting headmaster, Brother Leon, undertakes a fund-raising activity of selling boxes of chocolates, an activity he assumes will get him promoted to permanent headmaster. He enlists the help of the Vigils, a secret student society, the power of which lies in the hands of Archie, the assigner of tasks. One boy alone, Jerry Renault, refuses to sell the chocolates and fights the power structure, bringing on the wrath of Brother Leon and all the Vigils.

▶ Nonfiction

★ Landau, Elaine **Terrorism: America's Growing Threat** Dutton, 1992 ISBN 0 525 67382 2

The author explains the rationalization for terrorism, and the argument comes very close to the one Miro uses in *After the First Death*. She then provides information about some of the major terrorist organizations and their activities in this book aimed at a middle school audience.

★ Lawson, Don **America Held Hostage: The Iran Hostage Crisis** Watts, 1991 ISBN 0 531 11009 5

The author carefully lays the historic basis for the events in Iran, covering the U.S. involvement in Iran throughout the 20th century, before getting into the hostage crisis itself.

Catherine, Called Birdy

★ ★ ★ ★

by Karen Cushman
Clarion, 1994
ISBN 0 395 68186 3

▶ COMMENTS

This is the strongest book we've found about life in the Middle Ages which has a good story and character development, as well as good historical information.

▶ THE PLOT

The scene is a manor house in England in 1290, and Catherine, the willful, stubborn, and delightful daughter of Sir Rollo and Lady Aislinn, has been asked, by her brother the monk, to keep a journal, and these are her daily entries for one important year in her life. She has been promised in marriage to a knight who is wealthier than her father. Unfortunately, she finds her future bridegroom to be old, crude, and disgusting. Unlike most of her friends, Birdy rebels against women's work and life. She resents being bought and sold in order to make her father richer, and she has succeeded in driving off all previous suitors.

As we live through a year with Birdy, we learn about village, castle, and manor life. We attend fairs, weddings, morality plays, masses, and funerals. With Birdy, we visit a monastery. We learn about herbal medicine and the roles played by people in every station of feudal life. Jews are expelled from England, and some stop at the manor house, where Birdy, who has been warned about them, looks for their tails and wonders at their humanity.

The afterword sets Birdy's life in a larger context and contains a lot of easily grasped historical information within a few pages, as does the entire book.

▶ TAKING IT DEEPER

Birdy's relationship with her parents changes in this year of her life. What changes do you see? Why do you think this happens?

Perkin, the goat boy, also rebels against his role in medieval society. What do you think his chances are for success?

Luck plays a part in what happens to Birdy. Find some places where, if certain things hadn't happened or had happened, Birdy's life would have turned out differently. Has luck played a part in your life?

Make a list of words you would use to describe Birdy, and then find evidence in her journal to support each choice of word.

There are many scenes Birdy describes which must have been very funny to witness. Find and read aloud some of these.

Birds play an important part of this book and are used as a symbol throughout. Find as many allusions to them as possible and see if you can decide why and how Cushman used them.

Several characters in this book have conditions that today's medicine or knowledge could help: Birdy's poor eyesight, lepers, and Perkins' leg. What is the modern cure for these and other ailments?

Ladies of the manor were expected to heal the sick and wounded. Mostly, they used herbs as medicine. Find out about the use of herbal medicine today. Which herbs are still used?

Birdy is poor at embroidery (perhaps because of her poor eyesight). Examine pictures of needlework done in that time or visit a museum in which such work is displayed.

Birdy and Morwenna watch a play in Lincoln in which the roles of the Devil and God are acted out somewhat hilariously, and Birdy thinks about what God should look like for her paintings. What do you think either or both should look like?

Birdy spends a lot of time painting on her bedroom walls. Draw or paint one scene from her description.

What do you think of Birdy's poetry?

Jews are being expelled from England in this story. Did that really happen in 1290? Find out why. What others countries expelled Jews? How recently?

Birdy's brother has been on a Crusade. What were the Crusades? Which one would George have been part of, and what did they accomplish? Was George right in his opinion of them after his return?

Why do you think there's so much in the book about the saints and their martyrdom?

There are three weddings in *Catherine, Called Birdy*. Although it was created about one hundred years earlier, find Jan van Eyck's famous painting, *The Marriage of Giovanni Arnolfini and Giovanna Cenami*. The painting itself hangs in the National Gallery in London. On the Internet, you can find it at **http://sun-site.unc.edu/wm/paint/auth/eyck/**. The clothing of the bride and groom show the dress of the merchant class in the 15th century. Students can speculate about how the bride and groom seem to feel about their marriage and whether or not the bride is pregnant. There are also many symbols and details in the painting which are fun to ponder. A single candle is burning, although it is daytime, and there is an image of St. Margaret carved on the back of the chair. Van Ecyk's signature is in Latin, which translates to read, "Jan van Eyck was present," which probably means he was a witness at the wedding. An ornate mirror on the back wall of the room shows the artist himself, as well as a second man, who may have been another witness to the ceremony. A small dog stands between the couple in the foreground, and on the window ledge is a bowl of fruit. The bridal couple is barefoot, and there's a pair of sandals in the front left-hand corner of the picture. Students might like to write a story about the wedding in the painting.

Birdy resembles other characters in books by other authors: **Cat, Herself**, by Mollie Hunter, for instance (HarperCollins, 1986 ISBN 0 06 022635 8), is another female who insists on independence and refuses to marry the man others have chosen for her. Can you think of other people you've met in books who are similar?

➤ RELATED BOOKS

(See also the related books for **The Ramsay Scallop** on page 207).

▶ Picture Books

★ ★ Anno, Mitsumasa **Anno's Medieval World** Putnam, 1980 ISBN 0 399 61153 3

This picture book introduction to medieval history is centered mostly in Southern Europe, but most things were the same in England at the time.

★ ★ ★ Chaucer, Geoffrey **Canterbury Tales** Lothrop, 1988 ISBN 0 688 06201 6, adapted by Barbara Cohen, illustrated by Trina Schart Hyman

Hyman and Cohen have chosen four tales to retell and illustrate: "The Nun's Priest," "The Pardoner," "The Wife of Bath," and "The Franklin." The tales entertain and enlighten, but together with the illustrations, they come to life, revealing much about the times and the people.

★ ★ Gerrard, Roy **Sir Cedric** Farrar, 1984 ISBN 0 374 36959 3

In the age of chivalry, Sir Cedric defeats the evil knight and wins the fair maiden. The plot is a spoof, but the illustrations are very informative.

★ ★ ★ Goodall, John S. **The Story of a Castle** McElderry, 1986 ISBN 0 689 50405 5

This wordless book shows us the inner workings of a Norman castle at about the time of the focus book.

★ ★ ★ Hunt, Jonathan **Illuminations** Macmillan, 1989 ISBN 0 02 745770 2

This alphabet of illuminated letters is full of fascinating information about medieval times.

★ ★ ★ Lasker, Joe **Merry Ever After: The Story of Two Medieval Weddings** Viking, 1976 ISBN 0 670 47257 3

A peasant wedding and a knight's wedding offer two sides of life in the Middle Ages. Looking at this picture book gives us some idea of what Birdy saw at the milkmaid's wedding and at her brother's wedding.

▶ Novels

★ ★ ★ Branford, Henrietta **Fire, Bed & Bone** Candlewick, 1998 ISBN 0 7636 0338 4

This is a good, well researched novel of the Middle Ages whose narrator is an old hunting dog. The Old Dog gives us her perspective on the plague, the life of serfs, the unfairness and cruelty of the nobles and priests, the Peasant's Revolt, and what it did and did not accomplish—and it all rings true. The dog belongs to Rufus and Comfort, two serfs whose backbreaking work is endless and ultimately fruitless. The dog is not completely anthropomorphic—she mates, gives birth, and is concerned for the safety of her pups, but she also has great love and loyalty for her humans, and her concerns and concepts are more like those of a human.

★ ★ ★ Cushman, Karen **The Midwife's Apprentice** Houghton, 1994 ISBN 0 395 69229 6

This book presents life at the bottom of the feudal ladder in medieval times. It works as a counterpart to *Catherine, Called Birdy*, being set in the same place and era. Cushman propels us into the life of a girl living in the Middle Ages, makes us like and understand her, and shows us a lot about the times, and a little bit about ourselves. Birdy was the daughter of a minor baron and, through her, we had glimpses of the life of the higher classes in medieval times. Alyce is an insignificant, nameless child sleeping in a dung heap when we first meet her. We know her first as Brat, and she is usually ignored and sometimes taunted by the other people in the village. Her progress from a Brat working for scraps of food to Alyce, the Midwife's apprentice, is painful and thought provoking. By the end of these well-wrought pages, we know Alyce and accept her small steps toward respectability.

★ ★ Lewis, Naomi **Proud Knight, Fair Lady** Viking, 1989 ISBN 0 670 82656 1

These short stories are set in 12th-century France.

★ ★ Rosen, Sidney and Dorothy **The Magician's Apprentice** Carolrhoda, 1994 ISBN 0 87614 809 7

Don't be fooled by the title; this is not a fantasy. When Jean, a 15-year-old orphan, is accused of having a heretical paper in his possession, he escapes the Inquisition's rack only by promising to spy on Roger Bacon, who is performing suspicious scientific experiments in England.

★ ★ ★ Temple, Frances **The Ramsay Scallop** Orchard, 1994 ISBN 0 531 06836 6

Set in almost exactly the same time as *Catherine, Called Birdy*, this much longer novel tells about two young people whose marriage has been arranged against their will. A very wise priest sends them on a mission together, during which they, and we, see much about French life in the Middle Ages, learn a great deal about themselves, and end up pleased about their coming marriage. This is also a focus book (see page 207).

▶ Nonfiction

★ Caselli, Giovanni **The Middle Ages** Bedrick, 1988 ISBN 0 87226 176 X

With detailed drawings and other artwork, we get a glimpse of the life of the time.

★ Gregory, Tony **The Dark Ages** Facts on File, 1993 ISBN 0 8160 2787 0

Well-captioned photographs and drawings make this short book accessible as well as informative.

★ Howarth, Sarah **Medieval People** Millbrook, 1992 ISBN 1 56294 153 4

One of three volumes in a series, this one looks at the life of six representative people: a doctor, a monk, a knight, a lady, a bishop, and a heretic.

Sees Behind Trees

★ ★ ★ ★

Michael Dorris
Hyperion, 1996
ISBN 0 7868 0224 3

COMMENT

This very short novel is accessible by most readers but is not simplistic in any way. Much of this story is mystical and unspoken, and must be interpreted by the reader. It revolves around a Native American boy with very limited vision going through a rite of passage, learning from the elders, and finding success beyond pride. It is set in the time before the European settlers, although the strangers they encounter may have been white.

These elements make the book very useful for whole-class reading. It can lead to a study of Native American cultures (see page 23), of people and characters who are physically challenged, or to a study of rites of passage in various cultures.

THE PLOT

At the beginning of this short novel, Walnut is dreading the coming-of-age ceremony when boys perform archery feats and earn their names of manhood. His very limited vision prevents him from mastering the feat of shooting thrown moss with his arrow, even after constant coaching by his mother. She then encourages him to perfect the skill of seeing with his other senses to see what she could not. Otter, the weroance, sets one more challenge at the ceremony, that of seeing what can't be seen. Walnut "sees" Gray Fire, Otter's twin brother, coming toward them from far out in the woods and earns the name "Sees Behind Trees."

Gray Fire enlists Sees Behind Trees' assistance in relocating a mystical place he once found that was so beautiful it enchanted him. Once, Gray Fire had been the fastest runner of all, but in that "water place," he had to cut off two toes to free himself, thereupon losing his running skill.

On the way to the spot they seek, Gray Fire and Sees Behind Trees stop to visit with a couple of strangers and their baby, who are fleeing bad strangers from the south. Sees Behind Trees finds the magical place but, once the two arrive, Gray Fire runs to it and disappears. Sees Behind Trees must find his own way home, and he does so, using the skills Gray Fire taught him on the way.

He finds the place where the strangers were, only to find their home burned and the baby hidden among the leaves. He brings the baby back with him and hears Otter's tale of what really happened to Gray Wolf long ago.

▶ TAKING IT DEEPER

Various characters in this book express their great pride in an achievement or skill. List those characters and their talents.
In this village, the women have a lot of power. Is that true of many Native American societies? What other cultures are matriarchal?

His father says that he will not eat until Sees Behind Trees return. How do other cultures use fasting?

On the way to the water place, Gray Fire prepares Sees Behind Trees for the journey home. How does he do this?

Sees Behind Trees says that growing up is like going through an invisible doorway. Is that how you think of it? Are there better images to describe it?

In the book **Through the Gate** (see below) the young people walk through such a doorway. Also, in *Through the Gate* and in *Sees Behind Trees* there is transformation into wildlife, although in one book it's less literal. There are other similarities between the two books. Find and list some of them. Which book do you think speaks most directly to you?

Sees Behind Trees says that Gray Fire is the most grown-up person he knows, and he lists the qualities that make him seem so: he's calm, polite but distant, and content with himself, and he doesn't seem to need others. Do you know anyone with some or all of these qualities? Do you agree that they make a person more grown up? What qualities would you add to or subtract from the list?

Sees Behind Trees observes that most people seem to be two people, one being largely pretense and the other, real. Do you agree

with this observation? Are you two people?

The encounter with the strangers reveals that the village where Sees Behind Trees lives has not been visited by strangers. How do we know this? Who might be the dangerous strangers from the south?

What clues does Michael Dorris give us as to the time and place of this story?

Names have great meaning and importance in this story. Who named you? Why was that name chosen for you? Do any of your names have meaning? Would you change any part of your name?

Gray Fire and Sees Behind Trees communicate with the strangers through sign language and through laughter. How do we communicate with laughter?

Sees Behind Trees learns many life lessons in the course of this short novel. List the ones you think are most important.

If those lessons are important, how would you go about teaching them to young people in this culture?

Gray Fire's place of connection is the water place. For him it represents the greatest beauty he has ever seen. Even Sees Behind Trees can see more clearly there. Have you ever seen a place that comes close to that water place? Describe it in writing or in artwork of some kind.

Hillary Rodham Clinton wrote a book called **It Takes a Village: And Other Lessons Children Teach Us** (Touchstone Books, 1996 ISBN 0 684 82545 7). In it, she talks about the need for the whole community's involvement in raising children. In *Sees Behind Trees*, many people in the village seem involved in the main character's life. How does your community and family seem to feel about this concept?

Otter tells her story at the end of *Sees Behind Trees*, and we get some sense of her guilt and her pride. What lines that she speaks do you find most revealing?

Sees Behind Trees has very limited vision, and his mother teaches him to make the most of his other senses. Talk to people who are blind to find out how they use their other senses and if they find those senses sharpened because of their lack of sight.

This story emphasizes what Sees Behind Trees can do instead of what he cannot do. What implications does this have for people with handicaps or disadvantages?

Today, because of computers and other technology, there are many things some people with limited or nonexistent vision can do. Find out how technology helps visually impaired and blind people. Find out how it helps other physically challenged people.

In spite of his disability, Sees Behind Trees finds a productive place for himself in his society. How does your community deal with physically challenged people?

Michael Dorris killed himself. Find out about his death and the scandal that surrounded it. Does knowing about the charges in his case change your feeling about his work?

▶ RELATED BOOKS

▶ Picture Books

★ ★ Armstrong, Jennifer **King Crow** Crown, 1995 ISBN 0 517 59634 2

This is a dark but provocative story in which a blind king is imprisoned. There, he is visited by a crow that tells him enough about what is going on outside of the prison to make the king appear to be magic.

★ Maclachlan, Patricia **Through Grandpa's Eyes** HarperCollins, 1983 ISBN 0 06 443041 3, illustrated by Deborah Ray

John's grandfather is blind, and he encourages his grandson to experience the world through other senses.

★ ★ Martin, Bill **Knots on a Counting Rope** Holt, 1987 ISBN 0 8050 0571 4, illustrated by Ted Rand

A Native American boy is blind, and his grandfather has told him the story of his racing triumph over and over again using the knots on a rope as a guide.

★ ★ ★ Yolen, Jane **The Seeing Stick** HarperCollins, 1975 ISBN 0 690 00596 2, illustrated by Remy Charlip

In ancient China, an old man teaches a young, blind princess to see with her fingertips.

▶ Novels

★ ★ ★ Bloor, Edward **Tangerine** Harcourt, 1997 ISBN 0 152 01246 X

Like Walnut, Paul has very limited vision. He refuses to let his new classmates know this and manages to play soccer quite well by using his other senses and abilities to their fullest.

★ ★ ★ Dorris, Michael **Guests** Hyperion, 1994 ISBN 0 7868 0047 X

As in *Sees Behind Trees*, there are strangers in this book who come in contact with the protagonist as he is going through a rite of passage. In this book, these are white strangers who come to a Native American village.

★ ★ Gleitzman, Morris **Blabber Mouth** Harcourt, 1995 ISBN 0 15 200369 X

Ro is mute. Her father is anything but mute. He is strong, loud, and flamboyant, and he often embarrasses her. Her entry into public school after years of being in a special school does not go smoothly as she refuses to take a subservient role.

★ ★ ★ ★ Philbrick, Rodman **Freak the Mighty** Scholastic, 1993 ISBN 0 590 47413 8

Two handicapped boys join forces to become greater. This is a focus book (see page 200).

★ ★ ★ Riskind, Mary **Apple Is My Sign** Houghton, 1981 ISBN 0 395 65747 4

This story takes place in the 1900s when Harry, a deaf child, is sent away from home to a special school for the deaf. There, he is overwhelmed by homesickness. During a football game, which pits a hearing team against the school's deaf team, Harry learns more about communication. Later, his handicap nearly results in his death.

★ ★ ★ Taylor, Theodore **The Cay** Doubleday, 1987 ISBN 0 385 07906 0

During World War II, a ship is torpedoed, and two survivors, a West Indian man and a spoiled young boy are marooned together. The boy has been blinded in the attack and must rely on Timothy to learn how to survive.

The Tulip Touch

★ ★ ★ ★

by Anne Fine
Little Brown, 1997
ISBN 0 316 28325 8

COMMENTS

This story is a fascinating character study of a child from an abusive home who is so devoid of empathy that her asocial behavior puts her beyond the reach of the school authorities and of her friend. This is no "bad seed," however, and the reader is given reasons for this disturbed child's behavior, and there is an indictment by her friend of the people who failed to help in time.

THE PLOT

Natalie's family has just moved into an old hotel, which they will renovate and then operate, when Tulip appears for the first time. Immediately, Natalie and Tulip become a twosome, with Tulip the dominant one. So dominant is she, in fact, that Natalie finds herself coming alive only when Tulip is there. Natalie's father goes out of his way to make Tulip welcome, but refuses to let Natalie visit Tulip's home. Tulip and Natalie engage in a series of mind games, which are increasingly mean-spirited. At school, even the teachers seem afraid of Tulip, and Natalie finds herself excluded from other friendships. While we never see any actual abuse, it soon becomes apparent that Tulip's father is abusive, and her mother is apparently powerless to help.

Eventually, the games escalate to a level that frightens Natalie, and she turns away from Tulip, taking up the threads of her own life. For a while, Tulip allows this to happen, but, eventually, she retaliates, and her revenge is terrible.

TAKING IT DEEPER

Make a list of the games Tulip and Natalie played. Some of them are explained, and others only named. What might the rules have been for those games? Who suffered with each game?

We know why Natalie was attracted to Tulip, but why did Tulip want, or even need, Natalie?

When Tulip was at the hotel and behaving so sweetly, was she play-acting? What makes you think that?

Who knew Tulip was in trouble? List these people and the reasons why they failed to help.

There are several points in the story when someone might have been able to change what happened. Make a series of "If Only" statements, such as "If only Tulip's mother had taken her and left the father, Tulip might have been helped." "If only the authorities had put Tulip in a foster home, Tulip might have been helped."

Is Tulip evil? Sick? Disturbed? Give reasons for your decision.

Did Tulip reach out for help? To whom? What was the result?

What help is there? Make a list of the agencies and people in your community and in your life who are available to help kids in trouble.

There's a bit of irony in the title of this book. Find out what irony is and then decide how this title is ironic.

What's the meanest thing you've ever done? Who suffered as a result of your meanness? Who suffered as a result of Tulip's?

Tulip is a villain, albeit a sick one. How does she compare to some of the other villains, such as Aunt Bea in **The Village by the Sea**, Mikey and Margalo in **Bad Girls**, and Erik in **Tangerine**?

▶ RELATED BOOKS

▶ Novels

★ ★ Berg, Elizabeth **The Joy School** Ballantine, 1998 ISBN 0 345 42309 7

There are childhood villains here too, though ones certainly less ominous than Tulip. Like Natalie, Katie is newly moved in to a new community. Her father is distant, and the two kids across the street are meanness personified. She falls in love with a Mobile station attendant who turns out to be a jewel. Not only does he not laugh when Katie's crush is revealed, he handles it with tact and understanding.

★ ★ ★ Bloor, Edward **Tangerine** Harcourt, 1997 ISBN 0 15 201246 X

It's Paul's older brother Erik, football star, who is Tulip's equivalent in this novel. Paul is legally blind, and Erik may well have caused the accident that injured his eyes. His father is so caught up in Eric's football prowess that he refuses to see the evil side of his elder son and pretty much ignores Paul. Paul, however, becomes a soccer star in his new school and, as his success there grows, his brother's destructive behavior also increases.

★ ★ ★ ★ Fox, Paula **The Village by the Sea** Orchard, 1988 ISBN 0 531 05788 7

Emma's father is about to undergo heart surgery, and because her mother will be busy coping, Emma is sent to stay with her father's half-sister, Bea, and her husband, Crispin, on the Long Island shore. Bea turns out to be difficult, indeed. Apparently, she drinks, and she is mean and selfish in dealing with Emma and the next door neighbor friend Emma makes. An unreasonable adult character is not typical in children's literature, and Fox creates a full-sided villain here.

★ ★ ★ Hahn, Mary Downing **Daphne's Book** Avon, 1983 ISBN 0 380 72355 7

In this book, someone does help a child in need, but it costs dearly. Forced by their English teacher to work together in composing a picture book, Jessica and Daphne are both uncomfortable. Jessica is on the fringes of the class, but at least she's not a pariah, like Daphne is. As the two girls work together, however, Jessica begins to like Daphne and her younger sister, Hope. The two live with their demented grandmother under barely survivable conditions. Before the girls' book is finished, Jessica and Daphne have had to reveal their most vulnerable spots to each other, and Jessica has had to betray Daphne's trust.

★ ★ ★ Voigt, Cynthia **Bad Girls** Scholastic, 1996 ISBN 0 590 60134 2

Mikey and Margalo meet in Mrs. Chemsky's fifth-grade classroom. For a short time, they are rivals, but soon team up for disaster. Mikey is aggressive and defiant, while Margalo prefers a sneaky approach, but together they make up a challenge for an equally resourceful teacher in this school novel.

CHAPTER 11

The Borning Room

★ ★ ★ ★

by Paul Fleischman
HarperCollins, 1991
ISBN 0 06 023762 7

COMMENTS

Fleischman has done a masterful job of showing us more than 100 years of American history in the microcosm of one room in one house. In so doing, he personalizes history and makes us see it as a series of lives involved in a day-to-day process of survival. The book is not long or difficult to read, making it a good choice for whole-class reading. Students may not think that they will care about the characters because they appear for such brief times, but such is Fleischman's skill that they most likely will care.

THE PLOT

Georgina, an old woman who now lies in the borning room, is our narrator, and she tells us about the house her grandfather built in Ohio, in 1820, and about the events of her family's lives that were centered in the borning room. The borning room was the scene of the births and the deaths of the family. Georgina was born there in 1851, and eventually gives birth to her own children in the borning room. Her mother died there while giving birth to another child when a new drug, chloroform, was used to ease the birth pains. A slave passes through the house on her way to freedom and helps the family through a difficult birth. The room is also the place where her beloved grandfather dies after refusing to change his free-thinking ways. The sense of the role of birth and death in life is strong in this simply and beautifully told book.

TAKING IT DEEPER

Find a character from a book set in another time, that you believe would be a better friend for Georgina than Hattie.

The family learns about slavery from Cory. How much of what she tells them is typical of slave experiences?

For many years, births and deaths in America have taken place, for the most part, in hospitals. Recently, there has been a movement toward home births and the use of midwifes both in and out of the hospital. Research some of the pros and cons of these trends.

The rituals of death in our society usually take place away from home in hospitals, funeral parlors and churches. If you knew you were dying, where would you like to be? What would you like to be done with your body after death?

Georgina's family plants trees to commemorate each life. Does your family or any one you know have a ritual of commemoration?

If Georgina's family had been black, would their lives have been markedly different?

Family Bibles were once used to record a family's births, deaths, and major events. How do we usually record them today?

If you were to create a record similar to that of a family Bible, what would be in it for your family?

Make a time line showing the events in the book and add to it major events of the time in Ohio and elsewhere.

Bring the book up to date. How many people might have used the borning room from that day to this? What would they be like?

Visit a house, or view plans of a house that has a borning room. You can find a model of such a house on the Internet at **http://www.alden.org/Museum/ Model%20House/model.htm**. Another Web site, **http://mcnet.marietta.edu/~burkeh/ little.htm**, tells about the Underground Railroad in Ohio and also mentions a house with a borning room. Find other such references in books and on the Internet.

In what ways are the action and setting of this book similar to those in **Gathering of Days** (see below)?

▨ RELATED BOOKS

▶ Picture Books

★ Greenfield, Eloise **Childtimes: A Three Generation Memoir** HarperCollins, 1993 ISBN 0 06 446134 3, illustrated by Jerry Pinkney
Three African-American women tell stories about their lives in this stunning picture book.

★ ★ ★ Yolen, Jane **House House** Marshall Cavendish, 1998 ISBN 0 761 45013 0
This photographic essay shows old houses in a small New England town, as they were and as they are now. A little information is given about the families who live in these houses.

▶ Novels

★ ★ ★ Blos, Joan W. **A Gathering of Days** Aladdin, 1990 ISBN 0 689 71419 X
Although the setting here is New Hampshire, not Ohio, you will find similarities to *The Borning Room* in this diary of a 14-year-old girl living in the 19th century. During the course of a year, we witness the changes in Catherine as she aids a runaway slave and loses her best friend to death.

★ ★ Hamilton, Virginia **The House of Dies Drear** Aladdin, 1984 ISBN 0 02 043520 7
This house is also in Ohio, and it was a station on the Underground Railroad. Now it is haunted, and there are tales about a hidden treasure. Thomas explores the hidden passages and finds danger on the way to treasure.

▶ Nonfiction

★ ★ ★ Bial, Raymond **Frontier Home** Houghton, 1993 ISBN 0 395 64046 6
This photographic essay explores one house and its furnishings on the frontier.

★ ★ ★ ★ Lester, Julius **To Be a Slave** Scholastic, 1988 ISBN 0 590 42460 2
Lester has anthologized the direct testimony of many slaves and has arranged the interviews in a sort of chronology. This is a very useful source about slavery.

Dateline: Troy

★ ★ ★ ★

by Paul Fleischman,
Candlewick, 1996
ISBN 1 56402 469 5

COMMENTS

Fleischman's masterful retelling of the tale of the Trojan War is only aspect of this remarkable book. It's his juxtaposition of newspaper collages that makes this book startling and immediately relevant. In 80 pages, in the simplest of languages—accessible to many students who would not think of tackling other versions of the tale—Fleischman has done a masterful job.

THE PLOT

Homer's **Iliad** is the source for this retelling of the causes, battles, and aftermath of the Trojan War. Fleischman tells the story simply and dramatically. However, after an introduction stating that, "Though their tale comes from the distant Bronze Age, it's as current as this morning's headlines," Fleischman then places newspaper collages on each page reflecting the modern equivalent of those events.

Hecuba's nightmare, interpreted by the priest to mean that the child she was about to bear would bring ruin to Troy, set in motion the events that would cause the tale's gods, heroes, and mortals to engage in a deadly war that would, ultimately, fulfill the prophecy.

TAKING IT DEEPER

Gather as many versions of the story of the Trojan War and its extensions as possible. Don't forget the mythology of Greece, current geography, the history of Greece, and books about the archeological discovery of the ruins of Troy (see below). Decide which aspect you would like to investigate further and how you will convey your discoveries to the rest of the class.

Find other accounts of the Trojan War. Reread one page from Fleischman's book and then find another author's account of the same events. What material did Fleischman choose to omit? What would the inclusion of that material have done to the book's effect?

Make copies of the brief text in the book and use them to make an annotated time line of the events of the Trojan War. Illustrate your time line.

Look at Fleischman's choices for newspaper clippings for each event in the war. What other choices might he have made? Look through current issues of magazines and newspapers, as well as library archives, to find other possibilities. Place those clippings or copies of them on the time line. Make lines showing the relationship of those clippings to the events of the war.

One of the many tragic figures in the war was Cassandra, doomed to be able to see into the future and yet have no one believe her predictions. What other characters do you see as particularly tragic in Fleischman's book?

Make a series of "If Only" statements about the war, such as: "If only Hecuba had kept her dream to herself, Priam would never have ordered the killing of the new baby Paris."

Can you do the same (make "If Only" statements) about a more current conflict?

This story is referred to as only a "mythic tale," meaning that it contains many actions and reactions of the gods and goddesses. Reread the story and make a list of the events that you think could actually have happened. If Hecuba's dream and Paris's awarding of the golden apple to Aphrodite did not set in motion the events that were to become the Trojan War, what could have done it?

Mr. Fleischman's technique of finding newspaper headlines and stories that have parallels to the events in his book could be used with other books. Try it with such books as *The Giver* and **1984**, for instance.

▧ RELATED BOOKS

▶ Novels

★ Coolidge, Olivia **The Trojan War** Houghton, 1952 ISBN 0 395 06731 6

Coolidge's book has been around for a long time, but it's well done and much lengthier than Fleischman's, offering many details not included in either Fleischman's or Rosemary Sutcliff's accounts.

★ Edmondson, Elizabeth **The Trojan War** Simon & Schuster, 1993 ISBN 0 02 733273 X

This is a brief recounting of the events. The myths are interwoven with the facts.

★ Evslin, Bernard **The Trojan War** Scholastic, 1988 ISBN 0 590 41626 X

This account is longer than either Fleischman's or Sutcliff's, though less literary.

★ Evslin, Bernard **The Adventures of Ulysses: The Odyssey of Homer** Scholastic, 1989 ISBN 0 590 42599 4

The *Odyssey* covers the voyage of Ulysses after the Trojan War.

★ Little, Emily **The Trojan Horse: How the Greeks Won the War** Random, 1988 ISBN 0 394 99674 7

This version of the story will allow less able readers accessibility to the story, but it lacks the passion and literary quality of either Fleischman's or Sutcliff's versions.

★ ★ ★ ★ Sutcliff, Rosemary **Black Ships Before Troy: The Story of the Iliad** Delacorte, 1993 ISBN 0 385 31069 2, illustrated by Alan Lee

Sutcliff's book is almost the antithesis of Fleischman's account—it is more descriptive and, although Lee's illustrations are fine, its meat is to be found in Sutcliff's text, not the graphics. Sutcliff's story is more detailed and more human than Fleischman's. Her images are powerful, and she presents a more balanced account than the *Iliad*'s pro-Grecian one did.

CHAPTER 13

Out of the Dust

★ ★ ★ ★

by Karen Hesse
Scholastic, 1997
ISBN 0 590 36080 9

▷ COMMENT

Out of the Dust is written in free verse, which gives a sparity to the text, making it a fairly quick read, but the novel has great depth and a strong sense of time and place. Its setting is Oklahoma during the thirties, and so we know immediately that the dust, at least some of it, is from the Dust Bowl. The history connection is, therefore, a strong one, but there are strong characters and some discussion of sex roles. Music also plays a strong part in the story.

▷ THE PLOT

In 1934, life is already tough, and it's about to get worse. Billie Jo, her mother, and her father are struggling to run their farm despite financial hard times. Her father doesn't say much, but we know he loves his family and that he is a man of the soil. Her mother obviously comes from a more refined background than her father. Billie Jo says her mother has made herself over to fit her father. She plays the piano beautifully and, when she plays elegant pieces, Billie Jo's father stands in the doorway and watches her with something in his eyes Billie Jo is seldom privileged to see. Billie Jo plays, too. Her music makes her mother wince, but she's making a name for herself with the kids at school for her wild and exuberant music. Billie Jo hopes to ride that music out of the dust.

Billie Jo's mother is pregnant, and they're all looking forward to the baby's arrival. The dust comes before the baby does, and the fierce dust storms and their aftermath drive many of the family's neighbors off. They're heading to California where things are bound to be better. Billie Jo's father has lived through hard times before, and he says the family is staying.

The book's climax is the tragedy. Billie Jo's father leaves a pail of kerosene by the stove (we never learn why), and her mother, thinking it is water, throws it on the stove. The flames send her mother out the door screaming for her father, and Billie Jo grabs the pail and throws the remaining kerosene out the front door, just as her mother is rushing back inside. Immediately, the flames engulf her mother, killing her and the baby. They also burn and scar Billie Jo's hands, so that playing the piano becomes so painful as to make it impossible.

Billie Jo's already remote father becomes unreachable. Billy Jo fears that they are both turning into the dust that has covered everything and, after trying to carry on without support, she runs away, only to discover that her future lies back home.

▶ TAKING IT DEEPER

Before we start researching and talking about the Dust Bowl historically, stay within the book for awhile. Billie Jo's mother made herself over to fit her father. How did she do that? What sacrifices, unmentioned in the book, did she probably make?

What about Billie Jo's father? Did he make himself over to fit her mother? Why not? Why doesn't he help Billie Jo during those awful days?

Do you think Billie Jo's inability to play the piano after the fire was psychological or physical?

What about the decision Billie Jo makes to turn back? Was it something the man in the freight train said?

Billie Jo says that he and her Ma were like tumbleweeds, but her father is not. What comparisons would you make between those personalities? Is Billie Jo a tumbleweed?

Start with the Internet to obtain information about the Dust Bowl. You can find a wonderful site on the Dust Bowl by the Library of Congress, with photographs, interviews, and sound recordings, at **http://lcweb2.loc.gov/ ammem/afctshtml/tshome.html**. There's a great photo of a dust storm and its aftermath at **http://drylands.nasm.edu:1995/dust.html**.

There's a classic documentary film called *The Plow that Broke the Plains*, by Pare Lorenz, that was made in 1936 and is still available. Footage of a dust storm is particularly good in that film.

Speaking of films, don't forget *The Grapes of Wrath*, both as a film and as a book, for kids in middle school grades. It's not hard to read, and nobody said it better than Steinbeck.

It's hard to sing when your throat's that dry, but Woodie Guthrie wrote and recorded several songs from that era and place. His CD called *Dust Bowl Ballads* is still available.

What about the science of the Dust Bowl? Was it bad farming, freak weather, some of both, or more? Can it happen again? It's time to consult almanacs for information about droughts, to get someone from your state university to talk about farming then and now, and then to turn to more literature.

▶ RELATED BOOKS

▶ Picture Books

★ ★ ★ Booth, David **The Dust Bowl** Kids Can Press, 1997 ISBN 1 55074 295 7, with illustrations by Karen Reczuch

This is a picture book about a father who's so discouraged by current bad times on the farm that he wants to walk away, but Grandpa remembers the Dust Bowl. He stuck it out through that, and his memories remind them all that hard times do end, eventually.

★ ★ ★ ★ MacLachlan, Patricia **What You Know First** HarperCollins, 1995 ISBN 0 06 024413 5, illustrated by Barry Moser

In a farm on the prairie, a family is about to leave their home. Our narrator proclaims that she will not leave. She will stay here in the place she knows best. Moser's illustrations show us that this is a tale set in the Great Depression.

★ ★ ★ ★ Stewart, Sarah **The Gardener** Farrar, 1997 ISBN 0 374 32517 0, illustrated by David Small

This is a wonderful picture book. The illustrations go far beyond the text to create images of the time of the Great Depression as the story recounts the adventures of a very optimistic little girl. Lydia is sent by her parents and her grandmother to work in her uncle's bakery in New York City. Her uncle, a grim and unsmiling man, works hard, and Lydia resolves to make him smile at least once. She does so by transforming their tenement rooftop into a beautiful garden.

★ Turner, Ann **Dust for Dinner** HarperCollins, 1995 ISBN 0 06 023376 1, illustrated by Robert Barrett

This is an easy-to-read book in which we watch a family fall victim to the Dust Bowl.

▶ Novels

★ ★ ★ Koller, Jackie French Nothing to Fear Harcourt, 1991 ISBN 0 15 257582 0

Set far from the action in *Out of the Dust*, this Depression novel takes place in New York City. We watch the effects of the Depression on several families, especially the Garveys and the Rileys. Both are Irish immigrant families living in a New York City tenement. After his father leaves to find work, teenaged Daniel Garvey takes on an adult role, earning money for the family when he can, and begging for it when he cannot. Mr. Garvey takes refuge in the bottle. This is a strong and very successful novel.

★ ★ ★ Peck, Robert Newton Arly's Run Walker, 1991 ISBN 0 8027 8120 9

This sequel to Arly is set in Depression-era Florida. Arly survives a boat wreck on Lake Okeechobee. He is more or less shanghaied into a migrant worker crew and lives in the crew's subhuman camps, befriended by a drunken man named Coo-Coo.

▶ Nonfiction

★ Antie, Nancy **Hard Times: A Story of the Great Depression** Viking, 1993 ISBN 0 670 84665 1

This is a very accessible, personalized look at the Depression. One Oklahoma family loses its home in the Dust Bowl and become "Okies" heading west to California.

★ Burg, David F. **The Great Depression: An Eyewitness History** Facts on File, 1996 ISBN 0 8160 3095 2

Many primary sources and photographs illustrate the era and the wide-ranging effects of the Depression.

★ Farrell, Jacqueline **The Great Depression** Lucent, 1996 ISBN 1 56006 276 2

The concentration in this volume is on the various work programs constructed by the government to create work.

★ ★ Meltzer, Milton **Brother Can You Spare a Dime: The Great Depression, 1929–1933** Facts on File, 1991 ISBN 0 8160 2372 7

This is probably the most comprehensive work on this book list. Meltzer starts in the early 1920s to outline the causes of the Depression, and continues his careful account through Roosevelt's New Deal.

★ ★ ★ Stanley, Jerry **Children of the Dust Bowl: The True Story of the School at Weedpatch Camp** Crown, 1992 ISBN 0 517 58782 3

This excellent book focuses on a village created by a group of "Okies" when they got to California. There are numerous photos from the Dust Bowl era.

★ Stein, Richard C. **The Great Depression** Cornerstones of Freedom, 1993 ISBN 0 516 06668 4

This is a good, concise history of the events in the era.

★ Wormser, Richard **Growing Up in the Great Depression** Atheneum, 1994 ISBN 0 689 31711 5

These are varied personal accounts of the time, and cover many areas of the country, as well as the Dust Bowl.

Kinship

★ ★ ★ ★

by Trudy Krisher
Delacorte, 1997
ISBN 0 385 32272

 COMMENTS

This is a sensitive story about family and community. With the setting being a run-down trailer court, we deal with poverty and pride. Also, the time is 1961, and laws (such as abortion laws) were different then. The multiple narrators make it a challenging book to read, although the reading level is not difficult. There are several symbols in the book, and the glimpses one gets of the characters' inner thoughts and motivations are fascinating.

THE PLOT

Perty (Pert) Wilson has been the life and the darling of the trailer court in the town of Kinship, Georgia, where she lives with her big brother, Jimmy, and her mother, Rae Jean. Most of the book is seen from Pert's point of view, but intervening chapters use the voices of the other inhabitants of the trailer court. Pert longs to see and know her father, who left the family shortly after she was born, and now he's here. At first, James Wilson seems to be the father she's dreamed of. He's charming, fun, and full of ideas and seems to be the hero of the court as he comes up with a plan to keep the authorities from removing them from what they call "temporary" dwellings.

Soon, however, it becomes apparent that he is unreliable at best and a crook at worst. Pert is further troubled by her brother's romance with and approaching marriage to a pregnant teenager. Pert consults the family doctor about aborting the child and creates the suspicion that she is the pregnant one.

Challenged by the authorities to prove that their dwellings are permanent housing, the individuals in the trailer court get to know each other and themselves and to take pride in their community. There are lots of discussion about what makes a home, and of the difference between kin and family.

TAKING IT DEEPER

Krisher elects to begin and end the book with the voice of Alice Potter, a minor character in the book. Students might like to figure out why she did that and what voices they'd have chosen.

Finding references to Alice Potter in the story is not easy, but she is the one who taught Pert about ESP, which she has used to contact her father. Did it work?

Also, in the beginning and ending chapters, much is made of Ms. Potter's decorative and personalized bottles. What do they symbolize?

There are other symbols in the story—circles and rings, for instance. How does Krisher use them to tie the story together?

Pert's family is the only Roman Catholic family in Kinship. How does she feel about that? How do the others in the family react to her mother's faith?

Try doing reader's theater with just the other voice chapters in the book. Together do they frame the story? What do you end up knowing about each trailer family?

In most good novels and stories, characters change in believable ways. Who changes here and what causes those changes? Who doesn't seem to change at all?

Pert's father shows up at a most convenient time. Later, we find out why he might have come. Did Pert know that? Would it have changed her feelings about her father? What motivates him to do the hurtful things he does?

Look for ways that the people in Happy Trails became Pert's family before and during the action of this book. Did they think of themselves that way?

RELATED BOOKS

▶ Picture Books

★ ★ Perkins, Lynne Rae **Home Lovely** Greenwillow, 1995 ISBN 0 688 13687 7

Janelle and her daughter Tiffany have moved into an isolated and dreary trailer, but Tiffany starts a garden and is soon helped by their mailman to make things prettier.

★ ★ ★ Swope, Sam **The Araboolies of Liberty Street** Dragonfly, 1995 ISBN 0 517 88542 5, illustrated by Barry Root

Unlike the people of Happy Trails, the people in this community are conformists largely because of a bully. Their rebellion is led by newcomers, and in the process their unique individuality comes through.

▶ Novels

★ ★ Cottonwood, Joe **Danny Ain't** Scholastic, 1992 ISBN 0 590 45067 0

Like Pert, Danny lives in a dilapidated trailer, but he lives there alone, fearing authorities because they'll take him away. His father is in a VA hospital suffering from post-traumatic stress syndrome.

★ ★ ★ ★ Fox, Paula **Monkey Island** Orchard, 1991 ISBN 0 531 05962 6

Monkey Island is a village created by homeless people, and Clay Garrity ends up there after his father and mother wander off. The people of Monkey Island are subjected to harassment and beatings by gangs and by the same kind of mindless authorities as in Kinship.

★ ★ ★ McDonald, Joyce **Comfort Creek** Delacorte, 1997 ISBN 0 385 32232 1

In this novel, it's not the father but the mother who has left, and the out-of-work father has moved the family's trailer to an even more isolated spot. However, the neighborhood created by the phosphate mine workers is also threatened with extinction.

▶ Nonfiction

★ ★ Houston, Jeanne Wakatsuki **Farewell to Manzanar** Bantam, 1974 ISBN 0 553 27258 6

During World War II, when Japanese-American families were uprooted and sent to relocation camps, the author's family was sent to Manzanar. She tells how the displaced people, living in deplorable conditions, became a community.

CHAPTER 15

Alan and Naomi

★ ★ ★ ★

by Myron Levoy
HarperCollins, 1977
ISBN 0 06 440209 6

 COMMENTS

At the beginning, this story seems overly simplistic. As the reader continues, however, the
plot and characters take on more complexity.
The avoidance of pat solutions and the down-
beat ending lifts this above many young adult
novels, and the oblique view of the war and of
the Holocaust opens many avenues for dialogue and further research.

THE PLOT

Naomi and her mother have moved into an
apartment in the same building as Alan and
his mother and father. Naomi is deeply disturbed (she has witnessed the death of her
father by the Nazis), and Alan is asked to
befriend her and, as Naomi is being treated by
a psychologist, to take part in her therapy. We
never see the psychologist, but she often suggests the next steps for Alan to follow. At first,
Alan is an unwilling participant in Naomi's
therapy, but the two children gradually achieve
real friendship. Alan's commitment and
friendship eventually strengthen Naomi to the

extent that she is able to attend school. When
the school bully taunts them both for their
friendship and their Jewishness, Alan fights
him. The sight of Alan being punched and
bloodied is too much for Naomi's fragile sanity, and she retreats into her insanity. At the
end of the book, Naomi is beyond Alan's
reach, and is institutionalized. Alan believes
she is gone forever, but his father thinks there
may yet be hope.

TAKING IT DEEPER

At the beginning of the story, Alan is most
interested in gaining the admiration of his gen-
tile peers. At the end, he has a much different
outlook on life. Look for signs in the book for
his gradual reorientation.

Although World War II is the setting for
this book, it never occupies central stage. Make
a list of the characters in the book and then
find ways in which each of them was affected
by the war.

What changes in the treatment of mental
illness have been made since the time of this

novel? How would Naomi be treated today by the mental health community?

The role that Alan's physical activity takes in this book is, of course, a vital one. Were there any good effects of the fight?

This book is slightly marred by ethnic stereotypes. Can you find them? What changes would the author have to make to avoid them?

Naomi's life is irrevocably changed by the Holocaust. In what ways is she a symbol for others?

Many of the activities suggested in the theme on the Holocaust on page 30 are applicable here.

▶ RELATED BOOKS

(For other books about the Holocaust, see page 30.)

▶ Novels

★ ★ Bennett, James **I Can Hear the Mourning Dove** Houghton, 1990 ISBN 0 395 53623 5

In this frank novel, Grace is institutionalized, and we hear not only her story, but that of several other patients in the hospital as they are helped by therapy.

★ ★ ★ Bridger, Sue Ellen **Notes for Another Life** Knopf, 1981 ISBN 0 394 94889 0

Tom, Wren and Kevin's father, has been hospitalized for depression, and the children are staying with their grandparents. Although Tom shows marked improvement for a while, his hold on sanity is tenuous, and so is Kevin's as he becomes overwhelmed with guilt.

★ ★ ★ ★ Brooks, Bruce **The Moves Make the Man** HarperCollins, 1984 ISBN 0 06 020679 9

This is a focus book (see page 150).

★ ★ ★ ★ Hamilton, Virginia **The Planet of Junior Brown** Simon, 1971 ISBN 0 02 742510 X

Homeless Buddy becomes friendly with overprotected Junior Brown. Their friendship is strong, but Junior retreats into an unreachable fantasy world.

★ ★ ★ ★ Lowry, Lois **Rabble Starkey** Houghton, 1987 ISBN 0 395 43607 9

The relationship between Rabble and her mother is delightful and in direct comparison to the relationship between her friend Veronica and her mentally ill mother. The concept of family is central to the book.

★ ★ Neufeld, John **Lisa Bright and Dark** Phillips, 1969 ISBN 0 451 16093 2

Lisa's parents are oblivious to her descent into mental illness, although her friends and teachers try to warn them about it.

★ ★ ★ ★ Newton, Suzanne **I Will Call It Georgie's Blues** Puffin, 1990 ISBN 0 14 034536 1

This is another focus book (see page 191).

★ ★ ★ Voigt, Cynthia **David and Jonathan** Scholastic, 1992 ISBN 0 590 45165 0

David, a Holocaust survivor, moves in with Jonathan and his family, but David is suicidal and very ill, and his behavior threatens a friendship between Henry and Jonathan.

▶ Nonfiction

★ Lundy, Allan **Diagnosing and Treating Mental Illness** Chelsea House, 1990 ISBN 0 7910 0047 8

This is a brief explanation of many forms of mental illness and its treatment.

16

The Giver

★ ★ ★ ★

by Lois Lowry
Houghton, 1993
ISBN 0 395 64566 2

 COMMENTS

This book, which is part fantasy and part science fiction, might intrigue many middle school readers. Lowry received the Newbery Award for 1993 for it, and while not difficult reading, it contains so much food for thought, discussion, and writing, that it makes an ideal focus book.

THE PLOT

The society we find in **The Giver** certainly seems ideal. Everyone has a job for which he or she is emotionally, physically, and mentally suited. The elderly are lovingly cared for, as are the newest members of this society. Every family has a mother, father, and two children, one of each sex. There is much laughter and obvious joy. There is no rudeness, no crime, and no disease, and little hint of the society's flaws, except perhaps its regimentation, in the beginning of this book.

We see this society through the eyes of Jonas, a young boy who is about to receive his life's assignment, along with others of his age group. To his astonishment, he is given the most respected job of all. He is to be trained to become the "Receiver of Memory." In the utopian society Lowry has created, people don't want to be burdened with memories. However, they also don't want to make decisions or changes which, in the past, have led to disaster. Therefore, they have assigned one person to keep all the memories of history—their own and that of all societies. The Receiver's job is to listen to their proposals and tell them whether or not they are likely to succeed based on the lessons of history. The present Receiver now sets about giving the memories—all of them—to Jonas, thus becoming The Giver. He does this by transmitting all of the senses that make up that memory. Jonas learns of war and hate, of snow and trees and colors, all of which are absent in this society. In so learning, he realizes the price his society has paid—and continues to pay—for its "perfection." The horror all around him becomes apparent. His decision about what to do with the information exploding within him is the climax of the book.

The ending is enigmatic and should lead to speculation and further discussion.

▶ TAKING IT DEEPER

The cover itself of this book is intriguing and faintly menacing. Designed by the author, who is an accomplished photographer as well as writer, the cover shows a black-and-white photograph of a bearded man. The expression on his face, particularly his eyes, is one upon which to speculate. Is it wisdom? humor? wariness?

Looking further, we see something which seems to be a tiny piece of another book jacket in the lower left-hand corner of the cover. Here is a snatch of color and a brief glimpse of trees. Like a prologue, the cover of the book becomes meaningful as we read it. What meaning does it have for you?

The title of the book is also something to ponder. The story is at least as much about Jonas as it is about The Giver. Why didn't Lowry title the book "The Receiver"? What would you have called it?

The role of history is called into question here. The movers and shakers in that society use the past only as a reference to the possible success or failure of their attempts to better their own society. Is that the best use of history? the only one? Why do we study it in one form or another throughout most of our scholastic lives? Who chooses what pieces of history we study, and is that changing? Why do we learn so much about ancient Greece and Rome, but so little about Asia? Who slants our views of history?

Some people think Jonas is dead at the end of the story; others think he has found a society more like our own. What do you think? What makes you think so? Lowry won't tell what she thinks other than to say she is hopeful. What does that mean to you?

Many people have been intrigued by Lowry's use of religion in the book. Does the Christmas scene at the end of the book represent religion to you? What else might it suggest?

Lowry has also said that there will be no sequel to The Giver. How do you feel about that decision? Why would you like one, if, indeed, you do? What would you hope the sequel would resolve?

In The Giver, Lowry has created an ideal society. You may want to pause as soon as the students have discovered this to allow them to speculate in writing or in discussion upon the ideal society they would create if they had the power.

What if you were given the task of creating a new society in space or on earth? What would you need? want? like? in which order of priority? What sustains life besides the obvious food, shelter, water, and air? What role does literature take? What books would you bring? Which, if any, would you include as required reading for your society? Look at the names used for other ideal societies and then carefully choose one for your own.

Other students might like to investigate some of the real attempts at such societies and collectives: Brook Farm, Owens' New Harmony, Shaker villages, communes, communism, socialism, and democracy. Finding out if and how they failed or succeeded, what they have in common, and where they differ could be a long-term project in which history and language arts are combined.

Still another tack from The Giver is to assume the title role yourself. What would you transmit to someone who knew only what Jonas knew, but about our own culture? What priority of memories would you have? What do you need to know or have experienced to operate successfully in the present world?

Look at Lowry's techniques in writing The Giver. How does she convey the various moods of the book? What choices does she make for word use, sentence structure, and foreshadowing and flashback? Has she used those techniques before? Has anyone else? (See related books listed below.)

See *Hornbook Magazine*, Aug. 94, for Lowry's acceptance speech for the 1993 Newbery Award, which she received for *The Giver*. It may give you more insight into the book and into the author.

▶ RELATED BOOKS

▶ Picture Books

★ Arnold, Tedd **The Simple People** Dial, 1992 ISBN 0 8037 1012 7

This is a society in which everyone lives a blissful life until a first invention is developed. This leads to the building of a wall to protect it, which eventually leads to total darkness.

★ ★ Bial, Raymond **Shaker Home** Houghton, 1994 ISBN 0 395 64047 4

This largely photographic book portrays the Shaker ideals of functional simplicity in life and work.

★ ★ ★ Blos, Joan **Old Henry** Morrow, 1990 ISBN 0 688 09935 1

Neighbors with a different agenda drive a nonconformist from his home in an old wreck of a house.

★ Komaiko, Leah **My Perfect Neighborhood** Harper, 1990 ISBN 0 06 023287 0

This rhyming picture book depicts the enjoyment of a neighborhood's diversity.

★ ★ ★ Pinkwater, Daniel **Big Orange Splot** Scholastic, 1977 ISBN 0 590 41597 2

This picture book pokes fun at neighborhoods in which every house looks just alike.

★ ★ ★ Swope, Sam **The Araboolies of Liberty Street** Dragonfly, 1995 ISBN 0 517 88542 5, illustrated by Barry Root

In this town, the houses are all neat, people are well behaved, and there is safety. There is also fear, however, because of General Pinch and his wife, who are ever watchful for any deviation from the norm. Then, the Araboolies move in next door to the Pinches. Not only do they not understand the Pinches' language and the rules, they don't care!

Yoaker, Harry **The View** Dial, 1992 ISBN 0 8037 1105 0

In this town of look-alike houses, each family has a unique view, and all are happy until one owner decides to improve his own view, which results in chaos.

▶ Novels

Adams, Richard **Watership Down** Macmillan, 1974 ISBN 0 02 700030 3
This is a focus book (see page 139).

The Bible: Genesis

The Garden of Eden is an ideal existence, if not an actual society.

★ ★ ★ Christopher, John **The White Mountains** Macmillan, 1988 ISBN 0 02 042711 5

This is the first in the Tripod series of books about an ideal, futuristic society in which everybody, after being "capped," is happy and productive. Two boys decide to ask why and eventually discover the machines that run the society.

★ Hilton, James **Lost Horizon** Pocket Books, 1984 ISBN 0 671 54148 X

Shangri-La is a land where time stands still and life is blissful. To accept or reject it is a decision made by the main characters in this romantic adult novel, which was made into a movie in the late thirties.

★ ★ Hughes, Monica **Invitation to The Game** Simon and Schuster, 1990 ISBN 0 671 74236 1

Newly graduated from government schools, a group of friends are assigned to be permanently unemployed. The Game is a mysterious, computer-induced, alternate reality with which the group becomes totally obsessed. What is The Game? What will the youngeters' future hold? What will the world be like in 2154? This accessible novel provides one inroad to these questions.

★ ★ ★ Huxley, Aldous **Brave New World** Longman, 1973 ISBN 0 582 53033 4

Huxley's cautionary predictions for the future of technology are the focus of this brief, futuristic novel. The society is more transparent than that in *The Giver*, but the two novels identify and attempt to "fix" many of the same flaws in our society.

★ ★ ★ ★ L'Engle, Madeline **A Wrinkle in Time** Dell, 1976 ISBN

One of the several societies Meg sees is one in which there is entire uniformity.

★ More, Thomas **Utopia** Norton, 1992 ISBN 0 393 96145 1

The reading level here is quite difficult, and few students will want to read it all. Still, it is one of the early constructions of an ideal society on paper, and it is the source for the word to describe such societies.

★ ★ ★ ★ Orwell, George **Animal Farm** Harcourt Brace, 1954 ISBN 0 15 107252 3

This allegory examines the illusions of a utopian society of animals after farm animals revolt, drive off the humans, and put themselves in charge. It quickly becomes a totalitarian state. This is an adult book within the range of mature readers.

★ ★ ★ ★ Orwell, George **1984** Harcourt, 1948 ISBN 0 15 166038 7

This cautionary novel examines a society in which Big Brother watches our every action. The opposite of a utopian society, this is a hellish one. Written when 1984 was well in the future, students may enjoy seeing which of Orwell's prophecies have literally and figuratively happened.

★ Plato **Plato's Republic** Viking, 1955 ISBN 0 14 044048

For capable readers, this is Plato's view of an ideal civilization in which learned members lead others out of the cave of ignorance to the light.

★ ★ Steele, Mary Q. **Journey Outside** Smith, 1984 ISBN 0 8446 6169 4

Each of the people encountered by this traveler from an underground society seems to be living an ideal life, but each is terribly flawed.

★ ★ ★ Thompson, Jullian F. **Gypsyworld** Holt, 1992, ISBN 0 805 01907 3

Several teens are abducted from our contemporary world and brought to Gypsyworld, where people have succeeded in creating an environmentally sustainable society.

► **Nonfiction**

★ ★ ★ Conrad, Pam **Our House: The Stories of Levittown** Scholastic, 1995 ISBN 0 590 46523 6

These short stories are fictionalized fact and they revolve around the town built in 1947 as an attempt to make an ideal town after World War II. The houses were alike. There was racism (no nonwhites allowed) and great regimentation (no laundry hung outside on weekends). Still, it was home for many people who loved it.

⊳ RELATED FILMS

Animal Farm Phoenix/BFA Films & Video VHS ISBN 0 7919 2630 3

This color film sticks closely to the plot of Orwell's political fable.

Utopias, narrated by Jim Fleet. Agency for Instructional Technology ISBN 0 7842 0259 1

This is a historical view of some of the 40 utopian communities established in the United States during the last half of the 18th century.

⊳ RELATED SONGS

"Little Boxes," by Malvinia Reynolds. Recorded by Pete Seeger, among others.

CHAPTER 17

The Wall

★ ★ ★

by Elizabeth Lutzeier
Holiday House, 1991
ISBN 0 8234 0987 2

COMMENTS

The wall in the title is the Berlin Wall, and it is both a symbol and a focus for much of the action in this book, which takes place just before the Wall's destruction. The time and place make this a good book for a shared study of history and political science.

THE PLOT

Hannah's mother was shot and killed while trying to drive through the checkpoint from East to West Berlin. Hannah and her father must pretend that they are unmoved by her death, so that her father will not be arrested, and Hannah will not be put into a children's home.

Through Hannah, we live the life of one in a society where telling the truth can get you, and those near to you, killed. We see the pressure to lie about everything, especially at school, where the students must play by the rules, attend large pro-government parades, and join the Free German Youth in order to get a college education and a good job. We feel the constant sense of looking over your shoulder to

see who is watching and the constant presence of the secret police. This book is not pro-West Germany or capitalism. Hannah wants to stay in her country and make it a better place. She does not want to move to a country where there is homelessness and unemployment, but she also wants to be through with the lies, and with not being able to trust your best friend. More than anything, she wants to be able to tell the truth about her mother's death. Hannah is involved in the increasingly frequent demonstrations for peace and witnesses firsthand the violent attacks by the government of the demonstators. Eight months after her mother's shooting, when she hears the news that the borders will be opened at midnight, we share first her disbelief and then her joy.

TAKING IT DEEPER

Collect and display newspaper and magazine articles about the fall of the Berlin Wall.

Find articles and books about the building of the Wall and the U.S.'s involvement in it. Some say that the Wall prevented World War

III. What did it accomplish? Why did it come down?

Collect information about what was happening in other countries during the time period of this book.

What has happened to West and East Germany since the fall of the Berlin Wall? Was it advantageous for both parts of Germany?

Find recent interviews of East and West Germans. Which of them come close to expressing feelings that you think Hannah might be feeling now?

How important is the truth in your life? In what ways does lying affect you and those around you? What type of dishonesty would be most difficult for you if you were forced to endure it?

In what ways is honesty encouraged in our country? In what ways is honesty discouraged? What types of lying are sanctioned in our culture?

Keep a liar's diary for a few days, recording your own lies and those you suspect on the part of others.

▶ RELATED BOOKS

▶ Novels

★ ★ ★ ★ Avi **Nothing But the Truth** Orchard, 1991 ISBN 0 786 20131 2

This is also a focus book (see page 142).

★ ★ Degens, T. **Freya on the Wall** Browndeer, 1997 ISBN 0 152 00210 3

Although not as fast-paced as *The Wall*, this book is set in the same time and place and provides another look at the factors that caused the Wall to come down.

▶ Nonfiction

★ Cipkowski, Peter **Revolution in Eastern Europe** John Wiley, 1991 ISBN 0 471 53968 6

Here are the facts about the rise and fall of communism in Poland, Hungary, East Germany, Czechoslovakia, Romania, and the Soviet Union.

★ Symynkywicz, Jeffrey B. **Germany: United Again** Dillon, 1995 ISBN 0 382 39190 X

Illustrated with news photos, this book outlines the events that led to the taking down of the Wall, and provides a useful time line.

CHAPTER 18

Goodnight, Mr. Tom

★ ★ ★

by Michelle Magorian
HarperCollins, 1986
ISBN 0 06 440174 X

COMMENTS

Besides being an absorbing novel in which the characterization is very good indeed, this historical novel is set in wartime London, but has more to do with internal than external warfare. It is also about child abuse, which we tend to think of as only a current problem. The book is long and, therefore, daunting to some less skilled readers, but most will find it's well worth the effort.

THE PLOT

During the bombing of London during World War II, many children were sent by parents and authorities into the countryside, where it was thought they would be safer. William Beech is one such child, brought with a group of children to find homes in a remote Welsh village. The woman in charge walks the children down the street of the village stopping at every house until all but William have been taken in. The last house is the home of Tom Oakley, a bitter, gruff, and isolated man. Tom's wife and child are dead, and his grief has overwhelmed him.

Against his better judgment, Tom takes Will into his home. As the child undresses that night, Tom sees the signs of terrible abuse on his body. Together the child and man heal each other. It takes as long for Tom to let go of his grief for his wife and child as it does for Will to feel strong and free. Both are beginning to feel real love for the first time when Will's mother forces him to return to London. Will is hopeful that the abuse is over and that things will be different between them, but her madness and abuse are worse than ever. By the time Tom finds him, Will's new baby sister is dead, and Will is not far from death himself. Tom kidnaps Will, thus bringing the authorities down on him and forcing him to turn to others for help. In spite of the child abuse and the casualties of war, this is not a mournful book but a celebration of love and life.

TAKING IT DEEPER

In this book, the two main characters change a great deal. Look for small details that show signs of these changes.

Will's friend, Zacharias, is almost diametrically different from Will. Find graphic ways of showing those differences and the causes for them.

Make a montage of images from magazines and other sources to show the personalities and backgrounds of one of the characters in the book.

How do you feel about the fact that religious fanaticism is used as one of the reasons for Mrs. Beech's behavior?

The author uses flashbacks in this book. Find the places where this is so and decide why you think Magorian used flashback.

This whole book takes place in Britain, yet many of the characters have trouble understanding the other's language. Why is this so?

Investigate some of the reasons for child abuse. What social agencies will really help kids who are victims of it? How easy is it to get in touch with those agencies?

During World War II, the King and Queen of England did not send their children into the countryside to escape the bombing. Find out why they made that decision and what effect it had.

▶ RELATED BOOKS

▶ Novels

★ ★ ★ ★ Coman, Carolyn **What Jamie Saw** Puffin, 1997 ISBN 0 140 38335 2

This is a brief, very accessible and chilling book about child abuse. Such is the author's skill that we are captured from the first sentence and live with Jamie and his mother as they escape the abusive situation they were in and start a new life. The violence comes from Jamie's stepfather, Van. Although we see only one explosion of his violence, we are aware that it is not an isolated instance. Van hurls the baby through the air in the first paragraph of the book. Mercifully, Jamie's mother catches the baby and that is the end of their relationship, but now the family must heal.

★ De Vries, Anice **Bruises** Front Street, 1996 ISBN 1 886 91003 0

In this novel set in the Netherlands, isolated and mysterious Judith is befriended by Michael, who discovers that her strange behavior is caused by her abusive mother.

★ ★ Neufeld, John **Almost a Hero** Atheneum, 1995 ISBN 0 689 31971 1

Assigned to work in a day-care center for homeless children during spring break, 12-year-old Ben finds one child being abused, and he and his friends undertake a rescue of the child. In the process, Ben learns about homelessness, privacy, and social action.

★ ★ Ross, Ramon Roval **Harper & Moon** Atheneum, 1993 ISBN 0 689 31803 0

This raw and exciting novel also is set in World War II and also is about an abused child. The scene, however, is Washington State. The abused child is Moon, inarticulate and half-wild, who is rescued twice by Harper, his 12-year-old friend.

★ ★ ★ Voigt, Cynthia **When She Hollers** Scholastic, 1994 ISBN 0 590 46714 X

Voigt takes us through one day in the life of a sexually abused teenager as she faces her stepfather with a knife over the breakfast table, somehow gets through the day at school (although she breaks down during gym class), and finally tells a lawyer about it all.

★ ★ Wild, Margaret **Beast** Apple, 1997 ISBN 0 590 47159 7

In this brief novel, we see a child attempting to use ritualistic behavior to control fear Bullied and tormented during the day by a classmate, 11-year-old Jamie is equally terrified at night by a beast only he can see.

★ ★ Wynne-Jones, Tim **The Maestro** Orchard, 1996 ISBN 0 531 08894 4

This is a survival story with many twists. Fourteen-year-old Burl comes upon the remote home of the Maestro while running away from his abusive father. The Maestro, a gifted musician, gives Burl shelter and a great deal more, while Burl grows strong enough to confront his father.

▶ Nonfiction

★ ★ Hyde, Margaret O. **Know About Abuse** Walker, 1992 ISBN 0 802 78176 4

This very accessible and remarkably comprehensive book deals with many kinds of abuse and the many reasons for it. Hyde also gives specific advice on where and how to seek help.

★ Landau, Elaine **Child Abuse: An American Epidemic** Messner, 1990 ISBN 0 671 68875 8

This is a brief explanation of some of the causes of child abuse and a list of organizations that can help.

CHAPTER 19

Letters from Inside

★ ★ ★ ★

by Marsden, John
Houghton, 1994
ISBN 0 395 68985 6

COMMENTS

This book is raw. The language is sometimes graphic, and there are some allusions to sex. Also, because the author is Australian, some of the language is difficult to translate into American idiom, but that doesn't stop the reader from becoming immersed in the lives of these two young people. It should appeal to young adult readers in the same way that **Go Ask Alice** did or does. The bleak story is compelling and should lead to some good discussions about family life, and crime and its results, as well as the effect of violent behavior on society.

THE PLOT

This book is written as a series of letters between two girls who've answered a magazine ad for a pen pal. Soon, Mandy learns that Tracey is in a maximum security prison for young girls, and Tracey is told that Mandy has a "weird" and violent brother. Neither Mandy nor the reader ever finds out what Tracey has done, only that it was bad and that she feels she deserves her sentence. We also learn that when she is released, at 18, from her present prison, it will be to go across the road to the adult women's facility for two more years. As the letters proceed, the friendship deepens and each girl becomes the other's best friend.

For Tracey, Mandy is the only bright spot in her awful existence. However, Mandy's brother continues with his violent behavior, and has amassed some weapons. Eventually, his behavior gets so bizarre that even her job-involved parents have to admit that something is very wrong. In the meantime, Tracey's depression has deepened, and as Mandy's letters cease, Tracey loses it almost completely. The last letter is a hopeless one from Tracey, and we become aware that something very terrible has happened to Mandy. The author leaves us there.

TAKING IT DEEPER

Whose life is worse, Tracey's or Mandy's?

Why do you think the author chose letters as the vehicle to tell the story? Would you have done the same? What effect does this device have on the reader? How does the author make you care what happens next? Would the ending have been more powerful if he had resolved things more neatly?

Find other books with enigmatic endings like this one, such as *The Giver* (see page 180).

What do you hope for Mandy and Tracey?

Investigate crimes in your area committed by young people. How many convictions per indictment? How many prison sentences served? What's the average length of jail time for various crimes?

Given that research, what crime do you think Tracey committed?

What does the book tell you about life behind bars for young people? Does your research bear this out?

◤ RELATED BOOKS

▶ Novels

★ ★ ★ Alcock, Vivien **A Kind of Thief** Dell, 1991 ISBN 0 440 40916 0

Although this book's title and cover accent its mystery, there is more emphasis on family loyalty than on mystery here. Elinor and her brother and sister are confronted with their father's recent arrest for embezzlement or some related crime, their young stepmother's desertion, and Elinor's subsequent acquisition of her father's briefcase. Soon, the children are split up among unwilling relatives, and Elinor winds up with her timid Aunt Agnes, Agnes's cranky mother, Mrs. Carter, and their foster child, Timon. Soon, Elinor's loyalties are torn, as she learns that Mrs. Carter was one of the people from whom her father stole money.

★ ★ ★ Gilstrap, John **Nathan's Run** HarperCollins, 1996 ISBN 0 06 017385 8

We know from the beginning that 12-year-old Nathan Bailey killed a guard at—and escaped from—the juvenile detention center in which he was being held. The police know it, too, and Warren Michaels is in charge of the investigation. We, however, are privy to one more fact: the guard had been trying to kill Nathan and his murder was self-defense. For a long time, we don't know why Nathan was the intended victim, but we are on his side as Nathan takes flight. Soon, many others are swayed to Nathan's defense as he calls a radio talk show and tells his side. Excitement grows as a hit man takes on the task of finding and killing Nathan, and there are more killings, but Nathan eludes both the police and the hit man in a story slightly reminiscent of *The Fugitive*. Although this is the author's first book, he manages to make it all believable and suspenseful. Like many of the radio listeners, we cheer for Nathan. Some of the language will upset some people, although the profanity is not profuse.

★ ★ ★ Lowry, Lois **Anastasia at This Address** Houghton, 1991 ISBN 0 395 56263 5

Anastasia answers an ad in the personals column and neglects to tell her new adult pen pal that she is a child in seventh grade. She puts her mother's photo in the letter, and when Septimus Smith appears on her doorstep announcing that he has been corresponding with the woman in the photo, Anastasia has some fast talking to do.

▶ Nonfiction

★ Wormser, Richard **Lifers: Learn the Truth at the Expense of Our Sorrow** Messner, 1991 ISBN 0 671 72548 3

This book is a follow-up to the film *Scared Straight*. Prisoners tell their stories as warnings to the teenage population.

I Will Call It Georgie's Blues

★ ★ ★ ★

by Suzanne Newton
Puffin, 1990
ISBN 0 14 034536 1

➤ COMMENTS

This novel explores the differences between perception and reality, as well as the clash of parental authority against teenage rebellion. Other themes in the book include the power of music to heal and to inspire, religious hypocrisy, and the strength of family feelings.

➤ THE PLOT

To all outward appearances, the Richard Sloan family is ideal. The father is the minister of the local Baptist church. His wife, much younger than he, always appears cheerful and contented and their three children (Aileen, Neal, and Georgie) are well behaved and respectable. In the privacy of their home, however, we see a tyrannical father who has browbeaten his wife into submission, and is attempting to do the same with his children. Aileen stands a good chance of flunking school, and is involved with a less than desirable young man. Georgie, the youngest, teeters on the brink of sanity, and Neal, the middle child, is afraid to tell his father that he has been taking piano lessons

and is quite good at it. When Reverend Sloan discovers that his job is in jeopardy, he completely loses control, venting his rage on the most vulnerable link in the family—Georgie. It is Neal who later finds Georgie in a catatonic state and demands help for him. It is also Neal who plays out his heart in a composition of his own for the piano.

➤ TAKING IT DEEPER

Find out about some jazz musicians. Find a jazz recording that you think might reflect Neal's feelings at the end of the story.

Define child abuse. Should what Neal's father does be considered child abuse? How about his mother's actions? Where do you believe the line should be drawn and why?

What services are available in your town for people in Neal's situation?

Neal feels responsible for his part in not being there for Georgie. How much responsibility do you think we have for our younger brothers and sistersHow much responsibility do you take?

Where do we draw the line for what is an adult problem, and how do teens fit in, being neither adults nor children?

Where did Neal's mother and father fail in taking on the responsibilty of the adults in the family?

Neal says that in a normal family you shouldn't be afraid of your parents all the time. How else would you define a healthy family?

Much of the book is about facades and about hiding who we really are. Why do we have a tendency to hide ourselves from others? What are we afraid of?

Compare Neal's feeling about his music with those of Sib in **Midnight Hour Encores** (see below).

▶ RELATED BOOKS

(For other books about music, see the theme on Music on page 68.)

▶ Picture Books

★ ★ ★ Raschka, Chris **Charlie Parker Played Bebop** Orchard, 1992 ISBN 0 531 08599 6

This is a picture book tribute to jazz musician Charlie Parker.

▶ Novels

★ ★ ★ ★ Brooks, Bruce **Midnight Hour Encores** HarperCollins, 1986 ISBN 0 06 020710 8

Sib, a superb young cellist, takes a cross-country trip with her father to make the acquaintance of her mother, and to accept a music scholarship in California. Sib's feelings about her music and her ability to compose it are similar to those of Neal.

★ ★ ★ MacKinnon, Bernie **Song for a Shadow** Houghton, 1991 ISBN 0 395 55419 5

Although the music in this book is rock rather than jazz, Aaron's feeling for it is similar to that of Neal. The father is also important in this book, although it is his absence rather than his presence that propels the story.

★ ★ ★ MacLachlan, Patricia **The Facts and Fictions of Minna Pratt** HarperCollins, 1988 ISBN 0 06 024114 4

Minna's search is for the perfect vibrato on her cello, and the competition she enters with her music chamber group interferes with her first romance.

★ Thesman, Jean **Cattail Moon** Houghton, 1994 ISBN 0 395 67409 3

This ghost story also revolves around music and the idea that music is the bridge between Julia, a present-day teenager, and the ghost of a woman who left her home to pursue a music career.

▶ Nonfiction

★ ★ Monceaux, Morgan **Jazz: My Music, My People** Knopf, 1994 ISBN 0 679 85618 8

Poster-like illustrations are used with one-page bios of the people who developed and performed jazz music.

CHAPTER 21

Lyddie

by Katherine Paterson
Puffin, 1994
ISBN 0 140 34001 2

COMMENTS

Paterson has created her usual cast of believable characters, with whom we identify, while also giving us a strong historical context for the novel. The novel's setting of the mills in mid-19th-century Lowell, Massachusetts, can be part of a historical study of the time. It can also be an introduction to the Industrial Revolution or to the development of labor unions.

THE PLOT

Lyddie Worthen, an impoverished Vermont farm girl, is determined to gain both her independence and the money to pay off the debts on her family's farm. Three years ago, her father left to earn money and has not been heard from since. Her mother, crazed by her obsession with an End-of-the-World religion, rents the farm and hires out Charlie, age 10, and Lyddie, 13, into a kind of bondage. Charlie, accepted into his new family, does well. Later, Rachel, the third sibling, joins him. Hired out to Cutler's Tavern, Lyddie is befriended by the cook,

Triphena. It is here, after observing the apparently successful life of a young woman factory worker who stopped at the tavern, that Lyddie decides to go to the mills at Lowell, Massachusetts. There, she lives in company-owned housing, and lives the arduous life of a mill girl. The workers are exploited by the mill owners, and those who agitate are dealt with harshly. Illness is a major concern. Lyddie becomes friends with Diana Goss, Betsy, and Brigid. Fired for her association with dissidents, Lyddie decides to go to Oberlin College for an education, rejecting a marriage offer for now.

TAKING IT DEEPER

At the beginning of the book, when the Worthens have lost their farm in Vermont, Lyddie and her brother have been more or less sold off by their mother, and their father has gone west, Lyddie promises Charlie that they'll be back. It's a promise she clings to and saves for throughout the book. She does not really keep her promise, however. What things intervene to keep Lyddie and Charlie from having a home together again?

Their equally unschooled mother has written, "We can still hop," a misspelling of "hope." Later, when Triphena, the cook at the tavern, says, "Some folks are natural born kickers. They can always find a way to turn disaster into butter," Lyddie repeats, "We can still hop." That writing becomes a recurring thought for Lyddie and Charlie. Is that the theme of the book? Which of the characters are hopers?

Lyddie's quest is clear and unwavering throughout the story—she wants to get the family's farm back. Triphena aids her at the beginning of her quest. Does Lyddie achieve her quest? What does she achieve? Who besides Triphena aids or hinders her quest? What other characters in the book are on quests, and how close do they get to their goals during the story? (See page 116 for other activities concerning quests.)

Make copies of Lyddie's correspondence and watch her spelling, grammar, and use of words improve. What's causing the improvement?

Their kindly neighbors, the Stevens, are Quakers. What do you know about that sect that will help you understand the Stevens family's actions?

Lyddie's discovery of the runaway slave Ezekial Abernathy in her abandoned house is her first contact with a black person. Why did he have to hide even in Massachusetts? What were the slave laws at the time? He makes Lyddie rethink her own position. Is she a slave? Was her mother? Why does she give him the calf money?

Reference is made to the fact that the railroads are bringing cheaper wool to the mills from the West, eliminating most of the sheep raising in New England at the time.

Railroads had other effects, including the cessation of the canals in the area. Research New England canals of the 19th century.

Lyddie's experiences with the protest movements at the mill give us a glimpse of the beginning of labor organization in the mills. Find out about the history of the mills of Lowell and the growth of labor unions in them.

Some Web addresses which deal with the mills of Lowell, Massachusetts, are: **http://www.nps.gov/lowe/default.htm**. This is the Web site for the Lowell National Historic Park, which interprets the history of the American Industrial Revolution in Lowell. There are slides and a good deal of textual information. **http://www.bc.edu/bc_org/avp/cas/fnart/fa267/19_mill.html**, which has photographs of the Boott Mill Complex at Lowell, and **http://www.vetc.vsc.edu/shs/lowell.html**, which offers photographs and other information about the Lowell mills.

▷ RELATED BOOKS

▶ Picture Books

★ ★ ★ ★ Cherry, Lynne **A River Ran Wild: An Environmental History** Harcourt, 1992 ISBN 0 15 200542 0

This traces the history of the Nashua River from wild and unexplored wilderness to the time of development of the mills in Lowell.

▶ Novels

★ ★ ★ ★ Bos, Joan W. **A Gathering of Days** Aladdin, 1990 ISBN 0 689 71419 X

Set in about the same time as *Lyddie*, and in the state next to the one in which *Lyddie* is set, this novel is written in the form of a diary. Slavery also comes into play in this book.

★ ★ ★ Rinaldi, Ann **The Blue Door** Scholastic, 1996 ISBN 0 590 46051 X

In this third volume of Rinaldi's quilt trilogy, Amanda is sent by her grandmother in South Carolina to work in the Lowell mills. She does this in the hope that she and her great-grandfather will mend their estranged relationship, and that he will use the cotton from her plantation in his mill.

★ ★ Skurzynski, Gloria **Good-Bye, Billy Radish** Simon & Schuster, 1992 ISBN 0 02 782921 9

Hank and Billy Radichevych (Radish) live in Duquesne, Pennsylvania, during the time of World War I. As with many immigrants, adults and children as young as 14 work in the mills.

★ ★ ★ Walsh, Jill Paton **A Chance Child** Sunburst, 1991 ISBN 0 374 41174 3

This is a time-travel fantasy set in London, England, during both the present and the Industrial Revolution. More than most time fantasies, this one gets into the social and political issues of the past. Creep, an abused child of the present, follows a canal to the period of the Industrial Revolution in England. There, his abuse continues as he assumes the role of child laborer and gradually forgets the present. His half-brother, concerned about Creep's disappearance, searches early 19th-century documents to find evidence of Creep's life and death.

► **Nonfiction**

★ Colman, Penny **Strike: The Bitter Struggle of American Workers from Colonial Times to the Present** Millbrook, 1995 ISBN 1 562 94459 2

This book is, as its title suggests, a comprehensive look at labor unions and their struggle to improve the lot of the working people.

★ ★ ★ Fritz, Jean **Harriet Beecher Stowe & the Beecher Preachers** Putnam, 1994 ISBN 0 399 22666 4

The Beecher family lived in Massachusetts not far from the mills in *Lyddie*. Their lives were, by comparison, privileged, but the strong women in the family also have much in common with Lyddie.

★ Kraft, Betsy Harvey **Mother Jones: One Woman's Fight for Labor** Clarion, 1995 ISBN 0 395 67163 9

This story explains the life and actions of Mary Harris Jones, who energized the American labor movement.

★ ★ ★ Macaulay, David **Mill** Houghton, 1983 ISBN 0 395 34830 7

The mill that Macaulay builds for us in great detail is a forerunner of the mills of Lowell. We see how the various machines work at a much simpler level.

★ Sherrow, Victoria **The Triangle Factory Fire** Millbrook, 1995 ISBN 1 562 94572 6

Although this tragic fire took place 60 years after the setting of *Lyddie*, the conditions she experienced in the mills had not improved, and were the cause of many of the fire's fatalities.

Strays Like Us

★ ★ ★

by Richard Peck
Dial, 1998
ISBN 0 8037 2291 5

⊳ COMMENTS

We chose this book because it's easily accessible but very well written. While it is a school story, it also has a lot to do with home and family. The school part deals with bullies, friendships, teachers, and even a home-school arsonist. The family part deals with errant parents, drug addiction, AIDS, neighbors, and belonging. Two characters never appear, although they are frequently referred to. There are wonderful characters, such as Aunt Fay and Mrs. Voorhees, and there's the question of secrets kept for years that have a decided effect on the story.

⊳ THE PLOT

Molly has been dumped with her great-Aunt Fay. Her mother has left her many times before, but always turns up sooner or later. We get hints of what life with her mother, whom she calls Debbie, must have been like: homeless shelters and soup kitchens, and never belonging anywhere. Molly doesn't try to make friends because she won't be anywhere long enough.

Will lives next door, and he, too, is a stray. He's been dumped with his grandmother, and we get hints that his father is in jail, but there's something mysterious about that household. It's Will who reaches out to Molly, asking her to walk with him to junior high the first day. At least they'll know each other.

Aunt Fay is a practical nurse and treats patients in their homes. One of her patients is the spoiled and self-centered Mrs. Voorhees. Fay takes Molly to Mrs. Vorhees' home, and Molly and Mrs. Voorhees treat each other warily. Aunt Fay also spends a lot of time next door because of Will's father. We don't find out until much later in the book that he's in the house and dying of AIDS. Gradually, Molly abandons her feeling of being "just temporary," and she and Aunt Fay show previously unexpressed love for each other.

Molly meets Tracy Pringle, an almost perfect girl her own age who lives in a beautiful house and is being home schooled. Tracy's mother puts an end to that slight friendship when she finds out where Molly lives. Later, we find out that it is Tracy who set fire to the school.

Debbie, Molly's mom, doesn't return, and Molly finds out several of the above-mentioned secrets before the year is up. She's come to grips with her lot in life and discovered a grandmother who was there all the time.

▶ TAKING IT DEEPER

Although Peck writes simply, there are some loaded lines in this book. For instance:

"I hung on the edges of school and watched, learning the names of people who didn't know mine."

Aunt Fay's reply to Molly's question, "Can I stay here with you?", "There's a lot I can't do for you, but you're home."

Write about either of those lines or any others in the book that reflect your own experiences or feelings.

Molly says the white poinsettia on Mrs. Voorhees' table didn't look real, "but then maybe Christmas isn't supposed to be." She also reflects on Will's line in his song, "Is this what Christmas is?" What role does Christmas play in the plot? What changes occur?

Molly's fight with Rocky Roberts surprises them both and changes their relationship, although it doesn't seem to change Rocky. Why does Molly refer to him as another stray?

Some characters in this book change in the course of a year. Other characters remain constant. Find a graphic way of showing this.

Tracy Pringle is shown as a perfect child with an enviable life. Why do you think she breaks down?

Mrs. Pringle is a minor character with only two scenes, but both of those scenes tell you a lot about her. What is her motivation? What does she think is important? What do you think will happen to Tracy?

Mrs. Voorhees is a silly character when we meet her, but by the end of the story, Peck makes us see her as a sympathetic one. How does he do that?

There's a good example of a cliff hanger in this book. At the end of Chapter 5, Molly comes into the dark kitchen and sees the shadowy figure at the table. What does this do to the reader? Find other examples of cliff hangers in other books (see page 133).

There's also a clearly identifiable use of foreshadowing at the end of Chapter 12: "It was the last time she ever wrote on that blackboard." What does that do to the reader? Find other uses of foreshadowing in books (see page 131).

Peck has Mrs. Lovett, a sympathetic teacher, display three poems. Why do you think he does that? What do those poems mean to you?

There are some nice subtleties in this book. For instance, Molly begins to worry about Aunt Fay only when her aunt is out driving on an icy night, after Molly has given up hope that Debbie will return. What other such subtleties can you find?

At one point, Molly compares Mrs. Voorhees to an artificial Christmas tree. Find comparisons for the other characters in the book.

The gift of the gold chain from Mrs. Voorhees—"the plainest thing in the box, and the best"—takes on added significance later in the story. What other things come to have greater meaning as you read further?

There are some repeated statements in the book. Peck uses them at the beginning of the story and repeats them near the end. Aunt Fay puts her hand on Will's shoulder when he's telling Molly about his father. Molly says, "It always meant something when she did that. She didn't touch you for nothing." Find the place where it's repeated.

Another repeated line is Will's. Twice he says, "Listen, you want to walk to school together tomorrow? That way we'll both know two people." The circumstances are very different each time he says it. Find out how and why.

A third repetition is that of the "pod people." It's applied first to Will and Molly. The second time it's used, it means the tent caterpillars. How does that change reflect changes in Will and Molly?

Also, Will offers to sing "Achy Breaky Heart" twice. His feelings and the circumstances are different each time. Why do you think Peck uses it twice?

The notebook is used as a symbol in this book. What does it mean to you?

Although Molly has been through a tough year, she cries only once. When and why is that?

The last chapter is told in the present tense. What effect does that have?

Will takes himself off the team at school because his teammates are afraid of catching AIDS from him. How contagious is AIDS? How is it transmitted? How much danger are those kids in? Make posters about AIDS.

How do you feel about home schooling? Mrs. Pringle's reasons for doing it are not shared by all home schoolers. Do some research on the subject. How many home schoolers are there in your community? How do they interact with the community?

▶ RELATED BOOKS

▶ Picture Book

★ ★ Newman, Leslea **Too Far Away to Touch** Clarion, 1995 ISBN 0 395 68968 6

A little girl and her uncle have a close relationship, enjoying many things together, including a trip to the planetarium, where they see stars too far away to touch. The homosexuality of the uncle is touched upon with the introduction of his close friend, Nathan. We also learn that the uncle has AIDS, and he discusses this openly with his niece.

▶ Novels

★ ★ ★ ★ Avi **Nothing But the Truth** Orchard, 1991 ISBN 0 786 20131 2

This is an excellent novel with a school setting. It's also a focus book (see page 142).

★ ★ ★ ★ Cormier, Robert **The Chocolate War** Pantheon, 1974 ISBN 0 440 94459 7

The bullies in this novel are fully supported by the teachers. Indeed, Brother Leon, the assistant headmaster, uses the bullies to accomplish his goals. They beat Jerry, a newcomer, nearly to death over his refusal to sell chocolates.

★ ★ ★ ★ Fenner, Carol **Randall's Wall** Bantam, 1991 ISBN 0 553 48021 9

Randall's wall is an imaginary one that surrounds him. Filthy, frightened, and isolated, Randall is referred to social services, whose interest in helping are half-hearted. His mother is apathetic and his father is violent. He is shunned by everyone at school except Jean, who, together with the one sympathetic teacher, manages to help Randall tear down his wall.

★ ★ ★ Fox, Paula **The Eagle Kite** Orchard, 1995 ISBN 0 531 08742 5

Liam's father, who lives apart from his mother, is dying of AIDS, and Liam has been told that he got it from a transfusion. Later, he remembers a time when he saw his father embracing another man on the beach. Liam goes through anger, denial, grief, and empathy through the long months of his father's illness.

★ ★ ★ ★ Morpurgo, Michael **The War of Jenkins' Ear** Philomel, 1995 ISBN 0 399 22735 0

Redlands is a private school with strict rules. A new boy, Christopher, refuses to submit to the unquestioning obedience demanded. His friend, Toby Jenkins, begins to realize that Christopher thinks he's Jesus Christ. Soon, a war erupts between the town kids and the Redlands boys at a river which divides the town.

★ ★ Nelson, Theresa **Earthshine** Dell, 1997 ISBN 0 440 21989 2

Both Slim and Isaiah have a parent who is afflicted with AIDS. Desperate to help, they join a support group for families of AIDS victims. Learning of a healer, Slim and Isaiah make a pilgrimage to obtain a cure. The quest fails, but the boys come to grips with themselves and their dying parents.

★ ★ ★ ★ Paterson, Katherine **Flip-Flop Girl** Penguin, 1994 ISBN 0 14 037679 8

Mason Matthews has been mute since his father's death. He and his sister, Vinnie, have moved with their mother into the house of their father's stepmother, a woman who seems distantly cheerful. Mason's refusal to talk is a cause for much embarrassment at school for Vinnie. Vinnie's friend, Lupe, is her only solace at school, but Vinnie is an outcast there.

★ ★ ★ Voigt, Cynthia **Bad Girls** Scholastic, 1996 ISBN 0 590 60134 2

Like Will and Molly, Mikey and Margalo are new at school. For a time, they become rivals, but, eventually, a friendship grows between them. Their teacher is usually one step ahead of them. We get only brief glimpses of their home life.

CHAPTER 23

Freak the Mighty

★ ★ ★ ★

by Rodman Philbrick
Scholastic, 1993
ISBN 0 590 47413 8

COMMENTS

This short novel packs a real wallop. Two of society's cast-offs join forces to become something bigger (literally) than either of them can be individually. There is plenty of action in this very accessible book, and many who find themselves walking to a different drummer will identify with these well-drawn characters.

THE PLOT

Kevin, a gifted child with a warped and crippled body, joins forces with Max, an awkward, large, learning-disabled boy with a violent temper and a violent past. When Kevin rides on Max's shoulders, they become Freak the Mighty. Kevin provides the fantasies, usually Arthurian, for them to act out and, for awhile, he is Max's brain. Max provides the pair with strength, speed, and locomotion. When Kevin demands that Max be taken out of his special needs classroom and placed with him, Max begins to think for himself and to discover his own abilities.

The whole story takes place in one year, beginning with the boys' meeting and ending with Kevin's death. Max is living with his grandparents because his father is in jail for murdering his mother. Kevin is living with his mother because his father abandoned them.

When Kevin's father returns, the boys use their powers, together with an unexpected burst of courage from a neighbor, to survive and conquer. Kevin has told Max that he will soon have an operation, which will make him a bionic robot, because his insides are outgrowing his body. Unfortunately, this too is a fantasy; Kevin's heart, as the doctor says, grows too big for his body, and Kevin dies.

TAKING IT DEEPER

Examine Kevin's dictionary. Some of the words are defined as a normal dictionary would define them, some are puns, and some reflect the action in the story. Can you figure out which is which? What words would appear in your personal dictionary? How would you define them?

What point in the story would you define as the climax? Take that point and make a diagram of the story, showing the events leading up to the climax that bring each of the characters involved to that moment.

Max says, at the beginning of the book, that this is the "unvanquished truth." The usual expression is the "unvarnished truth." Why does Max change it?

The relationship between Kevin and Max might be called "symbiotic." There are symbiotic relationships in the animal world. Find out about some of them.

Some friendships and even some marriages seem to function as a single unit, with each person contributing something to the pairing that makes them both stronger than they would be individually. Do you know any such pairings? Could such combinations make the individuals weaker rather than stronger? How?

Reread the part of the story where Freak gets the best of the bullies on the Fourth of July, then reread the part where Max's father comes. Are there any parallels here?

One reviewer called this book "choked with clichés and stereotypes." Another says, it's "A wonderful story of triumph over imperfection, shame, and loss." What's your review? Can you defend your decision?

Talk to teachers in the special education department of your school. Ask them to read the book and tell you what they think about Max.

Is there a disease or defect that would cause the symptoms Kevin has?

▶ RELATED BOOKS

▶ Novels

★ ★ ★ Deuker, Carl **Painting the Black** Houghton, 1997 ISBN 0 395 82848 1

Ryan and Josh Daniels form a symbiotic relationship as catcher and pitcher on the high school baseball team. Josh's athletic prowess is phenomenal, and he is fiercely competitive, amost ruthless. Ryan is less colorful, but their connection during the games makes them invincible. The symbolic title (hitting the black line between foul and fair) takes on more meaning as Josh's arrogance and vengeful personality take him over that line.

★ ★ ★ Johnston, Julie **Hero of Lesser Causes** Little, 1993 ISBN 0 316 46988 2

Patrick becomes almost totally paralyzed after contracting polio, and his sister, Keely, becomes his goad and companion, along with friends Ginny and Alex.

★ ★ Turner, Bonnie **Haunted Igloo** Houghton, 1991 ISBN 0 395 57037 9

Jean-Paul, a physically handicapped boy, suffers the taunts of the other children in Arctic northwestern Canada in the 1930s. Challenged to pass their test of bravery, he is nearly killed.

★ ★ Voigt, Cynthia **Izzy Willy-Nilly** Fawcett, 1986 ISBN

After an accident caused by her drunken date, Izzy suffers the amputation of her lower leg. Previously popular, she is now virtually abandoned by her so-called friends and turns to Rosamund, an awkward, unpopular classmate she had ignored.

★ ★ Werlin, Nancy **Are You Alone on Purpose?** Houghton, 1994 ISBN 0 395 67350 X

Harry and Alison have long been enemies. Alison's twin brother is autistic, and Harry has been merciless in tormenting him. Now, Harry has become a paraplegic. Alison ends up tutoring him, and the two form a friendship after realizing that they are both victims of their parents' expectations. Together, they let go of the isolation each has been using to cushion their world.

Words by Heart

★ ★ ★ ★

by Ouida Sebestyen
Bantam, 1983
ISBN 0 553 27179 2

 **COMMENTS**

This strong novel deals with violence and racism in Missouri in the 1920s. There is also an emphasis on the value of education. It can be used in a theme on racism and prejudice.

THE PLOT

Lena Sills' preacher father has brought his family to an all-white town in Missouri hoping to escape the hatred and violence of the South. Lena attends a one-room school, where they have a Bible verse contest every year. Everyone is sure that the same boy will win as always, but Lena knows the Bible and takes him on. Much to everyone's surprise but hers, she wins, but the prize is a bow tie. Lena's hopes for acceptance are dashed, but her father, one of the great heros of children's literature, strikes a bargain to help Lena continue her education. The violence that their presence occasions results in his death, but not before he has taught Lena a valuable lesson.

TAKING IT DEEPER

Although she is a minor character in the book, Claudie is an interesting one. Piece together what the book tells us about her to do a character study of Claudie.

Lena wants to please her father, but her impetuous nature sometimes disappoints him. Find examples of these disappointments.

The character of Mrs. Chism is a strange one. What does she want?

What does the Haney family want?

Winslow Starnes changes during the story. What are these changes and what caused them?

There are some wonderful images in this book. The baby lay on Claudie's lap "hanging over limply like an untrimmed piecrust," for instance. Find and share some other images you like.

Examine the role that religion plays in the lives of all these people, villains and heroes alike. Can deep religious views and racial hatred go hand in hand?

The teacher is usually a wise figure in

books. What sort of character is the teacher in this one?

Make a list of connected statements starting with "Because" and ending with "Lena's father was shot."

Why does Lena refuse to tell who killed her father? What would you have done?

What were the effects of Lena's father's death?

▶ RELATED BOOKS

▶ Picture Books

★ ★ ★ ★ Lionni, Leo **Little Blue and Little Yellow** Mulberry, 1959 ISBN 0 688 13285 5

This deceptively simple book has a lot of say about racism and prejudice.

★ ★ ★ Littlesugar, Amy **Jonkonnu** Philomel, 1997 ISBN 0 300 22831 4, illustrated by Ian Schoenherr

This picture book is based on fact and concerns the reaction of artist Winslow Homer when he was told he shouldn't visit the part of town where the ex-slaves lived in 1874.

▶ Novels

★ ★ ★ ★ Armstrong, William H. **Sounder** HarperCollins, 1969 ISBN 0 06 020143 6

This powerful novel about a sharecropper family and their dog shows the effects of brutality and racism.

★ ★ ★ ★ Cohen, Barbara **Thank You, Jackie Robinson** Lothrop, 1986 ISBN 0 688 07909 1

A white boy and an African-American man form a friendship based on their love of baseball. The story takes place in the 1940s, so segregation limits their activities.

★ ★ ★ Hill, Anthony **The Burnt Stick** Houghton, 1994 ISBN 0 395 73974 8

America is not the only nation where racism is rampant. This novel is set in Australia and deals with the treatment of Aborigine children.

★ ★ ★ Hooks, William H. **Circle of Fire** Simon & Schuster, 1982 ISBN 0 689 50241 9

Set in 1936 in North Carolina, this novel deals with the actions and reactions of the Ku Klux Klan and its effects on the people there.

★ ★ ★ ★ Krisher, Trudy **Spite Fences** Delacorte, 1994 ISBN 0 385 32088 4

The small town of Kinship, Georgia, changes forever for Maggie during the summer of 1960, when she is given a camera. It allows her to focus on the hatred and abuse that she sees white neighbors heap on black people.

★ ★ Nelson, Vaunda Micheaux **Mayfield Crossing** Putnam, 1993 ISBN 0 399 22331 2

This novel deals with the forced busing of the 1960s and its effects on the children who were transported to schools in which they became minorities and threatened the previous population.

★ ★ ★ Taylor, Mildred D. **The Gold Cadillac** Dial, 1987 ISBN 0 8037 0342 2

This brief book is based on the author's memory of a trip her family took to Mississippi in the 1950s, when segregation still ruled.

★ ★ ★ ★ Taylor, Mildred D. **Roll of Thunder, Hear My Cry** Bantam, 1984 ISBN 0 8037 7473 7

Set in 1927, this story is the first in a series of novels about the Logan family. Lynchings and other racial violence that black sharecroppers and farmers dealt with is the crux of the book.

▶ Nonfiction

★ ★ ★ Beals, Melba Patillo **Warriors Don't Cry** Archway, 1995 ISBN 0 671 89900 7

This narrative is based on the diaries of one of the black students who entered Little Rock's Central High School in 1957 and changed segregation forever.

Wringer

by Jerry Spinelli
HarperCollins, 1997
ISBN 0 06 0249137

COMMENTS

We chose this book because, on one level, it deals with peer pressure and its effects. Some have called it a fable. On a surface level, it deals with pets, giving it yet another hook for middle school readers. Although the boy in this novel is just approaching his 10th birthday, the novel itself is probably best understood by kids from fifth grade up. The idea that the adults in the town are participating in a barbaric rite into which they bring young boys is the crux of the novel, and should lead students into discussions about other such rites in their own worlds. Like all Spinelli novels, this one is accessible and should appeal to boys at least as much as to girls. Large questions are addressed here, such as what to do when society (in this case one town) mandates behavior that we think is wrong, and how to deal with bullies and peer pressure. It deals with violence as condoned by society, and the choices we make in life. The dynamics of Palmer's peer group also make for good discussion. The need for face-saving, the need to torment someone perceived as weaker, and the effect of passive resistance are also part of the action.

THE PLOT

In this town, the residents kill pigeons, and the killing of the pigeons has become a yearly rite in which the whole community participates. On the green, as the pigeons are released from the cages where they have been kept since their capture, the townsmen shoot them. To the 10-year-old boys goes the honor of rushing out onto the green after the shooting, to wring the necks of any birds that are wounded but not yet dead.

Gaining acceptance by his peers has not been easy for Palmer. The neighborhood bully, Beans, has been particularly difficult. Palmer has even stooped to harassing his one-time-only friend, Dorothy—who handles his harassment by rising above it—and Palmer has earned a nickname: Snots.

Palmer is already dreading the day when he takes his place on the field as a wringer, when a pigeon appears at his window and demands entrance. Knowing that his friends will completely reject him if they know he has befriended a pigeon, Palmer names the bird Nipper and hides his attachment to it. It's the much-maligned Dorothy who helps him get Nipper out of town, but leaves him where he can be captured for the shoot. Spinelli tells his grim tale with a solid understanding of the rites of childhood and with flashes of humor to lighten the reader's load.

▶ TAKING IT DEEPER

Palmer has been thinking for years about the day when he must wring the pigeons' necks. Find evidence of this in the novel.

Make a list of the alternatives Palmer has regarding the pigeon shoot. Then, prioritize the alternatives in terms of feasibility and results. What would you do?

Palmer feels pressure from many people in this book. Make a list of these people and the behavior they expect from Palmer. Which of them have the greatest effect on what Palmer eventually does?

Is Palmer a hero in the sense of being a heroic character? What makes a hero anyway? Who do you know or know of that fits that name?

Among many other pressures on Palmer is the bullying by Beans. How does Palmer handle it? What are other ways that you have read about, thought about, or done that would help in dealing with bullies?

What do Palmer's parents know?

On the jacket flap, the book has a subtitle: "Not All Birthdays Are Welcome." In effect, Palmer is terrified of growing up. Make two lists of your own feelings about becoming an adult: good and bad.

On a piece of paper, place the name of each child in the book in a separate circle. Draw lines to other characters to which that character has some connection in the story. Along the line, write the events that brought the two characters together. Color the strongest characters differently than the others. Compare your paper to those of others in the class.

What price does Palmer pay for his actions?

The pigeon shows up at the bedroom window of the one boy in town who is thinking of rebelling against the custom of wringing the necks of pigeons. How likely is that? It's an almost magical event. Why do you think Spinelli uses it?

Although there are moments that tear your heart out in this book, and other moments that are almost unbearably brutal, there are also some very funny scenes. Find and read one aloud.

What's the difference between what the people in Palmer's town do and any organized hunt? What about the buffalo hunt on the Yellowstone boundary each year? Is that different?

Although the shooting ceremony described in this book is probably unique, there are many places where birds have become pests in a community and various steps have been taken to control them. Find out about those situations and their resulting effects.

Find out about pigeons. Where do they come from? Why do they hang around urban areas? Where do they fit in the food chain? Who are their enemies?

Find out about racing pigeons. Can any pigeon be trained to race?

RELATED BOOKS

▶ Picture Books

★ ★ ★ Baker, Jeannie **Home in the Sky** Greenwillow, 1984 ISBN 0 688 03841 7

Mike tends pigeons in a coop on the roof of the building, and we see what happens to one of his charges, Light, as he wanders through the city.

★ ★ ★ ★ Macaulay, David **Rome Antics** Houghton, 1997 ISBN 0 395 82279 3

Macaulay plays in and around the buildings and monuments of Rome in this pigeon's-eye view of it all.

▶ Novels

★ ★ ★ Anderson, Janet S. **Going through the Gate** Dutton, 1997 ISBN 0 525 45836 0

Although this book also involves a rite of passage, it is a far less violent one than Palmer faces. These are five sixth graders in a one-room school, who are led through the gate at the back of the school to be transformed into one of the animals they have been studying all year.

★ ★ ★ ★ Cormier, Robert **The Chocolate War** Pantheon, 1974 ISBN 0 440 94459 7

In this story, it's not a whole town, but a private school in which violence is condoned and encouraged, at least by Brother Leon, the assistant headmaster. It also revolves around one child, Jerry, who refuses to play by Brother Leon's rules.

★ ★ ★ ★ Dorris, Michael **Sees Behind Trees** Hyperion, 1996 ISBN 0 7868 0224 3

This is also a rite of passage book. The skills needed for those rites are not possible for a visually challenged boy in this story. This is a focus book (see page 163).

★ ★ ★ ★ Hahn, Mary Downing **Stepping on the Cracks** Clarion, 1991 ISBN 0 395 58507 4

Like Palmer, Margaret and Elizabeth face torment by a bully. They are next door neighbors and best friends, although they have vastly different personalities. Both girls have brothers who are in the service, and they, like the rest of their families, are worried about them. At the beginning of the book, each girl is convinced that the war is necessary and a little bit glamorous. When they are confronted with a sick deserter, a neighbor, hiding out in the woods, they are at first horrified and convinced he is a traitor. He's the brother of the bully who has been bothering them. Soon, their sympathy for anyone who is sick outweighs their distaste, and they end up getting help for the man and, in the process, become aware that there are some people whose ethics are violated by any kind of warfare, no matter how just the cause may seem.

★ ★ ★ Kinsey-Warnock, Natalie **The Night the Bells Rang** Cobblehill, 1991 ISBN 0 525 65074 1

This story is also set in a small town and concerns a bully. The town is in northern Vermont, and the time is 1918. Mason lives on a farm with his younger brother and parents, and much of the book describes such rural pastimes as sugar on snow and cider-making, but the heart of the book lies in the perceptions Mason has toward Aden Cutler, a school bully. It's Mason who bears the brunt of that bullying, and often bullies his own brother, in anger at his helplessness. He frequently wishes Aden dead. It is also Mason, however, who is sole witness to and recipient of an act of bravery and kindness on the part of Aden. When every bell in town rings out for the end of the war, it is Mason who approaches Aden's mother who stands alone grieving for her son, who was killed in battle. Knowing that no one in the celebrating town thought kindly of her son, Mason tells her what Aden did for him.

★ ★ ★ ★ Peck, Robert Newton **A Day No Pigs Would Die** Random, 1994 ISBN 0 679 85306 5

Like Palmer, in *Wringer*, our narrator in this book must confront the death of a beloved pet. This brief novel is tender at times, yet harsh at others. It deals with the abrupt end of a childhood (supposedly the author's) when the realities of farm life mean that he must kill his pet pig. There is fine characterization here, and the Yankee values of the thirties in Vermont come to the fore.

★ ★ Turnbull, Ann **Speedwell** Candlewick, 1992 ISBN 1 56402112 2

This book is about racing pigeons, and Mary becomes involved with them while her father is looking for work and Mary is at home with her mother and two younger children. It's the Depression, and Mary needs to work, but is too young. She races her father's pigeons, but her mother, in need of food for the family, cooks three of them, and Mary runs away.

▶ Website

http://www.jkinder.com/pigeon/pigeons.htm

This Web site features information about pigeons and links to additional pigeon information.

CHAPTER 26

The Ramsay Scallop

★ ★ ★ ★

by Frances Temple
Orchard, 1994
ISBN 0 531 06836 6

COMMENTS

This is a wonderfully wise novel, steeped in careful research and full of fascinating details about life in the Middle Ages. It evokes the time well, and the pilgrimage the main characters take gives the reader a chance to see the effects of the feudal system on many levels. Temple also offers ideas and dilemmas about such things as religion—Catholic and Islam—honor, heroes, dedication, the nature of sin, and the debts owed by human beings to each other.

The theme of searching for oneself in the reflection of others' lives is also an interesting one.

THE PLOT

Elenor and Thomas' marriage was arranged for them long before Thomas left on a Crusade. Elenor is a curious, lively, and joyful person who has been enjoying her life in the village. Now, however, Thomas has returned, discouraged and disillusioned about what he has done and seen during what should have

been a holy war. The other Crusaders who marched with Thomas as their leader are also overwhelmed by the brutality and lack of respect for life they have witnessed and shown. Neither Elenor nor Thomas is pleased with the life that lies ahead for them.

Father Gregory devises a pilgrimage to a shrine in Spain for Elenor and Thomas, to lay the sins of the entire village at the altar of St. James. Their trek takes them around Europe, joining up with other pilgrims, getting to know many others, each other, and themselves. What they see and experience on their journey gives us insight into the way of life for many people during the Middle Ages.

TAKING IT DEEPER

Look for signs that the friendship between Elenor and Thomas is growing.

What does the title mean? What would you have chosen for a title?

Elenor thought, "Thomas, who had seemed staid as a too-finished portrait, was scattering into a series of sketches." What do you think she means?

Look for acts of kindness in the book.

"What do women want?" is a question from the book. It's also a question asked by Freud. According to the old woman in the book, "A woman wants sovereignty, she wishes to direct her own will." Do you agree? How many women do you know who have achieved a kind of sovereignty?

The story of Roland is told and discussed in the book. Do you think he was a hero? What about the other heroes of legend: Robin Hood, King Arthur, Ulysses, and the like? Would they be looked upon as heroes in our culture? Would women feel the same about them as men would?

The stories told by the people Thomas and Elenor meet teach them and us a great deal. Which of those stories has any meaning for you? Read **The Canterbury Tales** (see below) for other stories told by travelers of that time.

The Jews are suffering cruelties even in that time. Find out where the Jews were being sent and what happened to them next.

Read other stories of journeys that produced wisdom (see below). Which of them do you think would have been productive for you to undertake?

Find out more about the Crusades. How did they start and why did they stop, and did they accomplish anything?

Thomas and Elenor have no trouble conversing with the people they meet in France. Could this be because they were Normans? Find out more about the Norman people and their role in the Crusades.

RELATED BOOKS

(For other books set in the Middle Ages, see **Catherine, Called Birdy** on page 159.)

▶ Picture Books

★ ★ ★ ★ Cohen, Barbara **Canterbury Tales** Lothrop, 1988 ISBN 0 688 06201 6, illustrated by Trina Schart Hyman

Four stories from Chaucer have been adapted: "The Nun's Priest's Tale," "The Pardoner's Tale," "The Wife of Bath's Tale" and "The Franklin's Tale." Each is tellingly illustrated by Hyman.

★ ★ ★ ★ Hendry, Frances Mary **Quest for a Maid** Farrar, 1990 ISBN 0 374 46155 4

In the 13th century, Meg accompanies her Princess on a voyage to Scotland, but is wrecked at sea.

★ ★ Steele, Mary Q. **Journey Outside** Smith, 1984 ISBN 0 8446 6169 4

A boy leaves the underground raft society, which is all he has known, and crawls through a crack to a surface world. Each of the people he meets seems, at first, to be living an ideal life, but he discovers their tragic flaws and returns to his previous existence.

★ ★ ★ Sutcliff, Rosemary **The Light Beyond the Forest: The Quest for the Holy Grail** Dutton, 1980 ISBN 0 525 33665 6

This is the legend of Sir Galahad and is, of course, set in the Middle Ages.

★ ★ ★ ★ Woodruff, Elvira **Dear Levi: Letters from the Overland Trail** Knopf, 1994 ISBN 0 679 84641 7

Austin, a young orphan traveling west with a wagon train, sends letters back to his brother Levi. The letters show Austin's growing understanding of the world and of the people he meets on the way.

▶ Nonfiction

★ Steffens, Bradley **The Children's Crusade** Lucent, 1991 ISBN 1 56006 019 0

This brief book also mentions other Crusades, and offers information about the era and about the Crusades' purpose.

★ Martell, Hazel **The Normans** Simon, 1992 ISBN 0 02 762428 5

This book covers a time span from the settling of Rollo, in Normandy, through the establishment of Norman influence in Britain and the rest of Europe, especially through the Crusades.

A Taste of Salt

★ ★ ★ ★

by Frances Temple
HarperTrophy, 1992
ISBN 0 06 447136 5

 **COMMENTS**

Providing a link between current events and literature, this is a fascinating and disturbing novel in which two young people reach out to each other during a time of great trauma. It's a hopeful book in spite of the brutality it contains, and should provide some readers with some knowledge of the events of recent years in Haiti.

 **THE PLOT**

Djo has been a worker for Aristide, having been taken into the care of the priest when Djo was young and poor. He has now been severely wounded by a group of Tonton Macoute and is fighting for his life in a hospital. Jeremie is a more recent devotee of Aristide's and is trying to record Djo's life story—partly for Aristide, partly for her own education, and partly to keep Djo focused on trying to live. Shortly after joining Aristide's group, Djo was kidnapped and taken to the Dominican Republic to be used as slave labor in the sugar cane fields. He stayed there for several years until making his escape back to Haiti. While he was gone, Aristide had risen from parish priest to a presidential candidate. Jeremie had been raised in a far more genteel manner and was in a convent school when she became more politically aware. As the two young people learn about each other, they fall in love and, at the end of the book, seem likely to pursue a life together.

 **TAKING IT DEEPER**

The title refers to a Haitian saying that the taste of salt is the only cure for a zombie, and in this case, that taste of salt is education. How does education change one? Is it always for the better?

The Tonton Macoute have beaten Djo nearly to death. What is their motivation? What are the equivalents of the Tonton in other cultures today?

Research the history of Haiti to find out if Duvalier had any positive effects on the country.

Does the author's use of dialect in the story make it harder or easier for you to understand? Why? Does the glossary help?

Jeremie held some elitist ideas, which her relationship with Djo helps to alter. What are they and how many do you share in some way?

In this book, storytelling is healing. Relate or write about your own experiences with this phenomenon.

To what extent do you think these characters are realistic?

Find out about life in Port-au-Prince today. Who is president of Haiti now? What happened to Aristide?

Jeremie and Djo have very different views of the world: Djo sees it in terms of black and white, and Jeremie sees it as being full of shadows and doubts. Find evidence in the book to support that statement.

RELATED BOOKS

▶ Picture Books

★ ★ ★ Van Laan, Nancy **Mama Rocks, Papa Sings** Knopf, 1995 ISBN 0 679 84016 8

Although intended for a much younger audience, illustrations show some Haitians' home life, and the text echoes the rhythms of Haiti.

★ Williams, Karen **Tap-Tap** Houghton, 1994 ISBN 0 395 65617 6

The Tap-Tap is a sort of communal taxi which takes Sasifi home from the market, where she's been selling fruit. The culture and customs of the island nation are revealed in the illustrations and text.

▶ Novels

★ ★ ★ Temple, Frances **Grab Hands and Run** Orchard, 1993 ISBN 0 531 05480 2

This novel is set in El Salvador, not Haiti, but the author is again dealing with cruelty—trickery that the disenfranchised must suffer in a country where the government offers little support or assistance.

★ ★ ★ Temple, Frances **Tonight by Sea** Orchard, 1995 ISBN 0 531 06899 4

This novel gives human faces to the Haitian boat people. Many of the horrors referred to in *A Taste of Salt* are further explained here.

▶ Nonfiction

★ Goldish, Meish **Crisis in Haiti** Millbrook, 1995 ISBN 1 56294 553 X

This book gives a brief history of Haiti, from Columbus to Aristide.

★ Lerner Editors **Haiti in Pictures** Lerner, 1987 ISBN 0 8225 1816 3

This volume in the *Visual Geography* series deals with Haitian culture and history.

★ Vehiller, Nina **The Haitian Americans** Chelsea, 1989 ISBN 0 87754 822 X

Using photos and extensive text, this volume shows the traditions and cultures of this large group of immigrants.

CHAPTER 28

Belle Prater's Boy

★ ★ ★ ★

by Ruth White
Farrar, 1996
ISBN 0 374 30668 0

COMMENTS

This novel is rich in atmosphere, vividly creating the small, coal-mining town of Coal Station. Equally strong, however, are the characters White has created, namely Woodrow and Gypsy. There is also the mystery of Woodrow's mother's disappearance, and the notion of someone caught between two worlds, which adds interest and focus to the novel. A favorite poem of Belle Prater's provides a theme.

THE PLOT

Belle Prater, the mother of Woodrow, got out of bed in their mountain cabin at dawn one morning and disappeared, taking nothing with her. The effect of this disappearance, ultimately, was to bring Woodrow to live with his grandparents in Coal Station, and next door to his cousin Gypsy. Gypsy's father is dead, and her mother has remarried, much to Gypsy's disgust. She refuses to have anything to do with her stepfather, even though she liked him a lot before he became her mother's suitor.

Woodrow—cross-eyed and unsophisticated—quickly charms his new neighbors and classmates with his sense of humor and story-telling abilities. The question of his mother's disappearance makes him the target of much curiosity and some cruelty, however. Woodrow confides to Gypsy that he thinks his mother is caught somehow between this world and the next, because he can almost hear her talking to him. Gypsy, too, is haunted by strange dreams and nightmares, and eventually must confront her own father's suicide.

TAKING IT DEEPER

The poem that Belle quoted so often to Woodrow appears throughout the book:

"The breeze at dawn has secrets to tell you.
　　Don't go back to sleep.
You must ask for what you really want
　　Don't go back to sleep.
People are going back and forth across the doorsill
　　where the two worlds touch.
The door is round and open.
　　Don't go back to sleep."

Does it have any meaning for you within the book? out of the book?

There are many books in which characters are caught between two conflicting worlds. **I Am Regina** (see page 27) features a heroine caught between the worlds of the settlers and the Native Americans. There's a point in **The Giver** (see page 180) at which Jonas is caught between the society he knows and the one he is fleeing to, and in **Julie of the Wolves**, we have a young woman caught between modern and traditional cultures. Do the wolves in that book represent a door for Julie? **The Double Life of Pocahontas** is a nonfiction book about the same concern. Two picture books by Allen Say give portraits of people caught between two worlds: **Tree of Cranes** and **Grandfather's Journey** (see page 79). Name some other books that are concerned with conflicting worlds.

What about people who "are going back and forth across the doorsill"? Can you think of any?

Reread the stories Woodrow tells. Do they tell you anything about him?

Can you understand why Belle left? Was that her only alternative? Didn't she care what happened to Woodrow?

Another book in which a woman leaves her home and her children is Marion Dane Bauer's **A Question of Trust** (see page 132). Are the women's motivations similar?

Find and read some other books set in Appalachia (see page 80). Why do so many authors write about that area?

Woodrow is a wise innocent in this book. Some books and movies have a similar character. Ida Early (see below) is one such character, also from Appalachia, as it happens. Charles Wallace, in **A Wrinkle in Time**, and **Maniac Magee** also have a sort of innocence. Can you name any others?

RELATED BOOKS

(See the theme on Appalachia for more books and activities.)

▶ Novels

★ ★ ★ Bauer, Marion Dane **A Question of Trust** Scholastic, 1994 ISBN 0 590 47923 7

Charlie and Brad are furious with their mother for leaving them, and when they suspect a mother cat of abandoning her kittens, they almost kill her.

★ ★ ★ ★ Burch, Robert **Ida Early Comes Over the Mountain** Avon, 1982 ISBN 0 14 034534 5

Ida Early comes out of the mountains to offer her services to a motherless family. Ida's outlandish behavior is a source of joy and embarrassment to the children.

★ ★ ★ ★ George, Jean **Julie of the Wolves** HarperCollins. 1972 ISBN 0 06 021943 2

Julie is escaping the arranged marriage of the Eskimo culture when she becomes lost on the tundra. The wolves, which become her saviors and family, are threatened by the same culture.

★ ★ ★ Keehn, Sally **I Am Regina** Putnam, 1991 ISBN 0 399 21797 5

Regina is taken captive by the Indians and slowly becomes a member of their society. When the time comes to be returned to her own family, she is not too sure which culture is hers.

★ ★ ★ ★ L'Engle, Madeleine **A Wrinkle in Time** Dell, 1976 ISBN 0 440 99805 0

Meg, her younger brother, Charles Wallace, and their friend, Calvin, travel through time and space to rescue her father and are caught between worlds.

★ ★ ★ ★ Lowry, Lois **The Giver** Houghton, 1993 ISBN 0 395 64566 2

Jonas' home and society seem ideal. There is no sickness, and each member of society makes a valuable contribution to it. When he is selected to become the receiver of the memories of that society, however, he sees its tragic flaws and makes his escape. This is a focus book (see page 180).

★ ★ ★ ★ Spinelli, Jerry **Maniac Magee** Little, 1990 ISBN 0 316 80722 4 7

Jeffrey Magee, a homeless boy, runs into a racially split town, where he becomes the catalyst for change. This excellent novel is about prejudice and love, and home and baseball, and fear and understanding. It's about Jeffrey Lionel Magee, sometimes known as

Maniac Magee, and about the people of the town of Two Mills. Jeffrey has spent the last eight years in the bizarre household of his Aunt Dot and Uncle Dan, who hated each other but refused to divorce, and lived in the same house without speaking to each other, using Jeffrey as their go-between. Jeffrey runs away. That's the beginning of his running and of his search for a real home. He ends up in the town of Two Mills, two hundred miles away from his aunt and uncle. Two Mills is a town divided by race into the East End and the West End. There Jeffrey becomes "Maniac Magee," the subject of legends that have lasted ever since. In his search for a place to belong, he eventually succeeds to some degree in uniting the town by forcing at least some of its black and white residents to get to know each other.

Only Opal: The Diary of a Young Girl

★ ★ ★ ★

by Opal Whitely
Philomel, 1994
ISBN 0 399 21990 0
illustrated by Barbara Cooney

COMMENTS

Sometimes a picture book can lead directly to a longer and more difficult book. The advantages of such a pairing are obvious. Readers of lesser ability can use the picture book source only, and still contribute to the dialogue. Readers with more skill can read both and get both visual and textual images. As always with Barbara Cooney's work, the illustrations in **Only Opal** are terrific. You have to spend lots of time just enjoying the book visually. See page 72 for other ideas for using picture books in the middle school program.

THE PLOT

When you read the title page, you find that the words are not Cooney's but are those of a real little girl, Opal Whitely. Further exploration of the book and its afterword tells you that Opal Whitely was born at the turn of the century in Oregon and that she wrote this diary when she was five and six years old. This is a very special little girl. Opal had very few of the niceties of life and was apparently, for the most part, unloved and unappreciated, but she had the soul of a poet and a precocious understanding and knowledge of the natural world around her. Orphaned before this diary begins, she remembers much of what her biological parents taught her. This knowledge sustains her in the home of a very demanding foster mother.

TAKING IT DEEPER

From the afterword in the picture book, we learn that the text in *Only Opal* is taken from a more complete version of the diary, called **Opal: The Journal of an Understanding Heart**, by Opal Whitely, adapted by Jane Boulton

(Crown, 1995 ISBN 0 527 885166 186). Locate and read all or some of that book.

The afterword also says that the original diary was torn into bits by a jealous foster sister of Opal's, but that she saved all the pieces and, many years later, carefully and painstakingly reconstructed the diary and brought it to a publisher. Where did she meet the publisher? How could she put it back together again?

What happened to the other people in her diary: Dear Love, The Girl Who Has No Seeing, and even The Mama?

In the longer version of the story, we find out that Opal claimed to be the child of a French duke, but that the woman Opal called "The Mama," and said was not her biological mother, always claimed she was. So did other relatives. What could be the explanation for this and other mysteries?

In the longer version, you can find the passages Cooney excerpted. Would you have chosen those? Are there other parts you think are more interesting? What illustrations would you make for those selections?

Then there's the question of whether or not Opal was telling the truth. Did she really write it when she was so young or did she create it as an adult? She was seen piecing it together over many months, so she would have had to painstakingly print the diary in child-like letters on aged and different papers, tear it up, and then piece it all together again. Did she? Is it a fraud?

What about Opal's heritage? Was she the illegitimate daughter of Henri, the Duke of Orleans, as she claimed? If not, how did she come upon her knowledge of French as a child in the lumber camps of Oregon? What about the intriguing code that some of her writings seem to reveal?

If you could hire a researcher or detective to pick up where Jane Boulton left off in her search for Opal, what pieces of information would you have him or her follow up on?

Investigate some other famous mysteries about such people as Anastasia, Judge Carter, and Amelia Earhart.

RELATED BOOKS

▶ Picture Books

Bunting, Eve **Train to Somewhere** Clarion, 1996 ISBN 0 395 71325 0, illustrated by Ronald Himler

Some of the children on this orphan train will find good homes, but others may end up in situations like Opal's.

★ ★ ★ Lasky, Kathryn **Marven of the Great North Woods** Harcourt, 1997 ISBN 0 15 200104 2

Based on the memories of the author's father, this picture book tells about life in a Minnesota lumber camp.

▶ Novels

Cassedy, Sylvia **Lucie Babbidge's House** Avon, 1989 ISBN 0 380 71812 X

Like Opal, Lucie is an orphan. Each day, she rushes home from school, away from the taunts of her classmates, to a perfect home and loving family—in a dollhouse.

Paterson, Katherine **Jip: His Story** Lodestar, 1996 ISBN 0 525 67543 4

Like Opal, Jip is an orphan, or might be one. When he was three, he supposedly fell off a wagon, which careened down a road, and no one ever claimed him, so he was sent to the Poor Farm. Because of his dark skin and hair, he was assumed to be a gypsy and so was named Jip. Jip has a natural affinity for animals; indeed, for anything or anyone who is helpless or injured. When a "lunatic" is brought to the poor farm and bound and chained to live in a cage there, it is Jip who befriends and cares for him. Put, short for Putnam, turns out to be a fine, gentle, and learned gentleman when violent spells are not on him, and he and Jip become the best of friends.

★ ★ ★ Paulsen, Gary **Cookcamp** Orchard, 1991 ISBN 0 531 08527 9

During World War II, a little boy is sent to his grandmother's cookcamp in the Minnesota north woods. The men of the lumber camp became parents of the boy.

Author, Illustrator, Title Index

Author, Illustrator, Title Index (continued)

Author, Illustrator, Title Index (continued)

Author, Illustrator, Title Index (continued)

Author, Illustrator, Title Index (continued)

Author, Illustrator, Title Index (continued)

Author, Illustrator, Title Index (continued)

Author, Illustrator, Title Index (continued)

Author, Illustrator, Title Index (continued)

Author, Illustrator, Title Index (continued)

Author, Illustrator, Title Index (continued)

Author, Illustrator, Title Index (continued)

Author, Illustrator, Title Index (continued)

Subject Index

Subject Index (continued)